Ecopreneuring

The Complete Guide to Small Business Opportunities from the Environmental Revolution

Ecopreneuring

*The Complete Guide to Small Business
Opportunities from the Environmental
Revolution*

Steven J. Bennett

John Wiley & Sons, Inc.

New York • Chichester • Brisbane • Toronto • Singapore

In recognition of the importance of preserving what has been written, it is a policy of John Wiley & Sons, Inc. to have books of enduring value published in the United States printed on acid-free paper, and we exert our best efforts to that end.

Text printed on recycled paper.

Library of Congress Cataloging -in-Publications Data

Bennett, Steven J., 1951
   Ecopreneuring: the complete guide to small business opportunities from the environmental revolution / Steven J. Bennett.
      p. cm.
   Includes bibliographical references.
   ISBN 0-471-53951-1. -- ISBN 0-471-53074-3 (pbk.)
   1. New business enterprises. 2. Entrepreneurship. 3. Recycling (Waste, etc.) 4. Marketing--Social aspects. I. Title.

HD62.5.B455 1991
628.4'458'068--dc20

90-27593

Printed in the United States of America

91 92 10 9 8 7 6 5 4 3 2 1

*To the memory of Lewis Paul Todd—
the environment has known no better friend.*

Acknowledgments

This book could not have come about without the hard work of the members of the Bennett Information Group: Tom Maugh, Richard Freerman, Bob Kalish, Nancy Schmid, and Dorian Kinder all made significant contributions to the manuscript. Mike Snell, my agent and also a member of the Group, was instrumental in conceptualizing the book and monitoring its progress. Thanks, folks!

Equally important, I'd like to thank all the ecopreneurs who took time from their busy schedules to share their experiences and wisdom with us. I'd especially like to thank Joe Hevener of Offshore Ventures; Peter Kinder of Kinder, Lydenberg, Domini, and Co., Inc.; John Schaeffer, founder of Real Goods Trading Company; Sally Malanga, founder of Ecco Bella; and Alan Newman, cofounder of Seventh Generation, for subjecting themselves to exceptionally lengthy telephone interviews.

Research assistant Catalina Girona did a fine job of assembling the resource guide. Hats off to Marcy Ketcham, who once again managed a mountain of messy word-processing details in record time.

Eileen Shapiro of the Hillcrest Group provided invaluable insights into the strategic issues facing ecobusinesses today, while John Graham, the "father of magnet marketing," gave us a wealth of suggestions for teaching ecopreneurs how to successfully market their goods and services.

Back in New York, my editor, John Mahaney, supported this book from the beginning and played a key role in taming it as it developed a life of its own. Publisher, Gwen Jones, was instrumental in getting the project from the idea stage to the action stage.

Back at home, in Cambridge, PageWorks, Inc. once again did a terrific job with production. Special thanks go to Art Director Beth McMacken for a fine design and to Andrea Greitzer and Tania Liepmann for composing the pages.

Above all, I'd like to thank my wife, Ruth, and my children, Noah and Audrey, for putting up with my physical and mental absence during the past six months while I assembled the manuscript. I hope you come to agree that it was all for a very worthwhile cause.

Contents

Introduction

Doing Well by Doing Right

On July 19, 1986, at 3:45 A.M., a foul odor drifted into Edwin Jason's bedroom, jarring the 33-year-old potato chip salesman and his wife out of a sound sleep. A strange bubbling sound emanating from the garage gave the unwelcome wake-up call an especially eerie feel. After stumbling out of bed, it took Jason only seconds to trace the stench to his workbench, where a steaming vat was oozing viscous brown goop onto the floor.

Erstwhile ecopreneur Edwin Jason and his partner, Joe Hevener, had been trying for weeks to find the right method for converting fish remains into the perfect organic fertilizer. That evening, the two had worked until midnight, whipping up a brew of cod carcasses and enzymes. Weary from another night of fruitless experimentation, they shut down the "lab" and turned in, hoping that the hydrolysis process might start by itself during the night.

As the oozing mass on the workbench proved, the hydrolysis had not only begun, it had reached critical mass. Jason called Hevener, who dashed right over and began heaving stabilizers into the vat in an effort to check the reaction before it turned into the Creature That Ate Cape Cod. Unfortunately, the stabilizers only made matters worse, and the stuff began spurting from the top of the vat like magma from Mount Saint Helens.

The saga might have discouraged less dedicated ecopreneurs, but it stimulated Hevener and Jason to hum a few bars from the old "Entrepreneur's Blues." The two doggedly continued with their experiments until they finally mastered the hydrolysis process and found a way to mask the fish odor. Two years later, their first product, Squanto's Secret (named after the Cape Cod Indian who taught the Pilgrims how to farm with fish fertilizer), hit the street, and today it has become one of the hottest-selling (and sweetest-smelling) organic gardening products on the market.

Hevener says with a laugh, "Five years ago, if anyone had told me that I'd be making a living grinding dead fish, I'd have told them they were nuts." Then he gets very serious, explaining that he and his partner had dreamed for years about starting their own business, one that could benefit more than just their own bank accounts. That sense of mission, combined with a generous helping of energy, ingenuity, and tenacity, guided them into creating one of the more intriguing (and profitable) ecobusinesses of the nineties.

Enter the Ecopreneur

Today, similar opportunities abound for anyone who wants to make a living and at the same time solve environmental problems. A new breed of environmental entrepreneurs may, in fact, provide our best chance for restoring the air, water, and earth on which all life depends. Of course, no single person or group of people can completely undo the damage that we've wrought on the planet since the Industrial Revolution. That will take a concerted and massive effort by legislators, heads of large corporations, and government agencies. Nevertheless, the ecopreneur can lead the charge into a greener future while at the same time building a profitable enterprise.

Each ecopreneur makes a small, but vital, contribution to the great environmental cleanup ahead. Hevener and Jason's Squanto's Secret reduces the need for people to use chemical fertilizers on their lawns, gardens, and house plants—the runoff from which can destroy streams and lakes and the fish that inhabit them. And it solves a pesky solid-waste problem for large fish-processing companies, too, which only use one-third of each fish and pay to have the rest carted away (most of them gladly give it to Hevener).

Two hundred miles north, in Milbury, Vermont, Arnie and Ron Koss's company, Earth's Best, is creating a national stir, by offering the first line of organic, pesticide-free baby foods.

Across the state, in Colchester, Vermont, Alan Newman and Jeffrey Hollender's mail order operation, Seventh Generation, can barely keep up with customer demand for environmentally friendly products.

Meanwhile, in the small town of Monticello, Iowa, landscaper Klark Hagan parks his used beer truck in the local grocery store lot, where residents can fill it with their recyclable trash instead of tossing it into what little landfill space remains. Hagan sells his collection to recycling operations.

Up in the Great Lakes region, Felicia Frizzell's Glass Aggregate Corporation, based in Grand Rapids, Michigan, converts crushed colored glass (of no use to glass recyclers) into erosion-barrier material.

Out in Big Sky country, Dan Brandborg offers state-of-the-art solar energy technology through his Hamilton, Montana-based company, Sunelco, thus helping in the war against global warming and soaring energy costs.

And on the West Coast, ecopreneurs are busily creating and selling a broad variety of green products and services. Nester Noe's AFM Enterprises in Riverside, California, offers a broad assortment of environmentally sound paints, sealers, stains, and cleansers. Donald Knapp's Urban Ore of Berkeley, California, salvages perfectly good furniture, appliances, and construction materials from the town dump and sells them for reuse.

In the Northwest, Paul Derdzinski's Ecology House Franchise, Inc., offers people the opportunity to set up and run retail stores that carry exclusively environmental gifts, and in Friday Harbor, Washington, Richard and Sharon Hooper's Nature Recordings distributes a soothing assortment of natural sounds (the seashore, waterfalls etc) designed to counter noise pollution in the home and workplace.

If enough ecopreneurs throughout the land join the movement toward creating environmentally safe products and services, thereby putting tremendous competitive pressure on large companies to follow suit, eventually we will not only improve the quality of our air, soil, and water, but we'll also find alternatives to overflowing landfills, expensive or dangerous energy production facilities, and those many manufacturing processes that contribute to acid rain, the depletion of the ozone layer, and the warming of the earth's climate.

What Ecopreneurs Do

Ecopreneuring covers a broad range of businesses. Some ecopreneurs turn other people's trash into gold by starting companies that:

- Haul recyclable materials to manufacturers who can convert them into new products.
- Sell finished products made from recycled materials to individual consumers and businesses.
- Turn used motor oil that might formerly have been dumped on dirt roads into high-quality lubricants.
- Recycle coolants from discarded and broken air conditioners for use in new appliances.
- Convert plastic milk containers into plastic "lumber" that never rot or need maintenance.
- Use old newspapers to make inexpensive and bacteria-resistant bedding for farm animals.
- Turn sludge or food waste into fertilizer or soil conditioners.

Other ecopreneurs take old product ideas and give them a "green" twist by creating and/or selling:

- Foods free of pesticides and synthetic chemicals, and packaged in recyclable or biodegradable materials.
- Non-petroleum-based personal-care products free of potentially harmful additives and unnecessary dyes, also packaged responsibly.

- Cleansers, polishes, and other household items that contain no petroleum products or harmful chemicals.

- Paints, stains, glues, adhesives, and other workshop items free of environmental and health hazards such as mercury or benzene.

- Yard and garden supplies that do not contain organophosphates and other chemicals largely responsible for water pollution.

- Reusable canvas shopping bags that replace paper or plastic grocery bags.

- Energy-efficient light bulbs, water-conserving toilets, and other simple household products.

- Solar-powered ovens that eliminate the need for charcoal and lighter fluid, two major culprits in air pollution.

- Environmentally sound alternatives to hard foam "peanuts" and other non-degradable packing materials.

Still other ecopreneurs give old services a green spin.

- They package tours to the Amazon and other environmentally sensitive areas to teach tourists the importance of ecology.

- They help companies assess their workplaces from the standpoint of environmental fitness.

- They offer carpet-cleaning and other services that use non-toxic chemicals.

- They sell advice on environmentally sound investments.

- They create games, books, and software packages designed to educate while entertaining.

These represent just a smattering of the kinds of businesses ecopreneurs start and develop every day. The possibilities for running your own ecobusiness are only limited by your imagination; the environment is a vast field, and so are the problems plaguing it. By keeping a watchful eye on the news, and paying close attention to your immediate environmental needs, you, too, can define and redefine profitable new market niches.

Green Business vs. Business as Usual

At this point you might ask, "Other than the fact that an ecobusiness involves the environment, does it really differ from any other type of small business?" It does, and it doesn't. On the one hand, a business is a business. The same general principles of good management apply: organizing employees and resources, keeping your overhead down, targeting market segments, maintaining profitable cash flow, and controlling growth. And ecobusinesses fail for the same reasons that conventional businesses fail. Working for a noble cause doesn't insulate you from all the tactical blunders, savvy competitors, and changing customer needs that force almost 80 percent of startups out of business after the first year.

Still, ecopreneurs encounter unique problems, because they must remain keenly sensitive to developments in environmental science, legislation, and public awareness. A shoe store owner doesn't have to worry much about technological advances or new regulations, but a recycler must constantly monitor all sorts of factors, from research findings to local, state, and federal legislation, that can have a direct impact on his or her business.

For example, a 1990 law in California mandates that glass bottlers use a higher percentage of recycled glass than in previous years. This, of course, creates a new market for glass recyclers and can potentially make their businesses more profitable. Other laws have the opposite effect. Many states have passed legislation requiring that state-funded agencies and institutions buy the least expensive products and supplies available. These laws significantly influence paper recyclers, since recycled paper tends to cost more than virgin paper. As a result, recyclers cannot count on selling to certain state-funded universities, even though they would normally seem to be the most logical candidates. In short, this morning's news may cascade directly to tomorrow's bottom line.

Also, environmental entrepreneuring represents a new frontier, one that requires more foresight and pioneering courage than run-of-the-mill businesses. In addition, it requires a set of values and ethics sadly lacking in so much of corporate America. The ecopreneur must therefore be sensitive to the effects that "ecoscams" and "ecomarketing campaigns" have on environmental business. The public has already become wary of false claims of biodegradable fast-food packaging, trash bags, and diapers. In the long run the truth will win out, but in the meantime the ecopreneur must be ready to fight fires started by people who join the field for a quick buck without regard to the validity or integrity of their products or services.

A related aspect of the ecopreneuring field is that many buyers of environment-friendly products and services are extremely knowledgeable, very vocal, and often activist. They're more likely to write letters with suggestions and criticism, and demand tangible feedback. If they don't see reasonable changes in your offerings, they spend their ecodollars elsewhere. Therefore, ecopreneurs must go beyond the traditional rules of customer service and view customers as partners who can help them shape better businesses.

Finally, true ecopreneurs are driven by a special passion—to heal the planet. That commitment often gives them an extra edge when it comes to weathering the psychological and fiscal storms they will inevitably encounter as they grow their fledgling enterprises.

ల

About Ecopreneuring

Beyond Eco Guilt

This book will give you a head start into the field of environmental entrepreneuring by teaching you the fundamentals of creating a strong business. "But is it really right to profit from the environment," some people might ask? The fact is, if you want to save the planet, you can't do it without making a profit. Your heart may be in the right place, but if your mind isn't wrapped around the core concepts of running a business, you'll never be able to achieve your goals.

According to John Schaeffer, founder of Real Goods Trading Company, the nation's leading mail-order supplier of alternative energy products, many ecopreneurs fall into the "guilt trap" and set their profit margins unrealistically low, causing them to become mere statistics in the annals of business history. Schaeffer himself admits that this very mentality almost did in his own company. "Most mail order businesses operate with 55 percent profit margins," he explains. "Our margins were 28 percent. While we felt good about offering low prices, we couldn't service our customers adequately. The more the business grew, the worse customer service got. So we raised our margins to 40 percent and a funny thing happened—customers got behind us and understood. They knew we weren't trying to gouge them, and that it was necessary for us to generate a profit if we were to provide them with high quality goods and top notch service."

Schaeffer says that every ecopreneur needs to get over the guilt trap and generate a profit: "If you're scared at the thought of making a buck off the environment, you'd better think twice about going into business. Being righteous but bankrupt isn't going to solve anyone's problems. On the other hand, once you've mastered the money issue, you can use your business to bring about change."

As an example of what you can do when your business succeeds, look at Anita Roddick's sensational hit, The Body Shop, a franchise of retail stores that sell environment-friendly cosmetics and personal-care products. Started with a $6,000 loan a decade ago, The Body Shop's sales exceeded $140 million in 1990, and there's no end in sight. Yet the business serves as far more than a means of generating cash; the profits enable Roddick to support financially a broad range of environmental efforts, such as helping to preserve rain forests and saving the whales. As Roddick demonstrates, a strong business sense can naturally complement a passionate commitment to the environment, enabling an ecopreneur to succeed beyond his or her wildest dreams.

Whatever your motive for starting an ecobusiness, your success represents a win-win situation; the environment gets a little cleaner, and you get to eke out a living and achieve your lifestyle and spiritual goals.

A Field Guide

Regardless of whether you're a novice or seasoned ecopreneur, this book can help. If you've never run a business, definitely read this first part—its five chapters offer a crash course in basic entrepreneuring, with discussions of special issues relevant to the ecopreneur. The first chapter covers skills—what it takes to become an ecopreneur, and how you can get the necessary training for the challenges ahead. Chapter 2 describes how to develop a viable idea for an ecobusiness; although the field of environmental business is growing fast, the ecopreneur must still make wise choices in finding a niche. The third chapter describes how to fund an ecobusiness—a key to survival. Chapter 4 presents techniques for marketing your business, while Chapter 5 offers tips for managing growth and keeping your enterprise on a course that will maximize its chances for a bright green future.

Parts II and III describe specific opportunities for starting a green business. The chapters in Part II describe ecobusinesses that can help solve existing environmental problems and prevent new ones through recycling and other solid waste reduction techniques, while those in Part III teach you how to provide products and services that promote the green lifestyle. The chapters in Parts II and III present market overviews; estimated short- and long-term potential; startup requirements—capital, equipment, etc.; special legal and compliance issues; marketing techniques; spinoffs and diversification potential; and case studies and testimony from successful ecopreneurs.

Part IV, "The Ecopreneur's Resource Guide," compiles a far-ranging list of additional resources, books, magazines, and associations that can help you as your ecobusiness grows.

If you're not sure what kind of ecobusiness makes sense for you, browse through Parts II and III to see what catches your fancy. If you're looking for specific information about a particular field, use *Ecopreneuring* as a reference tool.

Finally, bear in mind that *Ecopreneuring* focuses on small-scale startups. Consequently, you won't find information about starting a hazardous waste management firm or a heavy manufacturing operation, both of which require massive capital, technical expertise, and sophisticated business acumen. This isn't to say that the kind of businesses described in *Ecopreneuring* can't yield significant revenues—just look at The Body Shop. But in harmony with the belief that small-scale entrepreneurs offer the greatest hope for the environment, this book celebrates the low-budget tinker, the do-it-yourselfer, the self-taught expert who has taken it upon himself or herself to do something for the greater good. These are the people who will ultimately do well by doing right.

Part I

A Crash Course in Ecopreneuring

Chapter *One*

On Becoming an Ecopreneur: *Skills of the Trade*

Green Business or Risky Business?

Question: What one single factor determines every ecopreneur's success?

A. Technical working knowledge of environmental science

B. Prior business experience

C. Lots of money

D. High risk tolerance

E. None of the above

Answer: None of the above. You can always get the technical know-how you'll need by reading books and tapping experts; you can learn business skills from others, from books, or from small-business groups, or hire consultants; and you can (and should) start on a shoestring. But one thing that you can't get from anyone else or subcontract out is a willingness to accept risk.

People who start ecobusinesses must face the fact that at some point, in some way, they will fail. Talk to an entrepreneur in any

13

field and you'll hear about a string of setbacks that inevitably attend a startup enterprise. Just because you are fighting for a good cause doesn't mean that you will automatically succeed. At its core, a green startup works like any other small business, and most small businesses fail in the first 12 months. In fact, every year more than 400,000 entrepreneurs start new businesses in the United States. Of these, 350,000 shut down before the year's end. Of the remaining 50,000, many hang on by the skin of their teeth, with only a small percentage attaining ultimate success. Most enjoy a modest degree of profitability at best.

Even if you don't fail outright, you will fail at some aspect of your business. Perhaps you'll grow a successful ecofirm but develop a new product line that flops. Maybe you'll get blindsided by competition and suddenly find yourself without a customer base. Or perhaps a new technology or set of regulations will make your business obsolete or uncompetitive.

So why do it? For ecopreneurs, the twin opportunities to do something for the environment and to control their own destinies override the potential risks associated with starting a business. Even so, the first-time ecopreneur may find risk taking quite anxiety provoking, possibly even an impediment to getting a good business idea off the ground. So if you feel the "green calling," and have never struck out on your own in business, ask yourself the following questions:

- What if I fail outright in the first six months? How will I survive economically? Do I have enough cash reserves to hold me until I can start another business or find another job?

- If the business generates marginal profits but shows promise, can I afford to hang on until it takes off?

- How will I feel about myself if I fail? Will the failure of my business make me feel like a failure as a human being? What will my family think? What will my friends say?

- If I don't succeed, will I have the nerve to try again?

If this line of questioning gives you sweaty palms, you need to find a way to make the risks more tolerable psychologically. The realities of the business world are immutable; your perceptions are infinitely malleable. There are several techniques you can use to help channel your fears about taking risks in a positive direction.

Identify Reasonable Risks

If you're the head of a household of five, and you're thinking of quitting your job, investing your life savings in starting an ecobusiness, and can tap no other sources of income, you're probably looking at an unacceptable risk. If, on the other hand, you can start your company as a moonlighting venture, and can test or develop it quietly on the side without jeopardizing your family's next meal, then the risk may be acceptable for your particular situation.

Many ecopreneurs ease into their businesses. Initially, Joe Hevener and Edwin Jason, creators of the organic fish fertilizer Squanto's Secret, maintained their regular jobs while tinkering with the new idea in the evenings and on weekends (Hevener managed a video store, Jason was a marketer for a potato chip company). Eventually, when the business became strong enough to support them, they quit their jobs and became full-time ecopreneurs.

Similarly, Sharon Rowe began working part time at her Eco-Bags company, which she operates out of her home office in New York City. Eco-Bags markets cotton string bags that shoppers can tote to the supermarket instead of bringing home paper or plastic bags. Rowe wanted to devote plenty of time to her infant son, but she also wanted to do something to help the environment. The moonlighting approach allowed her to do both. But with orders for more than 70,000 bags (from $1.50 to $4.99 apiece) flowing in during the first six months, Rowe had to expand the business and consider it a full-time enterprise (she's also developing a new line of reusable cotton and/or nylon-mesh sandwich and vegetable bags.)

Separate Your Sense of Self-Worth from Your Business Judgment

Pick up any business magazine and you'll read about people whose well-funded startups foundered. In many cases, millions of dollars were involved. What happens to these entrepreneurs? Do they crawl under a rock and hide from the world in shame?

No, the best ones come back again for another round. And they do it because they don't derive their sense of self-worth from success or failure in the business world. Sure, it feels lousy to lose a business, but the true entrepreneur realizes that a tactical business mistake should not erode self-esteem.

Consider how computer entrepreneur Gene Amdahl picked himself up following a disastrous venture. After starting his own successful company, Amdahl Corp., he assembled one of the most heavily funded startups in history, Trilogy, Ltd., which raised some $230 million in cash. Trilogy was a major flop, which some experts attribute to organizational problems that prevented the company from getting new products out the door on schedule. In addition to losing more than $2 million himself, Amdahl anguished over the impact on the people in his organization. But he picked himself up again, learned from his mistakes, and went on to start Andor Systems, Inc., which is developing components for the mainframe computer market.

Accept Failure as a Teacher

Entrepreneurs can accept failure because they know they'll be wiser the next time around. Historian Arnold Toynbee once noted that the one thing we learn from history is that we don't learn from history. Perhaps that's true in love, war, and politics, but in the entrepreneurial arena, people can and do learn from their mistakes, especially when they've been financially burned. When they bounce back into the arena for another round, they do so ready for the unexpected, and prepared never to make the same mistake again. When you treat failure as a teacher, you really can't lose—you can only get better.

Take the case of one of America's most resilient entrepreneurs, Dal La Magna, a.k.a. "Tweezerman." La Magna, who at one time computed that he singlehandedly lowered the average income of his Harvard Business School class by $80 a head, tried more entrepreneurial ventures in five years than most people do in a lifetime. Among other ventures, he took a stab at starting a water-bed company, converting drive-in movie theaters into drive-in discos, a computerized dating service, and specially designed lasagna pans. He finally struck pay dirt with his company Tweezerman, which wholesales top-of-the-line tweezers to salons, drugstores, and department stores. In 1986, it an grossed nearly $80,000; in 1990, with two factories in Italy, that number skyrocketed to $3 million. According to La Magna, nothing works better than "failing to get ahead."

Finally, bear in mind that striking out on your own to start an ecobusiness (or any business for that matter) involves certain trade-offs, such as:

- A regular paycheck for the ability to create your future rather than hoping your employer will do it for you.

- Job security for the ability to control the "five W's": *where* you work, *when* you work, *whom* you work with, *what* you work on, and *why* you work.

- An old-fashioned, plodding career path for a path to financial and lifestyle independence.

Everybody's Business

While ecopreneurs express similar attitudes about risk, they possess strikingly different backgrounds. Some, like waste treatment experts John Todd and Walter Adey, hold Ph.D.'s in the natural sciences, but most, like Joe Hevener and Edwin Jason, have no special training in environmental affairs. Some have earned bachelor's degrees in history or psychology, others have worked in sales, and still others boast two decades of experience as homemakers. Regardless of your background, there *is* an ecopreneurial niche that you can fill—all you need to get going is the commitment to a green future.

Consider the possibilities:

- An English major or teacher could write articles about the field, publish an environmental newsletter, and package information for a world craving environmental knowledge.

- A homemaker might develop a line of environmentally safe cleaning or baby-care products.

- A carpenter or craftsperson could research and develop a line of nontoxic and nonpolluting glues, paints, and other items for home use.

- Someone with a flair for preparing food could pioneer a new line of foods grown without hazardous chemicals and packaged in a responsible way.

- A person with access to a truck and some storage space might establish a recycling service for local businesses.
- Someone with financial or investment counseling experience could easily become a consultant in environmental investing.
- An artist could create environmental gifts, a musician could create environmental recordings.

This list could go on for many pages, but the point is simple: never let your official title or degree box you in. Never assume that just because you're an "X," you'll always be an "X." A title, a job description, a degree simply captures your present position. Think about everything that your job or degree *doesn't* say about you, then tap your repertoire of "hidden" skills. That will prepare you to leap from being something to doing something. Here are some ways to expand your abilities and develop new skills and contacts.

Apprentice Yourself

On-the-job training (OJT) can be one of the best ways to learn the nitty-gritty of your proposed ecobusiness. As a plus, you can get paid for garnering information that will help you launch your own business. For example, Edwin Jason, coinventor of Squanto's Secret, took a job in a fish-processing plant, where he learned techniques for cutting fish. This proved immensely helpful in designing a system for converting fish remains into fertilizer. Paper recycler Angelus Androutsopolous worked for an established recycling firm before starting his own company. Likewise, plastic recycler Barry Shemaria spent four years working for another plastics recycling firm before starting out on his own.

Caution! If you do take the OJT route, beware of potential legal problems with your former employer. These days the courts are receptive to the arguments of companies seeking damages from former employees in whom they invest time, money, and energy—only to see that investment create archrivals. IBM, for instance, took a group of former employees to court after they quit and started a competing manufacturing operation. The courts sided with IBM, insisting that ex-IBM-ers hand over a portion of the salaries they earned while working at Big Blue. Texas Instruments also sued a group of employees who left to start Compaq Computer—although TI lost the case, and the expatriates countersued.

The issue often comes down to trade secrets. While you can't patent an idea, an employer can claim that you've stolen trade secrets. And the issue of trade secrets can come up in the oddest of circumstances. For example, when Hertz's president, Joseph Vittoria, changed driver's seats to become VP at Avis, Hertz sued its rival, claiming that trade secrets went out the door with its president.

Whether or not you win or lose in court is not the issue—the point is to *stay out* of court. Battling a former employer can consume vast amounts of time and money, and in the end won't make you a dime.

The solution? Be upfront if there's a potential conflict. In Edwin Jason's case, there was no problem; Jason's planned fish fertilizer venture in no way threatened the livelihood of the fish processor. Androutsopolous took a job with a recycler with the explicit intent of setting up a competing business. Androutsopolous told his employer of his plans, and the employer even helped Androutsopolous secure his first contracts.

Barry Shemaria also took the honest road with his employer, who insisted on a nondisclosure agreement by which Shemaria would set up shop in a different part of the state, recycling a different kind of material. Shemaria feels no regrets about the arrangement; he got paid for his training and wound up in a profitable segment of the market.

The moral? Be honest. Even if you want to risk potential legal problems by not telling your employer of your plans, consider the emotional stress of going to work each day as a potential turncoat.

Seek Out Trade Associations

Virtually every field has a trade association designed to help member companies. The plastics industry, for example, is extremely active in promoting recycling efforts, helping communities and private individuals organize recycling programs, and putting entrepreneurs in touch with brokers and other companies that will purchase plastic goods. (See page 287 for a listing of trade associations that can be useful to the ecopreneur.)

Joe Hevener and Edwin Jason began attending meetings of New England Fisheries Development Foundation (NEFDF) to learn more about the fish-processing industry. At one of the meetings they learned about an NEFDF plan for creating a fish fertilizer processing plant that would recycle the tons of dead fish that member processing companies were paying to have hauled away. Hevener and his partner used the plan as a model for a smaller-scale operation, effectively gaining a lead over potential competitors. Attending the meetings also yielded another benefit: an investor (see Chapter 3).

Join or Work for Nonprofit Groups

Today, one of the best ways to learn about environmental issues is to become a member or an employee of a nonprofit group. These organizations tend to serve as funnels for a broad array of information vital to ecopreneurs. For example, Dorian Kinder, an environmental consultant in Thetford Center, Vermont, worked for the New York Public Interest Research Group. She then became an administrator for a philanthropic organization that awards grants to environmentally responsible groups. Both experiences proved invaluable in providing her with information that she would later use as a consultant who specializes in helping people achieve a green lifestyle.

Attend Professional Conferences

More and more for-profit and private organizations and institutions are sponsoring seminars that relate to ecobusinesses. Jerome and Nora Goldstein, the publishers of *In Business*, sponsor annual conferences covering various aspects of environmental entrepreneuring, such as finding market niches, setting the right growth pace, and establishing cooperative marketing ventures. Seminars and conferences are great places to learn from other people's successes and failures. They're also excellent places to network with other ecopreneurs and experts in the field. A single conference might provide just the missing piece of information you need to make your business happen.

Ecopreneur Sally Malanga, founder of the highly successful mail-order company Ecco Bella (Caldwell, New Jersey), relied heavily on seminars and conferences to learn about the mail-order business. "The Direct Mail Marketing Association conferences were incredible learning opportunities for me, since I didn't have formal experience with direct mail," she says. "For a few hundred dollars I picked up critical information that saved me thousands in the long run—it was an instant education."

Read Key Business and Environmental Magazines

Visit your local newsstand and you'll find a number of general business and entrepreneurship magazines. It's worth flipping through these periodically; better yet, subscribe to one or two—you'll not only keep abreast of new business ideas, you'll also learn by reading about other people's successes and failures. If you're located in a larger metropolitan area, you may also find on your newsstand a variety of environmental publications. Some, like *Garbage* and *In Business*, contain a wealth of information related to ecopreneuring. Pages 295–299 lists key magazines that should be on every ecopreneur's regular reading list.

Tap the Government

Local, state, and federal government agencies can be marvelous sources of environmental information. First tap the federal government. The Environmental Protection Agency, the Fish and Wildlife Service, or other government arms might just give you the data you need for a market or feasibility study. State and local governments can also be information gold mines. If, say, you're thinking of getting into clean air consulting, you'll have to follow guidelines established by the Environmental Protection Agency and National Institute of Occupational Safety and Health. But in addition to setting up the guidelines, both agencies can provide current information about the state of the art in air pollution research.

Tap Local Experts

Scientists at local universities and colleges can be excellent sources of information, and may be willing to give you a crash course in chemistry, physics, or whatever field is related to your idea. When the inventors of Squanto's Secret is decided to modify the New England Fisheries Development Foundation plan for fish fertilizer, they tapped scientists at the University of Massachusetts for information on replacing all of the inorganic ingredients with organic ones. Interestingly, once Hevener and

Jason perfected Squanto's Secret, the university researchers returned the favor by asking *them* to supply fish fertilizer for testing in their agricultural program.

Ecopreneur Floyd Hammer (see Chapter 7) also turned to the scientific community to help him solve a pesky problem: how to provide 2 x 4 recycled plastic lumber. His agricultural customers found the plastic planking they had been buying from him to be perfect for making hog and other animal pens. The only problem was that the wooden 2 x 4's they used to hold up the planking quickly rotted. His German supplier of the plastic planking didn't have the technology to make the new 2 x 4's, so Hammer visited a British scientist, who quickly solved the problem. Today, Hammer makes his own recycled lumber, a lucrative new addition to his agricultural supply business.

Form Innovative Partnerships

These days, it is becoming more and more common for a startup business to link up with a larger, established firm. The startup brings a new technology, product, or service, as well as a fresh perspective on the marketplace, while the large firm can supply much needed capital, marketing muscle, and management expertise.

When you enter into a partnership arrangement, you must bring something to the other party in return for benefiting from that company's expertise and bankroll. As you'll learn in Chapter 3, Joe Hevener and Edwin Jason linked up with Boston-based Steve Connolly Seafoods when it came time to roll out their Squanto's Secret fertilizer on a national basis. Connolly provided a proven track record in the field, as well as the funding and overhead needed to launch a serious business.

While the logistics of joint partnerships and ventures can be tricky, they may be just the mechanism you're seeking to complement your knowledge and skill base, as well as your passion to make your product or service a success.

℘

These are but a few of the most common ways to supplement your training and experience. The key point is that there's no need to let a lack of formal training hold you back. Sometimes, in fact, a lack of formal training can even be an asset, because you don't know enough to believe that something can't be done.

As Joe Hevener put it, "If we'd gone by the books, we never would have made it. Sometimes you have to be a little ignorant of standard procedure to come up with innovations."

Chapter *Two*

Ecothink:
How to Develop Winning Ideas for Environmental Products and Services

Greener Pastures

There are two types of people in this world: those who read about a good idea and wish they'd thought of it themselves, and those who go out and top it. Since you're reading this book, you're probably (or would like to be) in the latter category. And now is a good time to start thinking about launching an ecobusiness; the environment has become a major public issue that's here to stay, and the possibilities for starting and developing successful companies are almost limitless. To succeed, however, you must pick a business that's right for you in terms of resources, skills, and geographical location. This chapter describes various techniques that you can use to zero in on the ecobusiness that best suits you.

Step 1: Think in Ecoterms

As varied as ecobusinesses may be, they all serve a common purpose: to help heal and maintain our fragile environment. To this end, all of the companies that you'll read about in this book—or find in the field—play variations on a set of core "ecothemes." Following the list below, you'll find out how to "explode" potential ecobusiness ideas into their broadest possible potential.

The Universal Themes

Ecotheme 1: Breathe new life into old trash.

According to Webster's Third International Dictionary, "trash" means "something worth relatively little or nothing." Like beauty, however, that's all in the eye of the beholder. In preindustrial society, nothing went to waste, for people consumed every part of every plant and animal or turned it into a tool or talisman. The ecopreneur can play an important role in helping our high-tech world redefine its notion of trash, in effect whisking us back to times when people couldn't imagine discarding anything. Ask yourself the question, *"What kinds of things do some people toss out that other people might be able to use?"* Then try to come up with an answer. Here are some ideas to get you started.

In recent years, recycling has become a commonplace activity in many communities. For the ecopreneur, though, recycling is anything but ho-hum; exciting possibilities abound for anyone who wants to see paper, plastic, glass, and aluminum reused rather than buried in landfills.

As explained in detail in Chapters 6 through 9, ecopreneurs can get involved in recycling many different ways. Some actually handle the recycling process. For example, Floyd Hammer's company, Hammer's Inc., started off selling agricultural products. Now, in addition, it manufactures plastic lumber for constructing animal pens. Other ecopreneurs, like Valerie Smith-Androutsopolous and her husband, Angelus Androutsopolous (Vangel Paper Company, Baltimore, Maryland) collect recyclable materials from businesses for transport to larger processors. Some ecopreneurs, like Daniel Jerrems (Atlantic Paper Company, Baltimore, Maryland) sell finished recycled goods to the public.

Others, like Douglas Turner, who runs Cancelor Corporation in Arlington, Massachusetts, have developed bin and rack systems for helping individuals and companies sort their recyclable trash, and still others, such as Lee Winder of Authentic Euthenics in San Diego, California, provide people with simple, low-cost recycling tools, such as can crushers.

But don't get boxed into thinking that only paper, glass, plastic, and aluminum can be recycled. Today, you'll find no end of opportunities, from recycling automobile tires, batteries, and used motor oil, to chlorofluorocarbons from air conditioning units. Do they pay off? Safety-Kleen Corporation, with operations in cities throughout the United States, reclaims solvents, used motor oil, and other spent fluids from 250,000 businesses. Gross sales in 1989: $478 million.

Finally, extend the idea of recycling to mundane household activities. For example, when the birthday candles have been blown out and the kids have gone home, what happens to all the wrapping paper? If it hasn't been mauled by over anxious children, it may get reused by ecologically-minded adults like Anthony Conigliaro, a manufacturing executive who, on the side, sells kits for converting wrapping and other paper into decorative envelopes through his Anthony's Originals (Natick, Massachusetts).

Ecotheme 2: Resurrect dead matter, extend the expiration date.
This ecotheme closely parallels the preceding one, in that it deals with people's perceptions of trash. But the first ecotheme involves consumption: people use a product and discard it when it no longer serves their needs (batteries, tires, or motor oil), toss out its container (beer, wine, detergent), or pitch out a part that the manufacturer designed for replacement (photocopier and laser-printer toner cartridges). In contrast, Ecotheme 2 involves reusing items consumers have given the heave-ho, either because the products have gone past their expiration date or they have lost their fashion appeal. In this case, the ecopreneur asks, *"What's heading for the dumpster that someone can reuse with little or no retooling?"* The answers can be surprising.

As sociologist-turned-ecopreneur Dan Knapp discovered, the town dump beats any library for studying people's consumption patterns. And he should know. The headquarters of the former university professor's company, Urban Ore, sits right next to the

Berkeley, California, town dump. Each day, Knapp and his employees "mine" the dump for goods that other people wanted to get out of sight, carting them to another area for display and resale. In 1990, Knapp sold approximately $800,000 worth of "discards." (As the times get tougher, Urban Ore seems to do better, which is not surprising; Urban Ore can reduce disposal costs as well as save on the purchasing end.)

At one site adjacent to the dump, customers can purchase an odd assortment of goods ranging from furniture and toys to clothing and radios. As one Urban Ore employee comments, "We have one of anything that's ever been made on this planet." The condition of the goods ranges from needing a cleanup or repair job to pristine. A second site, several blocks away, only sells building materials—doors, windows, toilets, and other fixtures removed from homes and buildings during renovations or demolitions.

Knapp's customers for finished goods vary from the poor to engineers and inventors in search of an unusual piece of metal or a particular printed circuit board. Flea market sponsors and antique dealers also frequent the site, looking for "bargain dumpster" prices. Contractors seeking inexpensive building materials often buy from Knapp's second site, too.

Urban Ore demonstrates how a clever entrepreneur can create a good business by challenging one of modern society's most cherished notions: the inalienable right to dispose of whatever we want, regardless of its condition or potential future use.

Another "mining" opportunity resides inside many laser printers. The Canon laser "engine" introduced in the early eighties represented a technological breakthrough: each time you ran out of toner, you simply inserted a new cartridge that replaced the part most likely to break down—the imaging drum. This gave the machines incredible durability and longevity.

From an environmental standpoint, however, empty toner cartridges represent a significant waste; each cartridge consists of a heavy plastic case, a metal drum, and various gears. Given the millions of laser printers currently in service, this adds up to a lot of waste. In fact, according to some experts, 15 million toner cartridges hit the dumps annually, enough to stretch a quarter of the way around the world.

In response to the problem, some ecopreneurs have pioneered the art of toner cartridge remanufacturing. People interested in the service can, for example, send their exhausted cartridges to Brian Chaney and Marvin Masson's Advantage Laser Products (Tuscaloosa, Alabama). For a fee, Advantage will remanufacture the spent cartridges and return them to the owners (the company receives about 800 cartridges a month). The cost for the whole process is generally less than half that of buying a new cartridge. The company will also buy empty cartridges, which can be cannibalized for parts. With this arrangement, everyone wins, especially the environment.

Ecotheme 3: Find a new home for scrap.

This theme focuses on using by-products previously deemed worthless. In traditional manufacturing processes, some unusable scrap inevitably occurs. Or so the conventional wisdom goes. But in fact, many "by-products" can be turned into "real products." All it takes is an ability to think in terms of "ecological processing." The ecopreneur asks, *"Who's tossing out babies with the bathwater?"* Answers start coming quickly.

One industry's scrap may be an ecopreneur's treasure. Take Squanto's Secret fish fertilizer. Squanto's is made from "scraps" that fish processors once considered worthless—they discard about 70 percent of the catch, incurring a significant cost to do so. Squanto's Secret uses 100 percent of these remains (fins, scales, and all), proving that it's worthwhile to take a fresh look at old definitions of scrap.

Some ecopreneurs are making a living buying woodchips from lumber companies and then selling them to power companies as fuel. Others turn sludge from municipal sewer systems into high-grade fertilizer. An ecopreneurial wing of the Milwaukee Sewer District, the Milorganite Division, has been doing just that since 1926. Each year the division generates 60,000 tons of "Milorganite," sludge that's been dried, sanitized, and pelletized, selling $10 million worth of the high-grade fertilizer to municipalities, golf courses, and individuals annually.

For the ecopreneur who wants to keep his or her hands a bit cleaner, there's always the possibility of collecting yard waste. The raw materials for a yard-waste composting company are free, and you'll do your town a favor—yard wastes make up 20 percent of the "trash" collected each week in America's cities.

Finally, think about recycling food waste. Every day, garbage collectors pick up tons of food from America's curbsides and deposit it into dump sites. By the time food reaches our curbs, it's almost certainly beyond reconstitution for human consumption. But to enterprising ecobusinesses like Top Soil Inc., today's food wastes can become tomorrow's soil conditioners.

Another possibility for recycling food waste has been demonstrated by Louis Wichinsky, who tinkered with his VW Rabbit so it will run on vegetable oil. His best source? The spent fry oil from fast-food joints, which he can usually get for free. Although Wichinsky has not marketed his conversion device, it proves that even the most apparently spent material can be given a new life if someone is willing to apply some brainpower and elbow grease.

Ecotheme 4: Eliminate the offending agent.

In the early seventies, we became deeply concerned about the harmful effects of various additives and components in common household and food items. Interest and concern in the subject waxed and waned throughout the late seventies and eighties as the public seemed to grow weary of all the bad news.

Now, in the nineties, with the environment weighing heavily on people's minds, harmful chemicals once again make headlines. Consumers are demanding products free of unnecessary or toxic components, and they're insisting on products packaged sensibly. To meet these demands, the ecopreneur asks, *"What common items can I reformulate to make them safer to use and easier to dispose of?"* The answers have already initiated some interesting businesses.

Until 1989, the terms "green product" and "environment-friendly product" were novel. Today, they're a part of our daily language. A stroll through the grocery or natural-food store will reveal a growing number of items that stand out because of their positive environmental qualities—recycled packaging, biodegradable contents, formulated without hazardous chemicals, etc.

The demand for green products will continue to rise throughout the nineties, creating a vast array of opportunities for those who wish to produce and/or market environment-friendly items for home and business use.

Some large consumer product manufacturers offer green products, but so do a host of small-scale businesses. Sally Malanga, for example, the president and founder of Ecco Bella, runs a leading mail-order company that produces a complete line of environment-friendly personal-care products. Started from her kitchen table, the company has won national recognition for its environmentally safe product line.

Likewise, Allen Conlon's company, Allen's Naturally (Farmington, Michigan), sells a complete line of nontoxic and safe cleaning products, from all-purpose cleaners to glass cleansers and dishwashing detergents.

Yet another ecopreneur, Kevin Harper, founded Autumn Harp (Bristol, Vermont), which offers, among other items, a complete set of baby-care products, including the Unpetroleum Jelly, a biodegradable moisturizer with a vegetable oil base. Also for the nursery, Becky Kubota's Family Club House Inc., (Asheville, North Carolina) manufactures Dovetails, a truly disposable paper diaper designed to be used with a diaper cover (parents can purchase them from mail-order outfits like Cynthia Van Buren's Baby Bunz in Sebastopol, California).

For the workshop enthusiast, Nester Noe's AFM Enterprises (Riverside, California) offers a variety of adhesives and glues, while Livos PlantChemistry (Santa Fe, New Mexico—the U.S. division of a 15-year-old German company) provides home owners with an alternative to petroleum-based and synthetic products.

Safer Products (Newton, Massachusetts) has introduced a number of environmentally safe fertilizer and pest control products for the gardener and home owner. Even pet owners can benefit from the green product revolution: some ecobusinesses, like Nature's Gate (Chatsworth, California), offer complete lines of shampoos and flea-control and other environmentally safe pet products.

The list of ecobusinesses that produce environment-friendly products could go on for many pages; the point is that proven opportunities and outlets abound for anyone who wants to offer the world a greener way of consuming.

As a complement to the production of green products, opportunities exist for selling and distributing green products through mail-order and retail outlets. The most well-known and successful startup in this field, Seventh Generation, in Colchester, Vermont, presents an extensive array of environmentally safe products, some under its own label, some from other companies. To meet a growing demand for the products, Seventh Generation has also opened a retail store.

Other ecopreneurs going the green retail route include Annabelle Ship, who owns and operates The Green Planet (Newton, Massachusetts), an outlet for environmentally sound products for the home and garden, and Charles Hugus, owner of Earthwise (Charlottesville, Virginia). The opportunities for such outlets will expand as consumers become ever more aware of the need for safer and saner options.

Is "organic" just for health-food nuts? Hardly. Although the idea of organic (pesticide-free) farming has been around for years, it has taken on new meaning in this age of heightened environmental consciousness. Organic farming now means "Earthwise" farming. Runoff of pesticides is a major cause of water pollution, and many experts also believe that they lead to cancer and other diseases. This boosts the appeal of organic food to supermarket shoppers.

Today, hundreds of ecopreneurs have plunged into the business of growing and distributing organic foods to supermarkets and specialty-food stores. One company with a unique niche is Earth's Best, which produces organic baby foods. Though a fraction of the size of such giant companies as Gerber and Beechnut, Earth's Best is gaining tremendous momentum. The company grossed $1 million in sales in its first full year of operation, 1988, and reached $5 million in the second. For 1991, annual sales were estimated at $10 million. The market for organic baby food is estimated to be more than $100 million a year, and Earth's Best is poised to become an industry leader, proving that the ecopreneur can succeed even when faced with well-entrenched and well-financed competition.

"Peanuts, popcorn!" Today the age-old cry heard for decades at ballparks around the country has taken on new meaning at Steve Sommer's Alexander Fruit and Trading Company (Geyserville, California), which grows A1 (highly expandable) corn kernels and then pops it—not for consumption, but for use as an alternate to plastic "peanuts" used as a packing material. The main advantage of this product, "Future Pop," is that it solves a major environmental problem—just feed it to the squirrels when you're done with it.

Buoyed by the success of Future Pop, the sales of which are sufficient to fund a plant in the San Jose area, Sommer cofounded Ecological Agricultural Systems, Inc., which has developed a line of 100 percent biodegradable packaging products made from plant material. Sommer's goal is to deal with products that go "dust to dust"—"We want to be selling products that start in the earth and end there, too," he says.

Ecotheme 5: Be a tiebreaker.

Despite the widespread interest in environmental issues, little consensus has formed on many issues, such as energy, solid-waste management, pesticides, and other controversial topics. But while the debates rage on, some ecopreneurs have already begun offering alternative solutions. When weighing the issues, ecopreneurs ask, *"What's the alternative course?"* Then they strike out on that course with a vengeance.

Environmentalists, policy experts, legislators, and various academic pundits continue to argue about the pros and cons of different energy sources and our dependency on foreign oil. But ecopreneur John Schaeffer didn't wait around for definitive solutions; he took action by producing and selling alternative energy devices. As a result, Schaeffer's Real Goods Trading Company has become the largest mail-order supplier of alternative energy products in the country. Other ecopreneurs develop and sell water conservation devices, solar heating panels, insulation kits, energy-efficient light bulbs, and various products designed to conserve energy.

When the grocery store clerk asks whether you want a paper bag or a plastic bag, what should you say? "Neither"—and you simply unfold your canvas or string bag. Paper doesn't degrade in landfills any faster than plastic, and paper bags may require more energy to make in the first place. Plastics, on the other hand, are not made from a renewable resource.

Grocery tote bags have been popular in Europe, South America, and other parts of the world for decades, especially in places where paper or plastic bags aren't even an option. Now they're coming into vogue in the United States. Peggy and Malcolm Carlaw's company, Blue Rhubarb (Harmony, California), manufacturer of the EcoSac, demonstrates that if you make a better bag, green consumers will beat a path to your door.

Ecotheme 6: Give a product or service a green twist.

Most positive environmental action comes from reevaluating and adjusting mundane activities—the way we cook, shop, wash clothes, take a shower, etc. Similarly, many ecopreneurs look about the day-to-day world and ask, *"What traditional services can I perform with the environment in mind?"* Their answers have spawned whole new industries.

Grocery delivery services have been around since the days of the first general stores, and even today, people too busy or too infirm to do their own shopping often rely on grocery-shopping services to bring food to their tables. Gregg Plympton's Express Lane (North Palm Beach, Florida) adds a new dimension to the delivery concept by selecting environment-friendly food, housewares, and personal-care products for its customers in addition to more traditional items. Express Lane also collects used plastic grocery bags for recycling and spotlights goods packaged in recycled paper to encourage people to buy "green."

Automobile service stations generally do not score high marks for their environmental consciousness, but Jeff Shumway is trying to change that situation. His Ecotech Autoworks (McLean, Virginia) serves as a collection point for used motor oil, as well as other automotive fluids that shouldn't wind up in the sewer or dump. He also recycles chlorofluorocarbons from automotive air-conditioning units. With more ecopreneurs like Shumway, the automobile may become just a little bit less of an environmental menace.

Finally, there's nothing new about investment advisory services. But "green" investing has become hot, with ecopreneurs like Carsten Heningsen (Portland, Oregon) and Joel Diskin (Birmingham, Michigan) helping people decide which stocks deserve investor support, on the basis of environmental track records.

Ecotheme 7: Satisfy an information-hungry world.

The old saw "Information is power" certainly rings true in the environmental arena. The more people know about the environment, about environmentally safe products and alternatives, and about the role each individual can play in helping to clean up the globe, the better our chances are for a bright green future.

Professionals, too, always need concise, quality information and the writer, researcher, or scientist who follows the field may be in the best position to fill the niche. Ecopreneurs promote the good fight by asking, *"What information holes can I fill?"* And they communicate their answers swiftly.

Not everyone who wants to do something positive for the environment can make it as an ecopreneur; some people need the security of a regular paycheck. To assist those who want to work in the environmental field, Gail Becker offers her weekly *Job Finder* (Grand Rapids, Michigan), which lists more than 2,000 jobs in areas ranging from forestry to hazardous waste management.

How do oil spill experts keep up with oil spill news? And how do hazardous waste experts keep abreast of developments in their field? By reading Richard Golob's *Oil Pollution Bulletin* and *Hazardous Materials Intelligence Report*. Both newsletters "crunch" large volumes of legislative and technical information into digestible form.

Opportunities also crop up for enterprising writers to start newsletters and magazines geared to individuals. Debra Dade, for example, publishes *The EarthWise Consumer* (Los Angeles), dedicated to exploring nontoxic alternatives for the home. In the magazine arena, Patricia Poore launched *Garbage: The Practical Journal for the Environment*. Will people really buy something with a title like *Garbage?* The numbers speak for themselves: a scheduled printing of 50,000 copies for the first issue quickly ballooned into a run of 126,000 copies to meet demand. Since then, the magazine has gone on to become a nationally acclaimed source of environmental information.

Ecotheme 8: Educate, entertain, ecotain!

Healing the planet will take more than adopting a green lifestyle—it requires a massive reeducation effort. Adults need to learn how seemingly mundane activities can have a major impact on the environment, and how simple adjustments in their daily living can produce beneficial effects. Children need to be taught good environmental habits so they develop an environmental consciousness early in life. The ecopreneur can educate through books and magazine articles, as well as through recreational activities that promote environmental awareness. The ecopreneur, knowing that "all the world's a school," asks *How can I creatively present environmental issues?"* The answers often entertain as much as they inform.

In an earlier stage of his career, Mark Baker imported tropical hardwoods from South America. But after spending years on the "frontier" in logging camps, he concluded that deforestation was indeed creating an emergency, so he closed his doors and began searching for ways to use his knowledge of the industry and Brazil's resources to do something positive. As a result, he founded Ecotours (Cambridge, Massachusetts), which takes groups of tourists on expeditions to tropical forests, where scientist-guides explain the ecology of rain forests. With this approach, Baker hopes to give people better insights into how tropical forests work and what can be done to preserve them.

What would happen if the greenhouse effect progressed unabated, if we deforested the entire continent of South America or if all developed countries ran out of landfill space? Now, anyone with a personal computer can find out for themselves by booting up Chris Crawford's "Balance of the Planet," a software program that allows users to simulate the fate of the earth by comparing various scenarios for the wise or foolish use of natural resources. According to Crawford, the program educates and entertains and, most important, gets people to understand that their decisions and actions can tip the scales in favor of improving the planet's future.

The Pyramid of Opportunities

Regardless of which ecotheme interests you, you'll want to find a niche that matches your resources, skills, and talents. This entails going from the most obvious and specific types of business that satisfy a particular ecotheme to the less obvious businesses that may represent more creative and far-reaching opportunities. To begin the process, draw a pyramid. The top of the pyramid represents a narrowly focused activity. As you move down toward the base, the ideas become more generalized, with more and more varied opportunities.

Let's apply this model to recycling. At the very pinnacle, we have isolated a precisely defined activity: reconstituting material A into material B. This generally involves some kind of manufacturing process, which, in turn, requires a large capital investment. It also means that companies already in the industry—paper mills, glass manufacturers, etc.—are best set up to handle the job. Therefore, if we only consider recycling from a standpoint of material transformation, we're looking at a limited number of opportunities for business startups.

But now let's drop down a level to some of the activities that support the actual processing of materials: the collection of recyclable materials, the sale of recyclable materials to processors, and the sale of recycled materials to other businesses and the public. Most notably, you can start businesses revolving around these sorts of activities with considerably less capital; to collect paper, glass, and other material from businesses, all you need is a truck and some storage space.

Finally, move down to the bottom of the pyramid, which contains simple business ideas that entail preparing materials for the middle-level ecopreneur. Business activities at the base level of the pyramid might include the construction and sale of bins and racks for organizing recyclable materials in the home or business, or the sale of can crushers and other devices for conserving recycling space.

As you can see from the foregoing analysis, we've gone considerably beyond the limited concept of recycling as a materials transformation business to recycling as an umbrella for a wide variety of activities, including transportation, brokering, storage furniture, and household appliances.

To carve out a niche for yourself, you can apply the same kind of thinking to any ecotheme. Whether you actually draw a pyramid or simply envision one, you'll engage in the same sort of analysis: break down specific activities until you have developed a complete hierarchy. Then pick one that appeals to you personally and represents a good match to your current resources.

Once you've begun thinking in terms of the universal ecothemes, you'll begin to see the world through green-colored lenses. Next you'll want to focus those lenses on the rich opportunities that surround each and every one of us. The following steps will help you do so.

Step 2: Perceive the World as an Ecopreneur

Ecopreneurs, like all entrepreneurs, see the world a little differently than the average person, instantly clicking on opportunities for satisfying one of the ecothemes. If you keep your eyes open you can begin to see a rich array of ecopreneurial opportunities in the course of your daily life.

Extrapolate from Your Personal Needs

Entrepreneurs in general, and ecopreneurs in particular, take note every time they say to themselves: "I wish I had an X, Y, or Z." The reasoning is simple: if you need a certain kind of widget or a product formulated or packaged in a particular way, others will too. Many green product companies started from the founder's dissatisfaction with existing products and services. Sally Malanga started Ecco Bella because she simply couldn't find the kinds of cleaning and personal-care products that met her environmental standards. After formulating them for herself, she realized that many other people shared her needs, and thus expanded a personal need into a thriving ecobusiness.

Similarly, Annabelle Ship wanted to find household products that wouldn't trigger her own allergic reactions. After locating green product makers who could meet her needs, she opened The Green Planet (Newton, Massachusetts), a retail store where customers can find a wide assortment of environment-friendly products for the home and yard.

Explore Your Own Backyard

Often, an excellent idea for an ecobusiness is lurking in your backyard or nearby—just follow your senses. Joe Hevener and Edwin Jason, makers of Squanto's Secret fish fertilizer, literally followed their noses one day to the edge of a pier where they found a mountain of fish remains. The person who normally got rid of the "garbage" had lost his disposal license, so the fish had sat there reeking for days. That experience catalyzed the two ecopreneurs into finding a way of making use of otherwise undesirable by-products.

Pay Attention to the "Cultural Media"

For example, the budding ecopreneur gets a balanced "cultural media diet," consuming all types of print and electronic publications. After learning about the problems with paper and plastic bags through various radio, television, and newspaper stories, David Ferry wanted to do his part by purchasing canvas tote bags. When he couldn't find any in his local area, he decided to get into the bag business himself. Today, Ferry runs Earth Bags Ltd. (Leesburg, Virginia) with the help of the Industries for the Blind, through its industrial-work sewing program.

General News Publications

Read at least one major daily, scan a weekly news magazine, and flip on the radio or television around news time to get a sense about public sentiments and trends. National Public Radio is an especially useful source of information and ideas, since its programming tends to include in-depth examination of issues relevant to the environment. How can such news watching benefit the ecopreneur? Many ecobusinesses got off the ground after the media reported on various polls demonstrating that the environment was rapidly becoming the Number 1 issue on the minds of Americans.

Pay attention to advertisements, too. On August 29, 1989, Wal-Mart ran a full-page ad in *The Wall Street Journal*, calling for manufacturers to join the company in a campaign to provide customers with environmentally safe products. This, too, sent a strong signal that middle America was ready to join the green product revolution.

Environmental and Technical Publications

The ecopreneur should regularly read the key environmental publications listed on pages 296–299 in Part IV of this book. Keep your eyes and ears peeled for new scientific discoveries with entrepreneurial potential. For example, when major environmental and scientific publications began reporting on the widening ozone hole in the atmosphere, forward-looking ecopreneurs seized upon opportunities to recycle chlorofluorocarbons—one of the major threats to the ozone layer—from air-conditioning and refrigeration equipment.

Also be on the lookout for new legislation that can lead to environmental opportunities. So-called "market development legislation" is designed to stimulate markets for recycled materials, such as glass. A number of states have accomplished such legislation by requiring manufacturers to use a certain percentage of recycled glass in their bottles. Some laws also provide tax incentives for companies that use recycled goods. If you stay on top of the legislative scene in your community and state, you may be able to turn a vote into a business.

Trade Magazines

Every industry association publishes a trade magazine that reports on trends, events, new products, who's who, and other topics of interest to people in the field. A trip to a well-stocked business library will reveal such titles as *Beverage World*, *Cemetery Management*, and a host of others.

These magazines can prove invaluable to the ecopreneur, because they often contain gems about an industry you are not likely to find anywhere else. You might learn about a pressing environmental issue in a certain industry, or a new technology that can help resolve long-standing environmental problems for small businesses or consumers.

Browse through the "trades" every six months or so just to see what's happening—you might just find the spark for a new business.

Step 3: Test the Idea, Assess the Competition

After stumbling on an idea for an ecobusiness, you must give it the acid test: sleep on it. If the idea still feels right the next morning, there are several questions you should ask yourself.

Are There Any Precedents?

This cuts both ways. If yes, then you'd better be sure that you can compete effectively. If no, don't throw a victory celebration yet—there may be a good reason why no one has done it. Either the market may be too small, or technical or legislative constraints may make it unfeasible. If the business involves an engineering or chemical preparation, check with an engineer or chemist. If the business might pose large or hidden liabilities, check with a lawyer. If it involves numerous permits, check with local and state officials. With any idea, look for the potential hurdles that may render it too difficult to implement profitably.

Is There a Market for the Product or Service?

You need only one thing to start a business: customers. You can hit upon the greatest idea in the world and enjoy plentiful startup capital and a superb sales organization, but if there's no market for your product, you won't stay in business very long.

Conduct an informal market test by asking friends and relatives if they'd buy a certain product or service, without letting on it's yours (that might bias the answers either way). If you're marketing a single product, contact local distributors and retailers to get their reaction. If you're marketing a service, contact an association to see what they have to say. Perhaps you're thinking of starting a "green" travel service. An association of travel agencies might be able to help you determine whether there's enough of a market in your area.

Remember, just because your cause is noble, don't assume that the world will flock to your mailbox or storefront. The more you pretest your idea on potential customers and experts, the more you'll avoid making costly mistakes.

Whom Are You Competing Against?

A common illusion among entrepreneurs is that "no one else could be doing what I'm going to do," or that "if they are, they aren't doing it as well as I will." This kind of thinking will almost always get you into trouble. Again, no ecobusiness is immune from the basic principles of entrepreneurship. Sure, every town should have a green products store, but can your particular market support two? Three? Four? If you enter a crowded marketplace in which customers feel relatively satisfied already, you'll be fighting an uphill battle; if you do survive, you may simply dilute the market for everyone.

Finally, get a second opinion. Bounce your idea off a businessperson you respect or someone from SCORE (Service Corps of Retired Executives). Even if you're planning a solo operation, you can't possibly maintain an objective position all the time; after all, your *passion* to help the environment motivates you, and by definition, passion often defies the rational. Therefore, the wise ecopreneur befriends or hires an adviser before planning a grand opening.

Step 4: Put It on Paper

Most entrepreneurs assemble a business plan because they need it to secure funding (see Chapter 3). But even if you're only starting with a credit-card line or the money in your savings account, you still should create a business plan. Even a sketchy one will help you spot holes in your logic or areas that need more careful thought. Whether you use a high-powered desktop publishing system to create a spiffy-looking plan (probably a waste of time) or scratch out your plan on the back of an envelope (probably a bit too loose), make sure you cover the following elements:

Mission: What will the new business do, and why does the world need it?

Market: Who will buy your products or services from the company (demographics)?
How big is the market?
How much will it grow?

Pricing: What will you charge for your products or services?

Competition: Who are your competitors and how successful are they?
What are your competitors' strengths and weaknesses (e.g., pricing, sales, service, support)?

Operations: What overhead (office space, equipment, employees, etc.) will you need to get started?
How will your product be manufactured and distributed, or your services be sold?

Budget: How much will it cost to launch and operate your business?
When will you break even?
When will you get into the black?
What is your projected annual growth rate?

Diversification: What spin-off products and services might you develop?

Most experts on business planning would encourage you to perform this exercise for a five-year period, sketching both best- and worst-case scenarios. Your actual success will probably lie somewhere in the middle and take longer than you imagine.

જ્જ

If you possess little or no business experience, you might want to read one or more of the excellent books listed in the "Basic Business Bibliography" (see page 285). Testing an idea, homing in on a market, and gathering competitive intelligence can make all the difference for any entrepreneurial venture. As you've seen throughout this book, your good intentions will not prevent you from fatal mistakes. If you follow the rules of sound business, though, your good intentions stand an excellent chance of turning into a profitable enterprise. The following chapter covers the art and science of funding an ecobusiness, the next step in turning your dream into a reality.

Chapter *Three*

Bankrolling an Ecobusiness: *How to Find Capital for Startup and Growth*

Many people's dreams of starting a business go up in smoke after they get burned by their inability to raise capital for starting or expanding their operation. Ironically, money is usually the smallest impediment to starting a business, as we'll soon see. If you have hit upon a great idea, you can probably find a way to make it work, despite your seemingly limited cash resources.

Some ecobusinesses will, by nature, require more capital than others. At one end of the spectrum, starting a plastics-processing plant requires several hundred thousand dollars. At the other, you can start a business that collects and sells paper to recyclers with little more than a $500 used van. Likewise, a hazardous waste cleanup company can entail millions in startup costs, while a low-budget salvage company only needs a beat-up truck and some space to display its wares.

If you don't have extensive resources, you'll want to focus on business ideas that don't require large investments for inventory or equipment, overhead, staff, and other big-ticket items. But if you do need money to grow your business, don't immediately turn to the obvious source, the bank; first consider all the alternative sources of funds.

Alternatives for Finding Cash

Invest Brains, Not Bucks

When personal computers first began dotting the desks of offices throughout the country, an enterprising fellow (who prefers to remain anonymous) realized that the new machines would generate an unprecedented volume of confidential financial data. So he went out to start a security-tight data shredding service for banks and other institutions. This entrepreneur could have tried to secure the funds needed for state-of-the-art shredding equipment, a classy office and lavish warehouse space, not to mention a fleet of new Mercedes trucks to serve his customers. Such an approach could have cost him a bundle (and given his lack of assets and business experience, it's doubtful that anyone would have invested a dime in his vision).

Instead, he went to the junkyard, where he spent a mere $35 for a contraption that, with a bit of cleanup and tinkering, would do the job, albeit not as efficiently or quietly as a brand-new, high-tech shredding device. Next, he looked around town for a small company whose panel trucks were idle on the weekends and quickly found a trucking service that was all too glad to let him use a vehicle for only $25 per Saturday, plus gas.

With his makeshift shredder in his garage and his weekend truck ready for action, he visited various banks in the area to plug his services. Those who signed on gave him a two-month deposit, enough to keep gas in the truck and food on his table while the business got going. Within two years, he commanded the entire data-shredding market in his metropolitan area.

What's the difference between the two approaches to funding? P-R-O-F-I-T. Moreover, this entrepreneur took all the time and energy he could have wasted making a formal pitch for money and invested it, instead, in actually rounding up customers and satisfying their needs.

Oh, yes, he gave the business a green twist, making himself an official ecopreneur—he sells the shredded paper to a recycler, adding additional revenues to his growing company.

The data shredder's approach should serve as a model for *all* ecopreneurs. Even if your business does require startup capital for manufacturing, marketing, or distribution functions, you can always find ways to start off with little or no cash.

Consider how Joe Hevener and Edwin Jason started their fish fertilizer business. The original plan they obtained from New England Fisheries Development Foundation called for $1 million worth of processing equipment, far beyond what either of the two ecopreneurs could afford. So they took the sensible road, scaling back the plans to a garage-sized operation. Instead of investing in an expensive industrial-grade fish grinder, for example, they bought a simple hand-powered meat grinder. (They earlier discovered, to the dismay of Hevener's wife, that mackerel remains will destroy a conventional kitchen blender in a matter of minutes.) Similarly, instead of a 1,000-gallon vat, they started off with a 10-gallon pot.

Rather than beating the bushes for cash, Hevener and Jason spent their valuable time working within their means, quickly and efficiently developing their product to the point where they could convert to a larger-scale operation. This became possible when the two linked up with the largest fish processor in New England, Steve Connolly Seafood, which provided space and equipment for the venture (see page 55). We'll talk more about the mechanics of such joint partnerships later in this chapter.

Personal Savings and Outside Cash

After creatively eliminating or reducing as many costs as possible, you may still need additional cash, which means turning to the outside world. Some people prefer to invest their own money and retain full control over their businesses. Jill Matlack and her husband, Jim, used their own means to found Matlack Environmental Services (Durham, North Carolina), which required $100,000 in startup capital for recycling equipment. Now that the company has grown, the Matlacks, seeking additional funding for expansion, will turn to outside resources.

Sally Malanga also launched her highly successful green products mail-order company, Ecco Bella, with personal funds, as did Mark Baker, the founder of Ecotours. Wanting to retain control over their companies, they took the risks associated with putting their savings on the line.

If that sort of personal risk bothers you, consider tapping outside sources of cash. That way, your house, car, and other possessions won't be on the line. You may have an important idea that can help save the planet, the underlying logic may be sound, the timing may be right, the marketplace and competitive arenas may be favorable, and the economy may be conducive—but you still may feel reluctant to put your assets at risk.

Does using other people's cash get you off the hook? No—the goal of using outside cash isn't to shun your responsibilities. If you borrow money and the business flops, you may well want to pay it back. But at least you can do so at a pace that won't place an excessive burden on you and your family. And you'll still have the nest egg that you've set aside for emergencies or your children's education.

Outside cash can come from many sources: money from relatives and friends; credit from customers, clients, and suppliers; customer investments; bank loans; and venture capital. Let's take a look at each one.

Tapping Family and Friends for Cash

Do relations and money mix well? That depends. Some entrepreneurs have enjoyed very positive experiences. Charles Hugus, for example, approached a group of his friends, acquaintances, and local folk with a letter soliciting money to fund his green products retail store, Earthwise, in Charlottesville, Virginia. For each $100 that the investors put into the store, they received a coupon for $120 worth of merchandise, provided that they didn't redeem it for 90 days. After 120 days, it was worth $130 in merchandise. Hugus personally guaranteed each investment, and submitted an audited statement along with his solicitation letters. Besides raising the $10,000 in startup capital Hugus needed to open Earthwise, the funding arrangement generated invaluable publicity and word-of-mouth referrals, giving the business an additional jump start.

Not all "friendly financing" arrangements work out so well. In a worst case, a failed business can result in the loss of longstanding relationships. Here are a few points to consider before accepting a check from a friend or loved one:

- *Are your friends or relatives playing with "match money"?* In other words, could they afford to hold a lighted match to the sum of money involved and watch it go up in smoke without undue anxiety? Sometimes friends and relatives are eager to help out but don't understand the risks involved—you have said the idea will work and they trust you. But what if the money involved constituted their own retirement fund or nest egg?

- *How would friends or relatives react in the event of a disaster?* Could you face your lenders if you failed and lost their money? Would these relationships be shattered? If so, don't borrow that money. In our short span of time on this earth, nothing is more valuable than a few loving human relationships, so protect them at all costs.

- *Do the funds come with hidden strings attached?* Even if your friends or relatives will gladly lend you the money and you don't fail, do they expect either tangible or invisible interest rates? Will you become subservient in some subtle ways? If you borrow from your parents, will you be reduced in some fashion to an adult child? Will you have to kowtow for the rest of your life? If you know the personalities, you'll know the answer to questions like these. If you don't know them well enough to answer yes or no definitively, then don't ask for a loan—money can liberate all sorts of monsters that can make life miserable for everyone involved.

A variation of the borrowing theme entails bringing family and friends into the business. This proposition tends to evoke a variety of responses. Some people say that working with friends or kin gives them great joy. They explain that the trust among family members can never be matched by unrelated partners, and that the bonds that hold the family together ensure that the business will weather the toughest of storms.

Others find that working with a spouse or family member has some negative aspects. Jill Matlack, who works closely with her husband, finds that their relationship helps bring out their complementary skills. But it also makes it difficult to separate their work life from their home life. The best part of working with a spouse, she says, is sharing a vision and set of goals for the business.

At the other extreme, family businesses can turn into vicious civil wars, brother against brother, father against son, husband against wife, friend against friend. The history of business is fraught with examples of mothers who fired sons; sons who fired fathers; and brothers who parted as bitter enemies.

Will it work for you? Rely on your judgment and apply the "least-doubt" principle: if you harbor the slightest doubt as to whether an arrangement with family or friends will work, avoid it—the potential risks far outweigh the possible rewards.

Getting Credit from Customers, Clients, and Suppliers

Your customers, clients, and suppliers can help float your business during the critical early stages. For example, you can ask for advance deposits on your goods and services. The entrepreneur who started the data-shredding service did just that, collecting for two months' worth of service in advance. Since the cost was not great for such a commitment, his customers easily advanced the money.

You can take the same approach with any ecobusiness. If you're selling an environmental newsletter or publication, or a new kind of environment-friendly product through the mail, take prepublication or advance orders (careful, though, the Federal Trade Commission says you have to come up with goods within six weeks of taking someone's money in advance). Similarly, if you're running an environmental consulting service, try to work out retainers with your clients so they're paying on the first of each month for a certain number of your hours. However you collect advance payments, bear in mind that you have to use the money to provide the goods or services that you've promised; if you sink the advance payments into your salary or the purchase of equipment that won't immediately fulfill your obligation, you'll soon be back on the road looking for other sources of outside cash.

Finally, not all funding comes in the form of hard cash—suppliers can, in effect, make you a loan by giving you more favorable terms. If your business plan for a green products retail store looks solid and you can make a strong case for its future profitability, you may be able to work out an arrangement under which you pay for goods in 60 days, instead of 30 days or COD. Perhaps you can work out a better discount rate—a break at 10 units instead of 25. What does the supplier get out of it? Answer: Suppliers want to keep you loyal and watch your business grow so you will buy more from them later on. If they believe in your capabilities, they face a win-win situation; they'll help you get off the ground and create more business for themselves in the process.

Frookies Corporation, which pioneered the "cookie you'd give your kids," has developed an interesting variation on the supplier-credit theme. Frookie distributors and suppliers were sold shares of the fledgling company, generating cash and, at the same time, creating a strong incentive for everyone to get the product on the supermarket shelves.

Seeking Grants

State grants and foundations represent another potential source of money for ecopreneurs. Many states have instituted low-interest loan programs for ecopreneurs who get involved with recycling businesses. Pennsylvania sponsors the Environmental Technology Loan Fund, Illinois the Recycling Grants Program. Many foundations, too, have established special programs for ecobusinesses. You may find, though, that some grants programs apply only to nonprofit organizations.

Borrowing Money from the Bank

Banks represent one of the great paradoxes of the business world: most will give you money only if you don't need it. In other words, if you have sufficient collateral, they'll be glad to lend you funds. Also, banks do not normally like to take risks, so they may be willing to lend you money only if you bring in a cosigner with a strong credit rating and sufficient assets.

If the bank is your only option for funding your ecobusiness, consider the following maneuvers.

- **Get a track record**. If you've never borrowed money from a bank, take out a personal loan for $200 or $300, or whatever the bank will give you. Pay it back the next day to reduce interest charges. With your excellent record, you can probably go back and borrow $500 or $1,000. Pay that sum back immediately, too. Keep doing this; and you'll eventually be able to take a sizable personal loan, which you can in turn lend to your company (make sure you document all your transactions and charge your business equivalent bank rates to keep the IRS happy). Bear in mind that you're still taking out a personal loan, and your assets may well be at risk if you default, even if the company swallowed the cash.

- **Provide hard numbers**. Bankers read statements from the bottom up. The numbers will set the tone for the rest of the discussion. Provide realistic projections that document your assumptions. Present a solid business plan that shows exactly how you will achieve your targets, and why your plan will work. The plan should also generate confidence in you as an ecopreneur—as someone who can make it happen and succeed even when the chips are down.

- **Develop a personal rapport with your banker**. Even though bank officers may act like aloof number crunchers, they're people, too, with families and feelings. Whenever you go to borrow money, visit the same officer. Get to know the officer personally—ask about his or her family and personal life. Show the officer what you're doing—bring in samples of your products, your ads or brochures. Get the person emotionally involved with you and your activities. If you have an office, an invitation to tour it—even if it's only one room—will help. No, you're not transparently bribing the bank officer but substantiating your work and capabilities; if the numbers are teetering on the margin, the officer's personal knowledge of you may be the deciding factor in swinging things in your favor. Ultimately, you want the banker to feel like a partner, so that the issue becomes not one of: "Will you give me X dollars," but "How can we work together to make this business grow?"

- **Don't just mail in a loan application**. Make an appointment to give a brief presentation, summarized with a few charts and graphs. While the banker will no doubt want to review the numbers and possibly confer with colleagues, that final little personal touch and burst of enthusiasm will set the review process on a positive track.

An indirect way of borrowing from the bank involves drawing advances on your credit cards. These days, even people considered to be high credit risks are bombarded with solicitations for preapproved credit cards with high limits, and most banks are eager to give them to those who apply and come close to their criteria. Be aware, though, that "plastic financing" is risky; if the business doesn't perform as you expect, you may be saddled with huge monthly payments at onerous interest rates. And if you miss even a single scheduled payment, it will go into your credit history. If you go 60 or 90 days past due—or worse, default—your record may become permanently scarred. Therefore, only use plastic financing in the following circumstances:

1. When you need a small supplemental loan that you know you can repay in the next three to six months.

2. When you need to purchase inventory that you are sure will move within 30 days of hitting your shelf.

3. When you need to acquire a piece of equipment that will pay for itself fast enough to generate the monthly payments plus interest.

Never use plastic to:

1. Meet payroll.

2. Carry you through a down period of six months or more.

3. Pay for basic capital investments (chairs, desks, etc) that will never pay for themselves in any tangible way.

Turning Customers into Investors

Every successful new venture passes through three phases of natural evolution. The first phase, the startup phase, is the most critical. In the next phase, growth will happen naturally if the business gets on the right track. The third phase, expansion, usually requires an infusion of cash—the business typically can't afford to diversify or increase its base solely on its current revenue stream.

The third phase is where customer offerings can come in quite handy, as John Schaeffer discovered when his alternative energy product firm, Real Goods Trading Company (Ukiah, California) needed to raise cash in order to build its inventory. In 1986, Real Goods, a mail-order operation, generated sales of $80,000. By 1989, annual sales had jumped to more than $2 million. But the company's inventory levels could not keep up with the orders; according to Schaeffer, inventory would turn over 30 to 40 times a year, which wreaked havoc on the company's ordering system—nothing stayed in stock for more than several days.

Schaeffer needed $150,000 to bring inventory turnovers down to four or five times a year and keep product in stock. When he heard about a co-op grocery store that had raised money through its customers, he decided to try the same approach, placing a one-paragraph blurb in the company's catalog explaining why Real Goods needed the money and exactly how it would be used. The blurb also explained the investment's structure. Customers could invest a minimum of $3,000 for two years, at a 10 percent return. Customers who invested more than $10,000 for the two-year term would get 12 percent interest.

To Schaeffer's astonishment, the catalog blurb stimulated a flood of money over the next 30 days, with the largest check made out for $25,000. The only problem was that the flood didn't stop, and Schaeffer had to send back the "excess" checks.

With $150,000 in hand, Real Goods was able to maintain the kind of inventory flow it needed. But Schaeffer found that the increased business required an expanded operation and a new computer system, all of which carried a price tag of $100,000. So he went back to his customer file, sending letters to all of the people who had previously sent money, as well as those whose money he had returned. This time he offered a flat interest rate (10 percent), raised the minimum from $3,000 to $5,000, and stipulated a minimum three-year term. Again, the floodgates opened, and he ended up turning people away. Months after he closed the offering, money still dribbled in from places as far away as Singapore.

According to Schaeffer, the investment drive succeeded beyond his wildest dreams and reaffirmed his faith in people. Still, he warns that not every ecobusiness can use this fundraising approach; Real Goods had been around since 1978 as a retail operation, and since 1986 as a mail-order company. Thus, his company had built a long track record and a dedicated following. A startup simply can't expect that kind of customer loyalty.

A variation on the customer-as-investor theme has been used by small organic farms. Brookfield Farm, in South Amherst, Massachusetts collects several hundred dollars and a small amount of labor from 85 families who in return receive supplies of organically grown food. Other farms simply charge a flat rate for an annual supply of organic produce.

Whatever arrangement you strike up with your customers, bear in mind that if you're doing a good job satisfying their needs, they will feel a vested interest in helping you grow. Take advantage of the strength of this win-win relationship whenever you can.

Seeking Venture Capital

Venture capital forms the backbone of high-level research and development. Unfortunately, it's the hardest kind of money to obtain, and you won't get it with just a business plan or an application. Venturists take very selective risks, seeking a quick return on their investments (five years or less), so they scrutinize proposed companies with a microscope. Also, many venturists aren't interested in entrepreneurs seeking less than $500,000—the amount of energy spent cultivating the company simply isn't worth the potential return.

In addition to a good idea, you'll also have to present a strong management team that includes financial, marketing, operations, and R&D people. In some cases, however, the venturist will assemble the missing players of the team. Scientists and engineers are often surprised when this happens; they believe that since their work and ideas are unique, the venturist will simply hand over a blank check with no questions about who will manage the business.

Venture capital comes at a price. For one thing, the venturist may not share your goals. You might be in it for the long haul, because your product or technology can help serve the environment. But the venturist may want to see research sped up and focused on products that can be brought to market as quickly as possible, which can result in a bitter clash that leads to your leaving the company. This happened to nobel laureate Walter Gilbert, who eventually left the biotechnology firm he founded, Biogen. Gilbert wanted to do more long-term research; his investors, however, insisted on research that would offer a faster return.

Despite its drawbacks, venture capital can be an excellent (or the only) source of cash for some types of undertaking. For example, Ecological Engineering Associates (Marion, Massachusetts) needed $5 million to fund the development of its revolutionary water treatment technology—that kind of cash is generally not anted up on the kitchen table from friends and relatives, and venture capital proved to be the best route.

In addition to being a viable way to fund certain types of business, good venturists can provide invaluable management assistance based on years of experience with a wide range of companies. If your startup idea or expansion requires a great deal of money, and you can demonstrate an enormous potential for returns, then venture capital may be the route to follow.

Join Forces with a Larger Friend

Nature is full of symbiotic relationships, where two dissimilar organisms live together in a mutually beneficial relationship. In ecopreneuring, symbiotic relationships can make all the difference in helping a business idea see the light of day. In a symbiotic business arrangement, everyone wins by sharing. For instance, a group of lawyers might sublet space as well as secretarial time to a group specializing in ethical and environmental investments. The investment counselors pass along clients who need legal work or advice, while the lawyers pass along clients who need investment advice.

You can run many kinds of ecobusinesses along similar lines. If you have a business that sponsors ecological tours, you might join forces with a conventional travel agency with an infrastructure already in place—the space, the agents, computer system, mailing lists, and, most important, the customer base. While you'd give up a piece of the business or a percentage of gross revenues, you'd also reap tremendous benefits from your partner's people, equipment, and systems. The agency, in addition to some revenues from your business, would enjoy business from your ecotravelers, who would begin to use it for their routine ticketing.

Let's say that you want to start a business that recycles chlorofluorocarbons from automobile air conditioners. Rather than securing garage space and equipment, you link up with a receptive service station. You provide the know-how and perform the recycling process, while the service station, for a percentage of your revenues, draws the customers, advertises the services, and provides the equipment.

This sounds good on paper, but do such arrangements really work in the real world? Look at how Joe Hevener and Edwin Jason answered that question by turning to a larger organization to help achieve the production levels they'd need for national distribution. Once the two ecopreneurs had perfected the process of generating high-grade fertilizer from fish remains, they described their progress at a New England Fisheries Development meeting. NEFD wouldn't consider backing the enterprise, because it required less than $100,000 for startup. But Steve Connolly, the president of Steve Connolly Seafoods, the largest fish processor in New England, loved the idea. He called the next day, and within weeks the trio had formed Offshore Ventures, a joint venture between Hevener and Jason, and Steve Connolly Seafoods.

Hevener and Jason provided their knowledge of the process for creating Squanto's Secret, while Connolly provided the space and equipment necessary for large-scale production. And Offshore Ventures needs it—the demand for Squanto's Secret has skyrocketed. On the other side, Connolly Seafoods not only benefits financially from participating in a lucrative arrangement, but it solves a pesky disposal problem as well; the Squanto's Secret manufacturing operation consumes the fish remains that Connolly Seafoods would normally have to pay to have carted off.

If you're thinking of embarking on a joint venture, bear in mind the following points.

- **Talk is cheap—you can't walk into this type of relationship with just an idea.** You need a critical piece of the puzzle, something that the larger company wouldn't normally be able to obtain on its own. If you simply bring an idea to the party, you'll either get a small piece of the cake, or you might even starve. Remember, there's no way to protect an idea; your only insurance is to become indispensable. Hevener and Jason had the goods—they'd spent hours perfecting their formula and had reached a point where scientists from the University of Massachusetts relied on the two ecopreneurs to provide fish fertilizer for their meticulous tests. The bottom line is that the more you can contribute, the stronger your position in the partnership.

- **Make sure the partner makes a strong contribution.** This is the flip side of the foregoing piece of advice. Seek a partner who can bring valuable assets (tangible or intangible) to the table. If the partner has a computer system that would benefit your operation, that's a poor reason for giving up a piece of the action—you can always lease or rent a computer until you can afford one yourself. On the other hand, if the partner provides a customer base that would respond enthusiastically to your product or service, you win instant sales, which may prove essential to getting your business off the ground.

- **Never box yourself in forever**. You should carefully review the structure of a proposed joint partnership with your attorney. Make sure that if the relationship goes sour, you can pull out without losing everything you've built.

You might consider another very special form of partnership: the business "incubator." You won't find one in every city, but they are becoming more commonplace. Business incubators can reduce the overhead expenses of startup businesses by providing low-cost office space, office equipment, and administrative support. One private incubator in Brattleboro, Vermont, Envirologic, provides administrative assistance to companies working in the environmental field. After spending a year in the Envirologic incubator, one company, the Energy Recycling Group, which recovers landfill gas and uses it to generate electricity, went out on its own and realized $300,000 in sales during its first year of independent operation. The company sells its electricity back to Central Vermont Public Service Company. Other "hatchlings" that plan to walk on their own include a company that converts food scraps and municipal wastes into soil conditioners.

To find out about business incubators in your area, contact the National Business Incubator Association (see page 294).

Finally, if funding represents a major difficulty, consider contacting a financial advisory firm like the Catalyst Group of Brattleboro, Vermont, which not only may be able to help you locate sources of cash for your ecobusiness, but also can lend their experience with marketing and development issues.

Keeping Costs Down

Contrary to conventional wisdom, undercapitalization is *not* the most common cause of premature business death. If anything, having *too much* cash can croak you even faster. Entrepreneurs with access to deep pockets often spend the money on dumb things that won't help them grow, such as fancy furniture and an executive fleet (more on that in Chapter 5). In the final analysis, however, entrepreneurs succeed on their ingenuity and ability to run a lean operation. Too much seed money can dull your creative impulses and allow you to run fat.

Even if you're swimming in cash, "think poor" and observe some general rules designed to help you concentrate your resources on what really counts.

Go Second Hand or Bargain Basement Whenever Possible

Unless you legitimately need to impress clients, take the cheapest route you can when setting up shop. That means hanging out your shingle in your garage or basement, or subletting a corner of someone else's office until you really need space. As an alternative to committing yourself to a lease, you might be able to find an office-park setup where you pay a relatively low monthly fee and in return get your telephone professionally answered and have access to a respectable conference room when you need it.

Running lean also means buying secondhand furniture and office equipment when you do acquire an office. (You can get all the low-cost computer gear and general office equipment you'll need through the Boston Computer Exchange in Boston, Massachusetts.) You might want to visit a few bankruptcy auctions or storage liquidations, where you can often pick up handsome office furnishings for a song from people who didn't pay attention to their own knitting.

(Note: a must-read on this topic is Arnold Goldstein's *Starting on a Shoestring*. See the "Basic Business Bibliography," on page 285.)

Network to Obtain Products and Services

Bartering may be as old as civilization, but it still works beautifully for today's ecopreneur. Perhaps you can share space with another business and split the cost of a computer and a secretary or receptionist. Or perhaps your service can complement another's—a green products retail store on one side, a green lifestyle consulting firm on the other side—the two wouldn't compete, and at the same time could act as referral services for each other.

You can trade for mailing lists, equipment, materials, and other items that otherwise might drain your cash. A supplier might make a good customer, and vice versa. Such noncash transactions can save you more than money, creating a network that can form a foundation for continued growth.

Never Hire an Employee Until You Need One

Employees are expensive on various counts. First, they require a regular paycheck, usually once a week. That can put undue constant pressure on you to keep cash flowing positively. Second, payroll taxes, workman's compensation insurance, and benefits can add 20 percent or more to the base cost of salaries.

What's the alternative? Hire people as independent contractors—for accounting, word processing, research, etc.—until you need them on a regular basis. When you do need to hire support people, make sure they can take full advantage of whatever equipment you might have. State-of-the-art computer technology, for example, makes one person with the right software able to perform the tasks of an entire typing pool and production department.

In addition, as the price of information continues to drop, make sure that your staff know how to access online databases—for a very small sum and a few minutes of time you can quickly scan a mountain of magazines, newspapers, and journals that would take a person hours to cull through and photocopy manually.

As an example of how to operate with independent contractors, consider this author's research consortium, the Bennett Information Group, which includes a half dozen writers and researchers located from coast to coast. The group members fulfill assignments in their own offices with their own equipment. They're responsible for their own taxes and set their own hours—key definitions of an independent contractor. Responsibility for production of reports goes to other independent contractors, who also have their own offices, computers, etc. Obviously, you can't do this with receptionists and other people needed on site on a regular basis. But whenever possible, strike up arrangements with people who can cover their own overheads and provide their own benefits.

Incidentally, all members of the Bennett Information Group use modems whenever possible to transmit word-processing files, thereby eliminating the need for paper, envelopes, and the energy needed to move the mail via courier planes and trucks. This creates an ecological organization that practices what it preaches.

Go Easy on Supplies

Sure, you can get a great deal when you buy in bulk. But what are you going to do with 400 felt-tip pens or 50,000 envelopes if you have no invoices to write up? One ecopreneur, who shall remain nameless, actually drove his environmental publishing company to the brink of extinction by ordering a five-year supply of envelopes, stationery, and various printed paraphernalia.

Put your money where it will make money, in such activities as sales and service. When you've built up a financial base, you can enjoy the luxury of buying in larger quantities.

Avoid Consultants like the Plague

A startup enterprise needs a good lawyer (again, one who specializes in small businesses) to make sure that the company is set up properly. An accountant will help set up a chart of accounts and teach you how to handle the books. After that, steer clear of people offering their advice for a fee. Read books (see the "Basic Business Bibliography," on page 285) and join small-business groups where you can learn from other members and share your own experiences.

You might also be able to obtain free help from your local chamber of commerce or the Small Business Administration. In addition, women and minority entrepreneurs can gain access to numerous associations, government agencies, and nonprofit organizations designed to help them get going and succeed.

In general, never spend money on advice you can get for free, especially in the early stages, when every penny counts. At some point, you might need a professional ad agency, PR firm, or financial adviser. Until then you can rely on the many excellent how-to books on advertising, sales presentations, publicity, creative financing, and cash management listed in Part IV.

ᗈᎤ

At this point you've gotten a feel for the variety of funding sources available to the ecopreneur. Use these as general guidelines for organizing your effort to bankroll your business. Every startup situation is unique, so you might need a hybrid approach to raising cash. However you decide to go about securing money, protect every cent and make sure you direct it toward making the business grow. In the next chapter we'll take a look at the most critical growth element, marketing.

Chapter *Four*

Cultivating Customers:
How to Market Green Products and Services

New Thoughts on an Old Subject

Mention the word "marketing" and most people assume you mean "selling." Mention the word "sales" and most people think of Willy Loman, beating the street and making "cold calls" on prospective customers. Beware of these misconceptions. They can kill your ecobusiness, because without the right kind of marketing and selling, your company will never move past the idea stage. Remember, the only thing you really need to start a business is customers for your product or service. But you'll never attract those customers unless they know that you exist and that you can satisfy their needs. In this chapter, you'll learn about some basic tools for building a strong and loyal customer base. Some of the tools will cost you little or nothing, while others require a bit of a bankroll.

Understanding Marketing and Sales

Traditionally, people have assumed that marketing and sales are synonymous. Or, as marketing expert John Graham of Graham Communications (Quincy, Massachusetts) puts it, "They think marketing is a closet where a company stores brochures or flyers. When it's time to do marketing, the marketing director—often a secretary—mails out a brochure to someone who's requested information." In his innovative book *Magnet Marketing* (see "Basic Business Bibliography" on page 285), Graham explains that marketing entails far more than distributing brochures; rather, it involves cultivating customers and clients so that they're naturally predisposed to buy from your business. Selling, on the other hand, is the art of positioning yourself so that you are there when the customer decides to buy, and then closing a deal. This doesn't mean that the salesperson is merely an order-taker. To the contrary, marketing and sales people work hand in hand to attract customers. The salesperson serves as a problem-solver who works with prospective and regular customers to satisfy their needs and ensure that they'll remain loyal for years to come.

When a business uses magnet marketing, there's no need to make cold calls on people who'll slam the door in your face because they feel more pressing needs, such as tending to their own business or spending time with their families. (How many times have you winced at the phrase, "If I could only have twenty minutes of your time...?" Anyone in business who has 20 minutes to waste on a cold-calling salesperson won't be in business very long. And don't you resent the invasion of your privacy?)

Also, the idea of cold calling stems from a very presumptuous notion—that people will trust someone who has just dropped in out of the blue. Why *should* anyone buy your wares or services if they don't know anything about you or your company in advance? It's hard enough to sort through companies and product offerings that you've thoroughly researched—who needs an additional complicating factor?

These points apply especially to ecopreneurs; just because your product or service may save the planet doesn't mean that everyone on the planet wants to hear about it, let alone buy it. Yes, the market for environment-friendly products and services will continue to expand at the speed of light throughout the nineties. But you must still observe proven rules of marketing that can make or break any business.

A Magnet Marketing Program for Ecobusinesses

An effective magnet marketing program constantly cultivates customers by reminding them that your ecobusiness exists, that it offers high-quality goods and services, and, most important, that it is the *vendor of choice!* You accomplish this through a combination of publicity, self-promotion, media activities, and paid advertising.

Before describing each component, let's assume that your ecopreneurial enterprise is, at first, a one-person band. Even if you're doing it all yourself, you need to remember the importance of switching your marketing and sales hats; first you establish a reason to buy from your company with customer cultivation techniques (marketing), then you get down to the business of closing sales.

This sort of one-two punch will prove most effective when you use all components simultaneously. You can conduct media relations quite inexpensively, and they may yield dramatic results. Self-promotion will cost you some money if done properly, as will paid advertising. Regardless of the expenses involved, however, the ecopreneur must pick and choose wisely—think of it as a recipe for a healthy diet, making sure that you get nutrition from each of the basic food groups.

Finally, customer education plays a critical role in any magnet marketing program. Customer education means that instead of blabbing about having the "mostest and the biggest," you focus on conveying useful facts. This validates your company as an expert provider of products or services, which in turn builds customer confidence. When the customer decides to buy, who automatically comes to mind? You, of course.

For example, in the international travel arena, Northwest Airlines demonstrates the effectiveness of this approach with its ads that teach customers how to do business in Japan and other

Pacific Rim countries. The headline of one Northwest ad aimed at business travelers reads, "Women doing business in Asia shouldn't reveal too much of themselves." The ad then describes potential cultural pitfalls that women should avoid when doing business with Asian companies. At the bottom of the ad, readers learn that Northwest "can offer something no other airline can: the knowledge, insight and understanding that comes from more than 40 years of helping people do business in Asia." To frost the cake, the ad even provides a toll-free number travelers can call to get a free booklet loaded with hints for successfully doing business in the Pacific Rim.

The Northwest Airlines ads exemplify a mode of marketing that every ecopreneur should incorporate into his or her business thinking. Granted, you may not possess the capital to run expensive ads in high-priced magazines, but one way or another, you can always build customer education into your marketing activities.

Seventh Generation, the premier green products mail-order operation, packs its catalog with useful hints for environmentally conscious consuming. One catalog contains a sidebar "What you should know about cleaners," which addresses issues such as "Why are vegetable-based cleaners better for the environment?" "What's wrong with regular cleaners?" "What's the problem with phosphates?" and "Do non-synthetic cleaners work?" Readers of the catalog learn *why* they should prefer environment-friendly cleaning products, not just what products they can buy. The information approach further positions Seventh Generation as the expert in the field and the vendor of choice.

In the following sections, which explain the individual components of a magnet marketing campaign, you'll learn how to weave a strong customer-education theme through all your marketing activities.

Media Relations

In this age, sometimes called the Communications Era, with all its sound-bites, photo opportunities, and spin doctors, media attention can make a company, and the lack of it can break a company. You can use a number of cost-effective, even "free," techniques to get the media working for your business.

Press Releases

Ecopreneurs find themselves in an enviable position with regard to the press: as public concern about the environment grows, so does the interest of magazine, newspaper, radio, and television reporters. Their stories about your business can be worth tens of thousands of dollars in paid advertising. In fact, a story in a newspaper or magazine, or a spot on a radio or TV newsmagazine carries an implicit third-party "Good Housekeeping" seal of approval that no ad or brochure can generate. As a result, stories about you, your company, or your products and services establish important credibility with prospective and existing customers.

Anything you do to promote your business can ignite a chain reaction of publicity. Joel Diskin of Worldview Financial Services, Inc. (Birmingham, Michigan), has done just that with his press releases. One of them led to an article in a local paper. This, in turn, attracted the attention of someone who mentioned it to an editor at *Michigan Business* magazine, which ran a page two article on socially responsible investing that featured Diskin's company, complete with his photo. Other newspaper articles led to contacts with a local public-access television network, and that sparked a half-hour interview on *Global Connections*, a weekly interview show. Diskin has combined a videotape of the interview along with reprints of the articles into a promotional package that he presents to nonprofit organizations to promote his educational seminars on ethical investing.

The following techniques can help you garner media coverage. Before delving into them, though, bear in mind that reporters, editors, and producers are extremely sensitive about being exploited as free advertising vehicles. If your material or approach looks like a thinly veiled attempt to get free print space or air time, it will turn off the media. With that in mind, let's talk about how to write a compelling press release.

A good press release begins with a grabber headline—if you can't interest editors, reporters, or producers from the first glance, you've lost their attention. The release itself should contain *news*—not self-serving hype about your product or service. For example, if you've opened a store selling alternative energy devices, describe the most exotic gizmo you stock and toss out some mind-boggling facts that could interest anyone.

Or, if you're starting a green travel agency, announce some surprising fact—such as the greenest tourist resort in America. The Cape Cod Chamber of Commerce has done just that, touting the National Seashore as one of the most environmentally pristine vacationlands on Earth. Whatever you do, avoid making your grand opening or fifth year in business the focal point of the argument—slip that kind of ho-hum information in at the end. If you give media people news, stories will follow automatically. How do you give your product or service a newsworthy twist?

- Challenge the status quo or conventional wisdom (such as the false notion that paper degrades in landfills).

- Describe something outrageous or unusual (such as a solar-powered computer).

- Present shocking findings from an informal survey or study (such as the fact that if you took all the toner cartridges tossed out each year and strung them together, they'd stretch a quarter of the way around the world).

- Stage an event that dramatizes a point (such as a "trashathon" at which people can dump their refuse in your hands and watch you organize it into recyclables, compostables, and reusables).

Regardless of your interest-sparking gambit, do something that differentiates you from the pack and catches the imagination of a reporter or producer. Find the old "man bites shark" approach that attracts attention and stimulates people's interest in your operation.

Here are two more points to consider:

- Send your release to the right editor, reporter, or producer. A label made out to "news desk" will quickly find its way to the bottom of the stack or the wastebasket. To avoid that, conduct a bit of research and target your mailing list (see page 287 for a listing of national media guides). For local media, pick up the phone and get the names of the specific people who might cover what you have to say.

- Never let rejection get you down. There's no guarantee that your first release will create screaming headlines. In fact, it probably won't, even if you offer an astonishing product or service. Smart ecopreneurs keep mining the media with press releases until one strikes pay dirt. In any case, *never* pester an editor, reporter, or producer. If they see you as a nuisance, you'll never get your name in print. People in the media tend to have elephant-sized memories.

Why go through all this effort? Because print space and air time is finite, and you're competing against pros who do everything right. But your effort can produce a huge payoff, and you might even find yourself being tapped as an expert when a story breaks in your field.

Oil spill specialist and newsletter publisher Richard Golob, for example, has carved out a niche as the expert of choice whenever a spill hits the headlines. During the Exxon Valdez incident, he FAXed a series of well-timed press releases containing hard-to-find information that he knew reporters would appreciate for their stories. One release provided data that newshounds could use to compare the Valdez spill with others in U.S. waters. As Golob made the reporters' jobs easier, they began clamoring for more information.

Golob's media efforts landed him appearances on prime-time NBC, CBS, and ABC news shows, as well as mentions in *The New York Times, The Wall Street Journal, Time*, and *U.S. News & World Report*. But the real results for Golob came in a 30 percent sales increase for his *Oil Pollution Bulletin* and a permanent place on the Rolodexes of editors, reporters, and producers across the country. The next time oil spills on troubled waters, Richard Golob will be one of the first people members of the media call for a story.

If you persist, you, too, can gain excellent media coverage for your ecobusiness. It doesn't matter what you make or sell as long as you continually pump out press releases to catch the roving interest of media people. Eventually, you may become a favored information source and enjoy a certain amount of celebrity that can cascade right down to your company's bottom line.

Bylined Articles

An alternative approach to media relations, the "bylined article," involves a publishable newspaper or magazine article written by you (or a ghostwriter) discussing an important issue related to your business.

For example, if you're running a paper-collection business, you might write an article designed for a regional business magazine or national trade journal that explores ways businesses can profit by selling their paper instead of tossing it out (don't appeal to business people on the basis of saving the environment—cast your arguments in terms of their profitability).

Or, if you're running a green products retail store, try to place an article in community newspapers about how consumers can select environmentally sound products, read labels for environmental hazards, avoid overpackaging, and make other decisions that will help them clean up their own backyards.

Environmental investment adviser Carsten Henningsen of Progressive Securities Financial Services (Eugene, Oregon) has successfully used the bylined article to promote his cause. Individuals on his staff regularly contribute columns to newspapers on news topics related to investing. Henningsen also parlayed his articles on socially responsible investing into a weekly guest spot on *Talking Stocks*, a daily radio program on a local National Public Radio affiliate.

To help ensure getting your own articles into print, keep your focus on the subject matter. Be satisfied with a little biographical blurb at the end of the article. Editors will instantly reject your article if it reads like an advertisement. Just as a press release must not seem self-serving, a bylined article must talk about topics, problems, and issues of interest to a publication's readers.

How do you get an article published? First, target a publication or magazine that reaches your customers. You can use the periodical directories on page 287, such as *Bacon's Publicity Checker*, which lists just about every publication and newspaper in the country. If you run a small local business, then focus on community newspapers and the major daily. If your business caters to a national audience, you enjoy a much broader potential (and will find it harder getting your articles published—the competition is stiffer and so are the criteria of the editors).

Next, write a query letter to the editor, explaining what you want to write and your qualifications for doing it well. Carsten Henningsen advises, "Be credible, be direct, and be specific." It helps to make a specific proposal, whether it's for a single article, a series, or a radio or television program. Offer a sample of what you have in mind, and propose any ambitious project on a trial basis. Above all, don't make it sound like a commercial for your business. Again, an educational approach will be more credible and more readily accepted. Once you submit your proposal or query letter, you'll get one of three replies: Yep (send it in), Nope (don't bother), and Maybe (send it in, but no promises). Be flexible—an editor may even suggest alternatives.

Finally, get down to work writing the article or hiring some writing assistance. If you must meet a deadline, hit it—if your articles work for the publication and arrive in a timely fashion, you'll most likely be invited to write more.

While bylined articles require work on your part, they can add an important tool to your marketing mix. Even though you've written the article, its publication by an independent party builds credibility with your customers and prospects. Bylined articles also establish your expertise, a crucial step toward predisposing people to buy from your firm.

If you succeed at getting bylined articles published, or at least being mentioned in or interviewed for articles, send copies to your prospects and customers. The credibility they radiate can never be matched by anything else you do or say. For special customers, write on the article something like "FYI," or "Thought you might be interested in this." Your real message: "Just a reminder that we're experts in the field, so you should feel confident about buying from us."

However you structure your media campaign, you can significantly boost its effectiveness with a strong self-promotion campaign, as we'll see in the next section.

Self-Promotion

A self-promotion campaign mirrors a media relations campaign. With a media relations campaign you take your best shot at getting members of the media to write about you, but you really hold no control over what the media do. With a self-promotion campaign, on the other hand, you function as the media, because you'll be publishing materials that directly tout your capabilities, products, and services. Of course, since you're promoting yourself, your campaign will not benefit from the implicit third-party endorsement and seal of approval of media coverage. But you can still generate a constant flow of marketing materials on your own schedule, thereby keeping yourself positioned in your customers' minds even when they are not ready to order or reorder yet.

Self-promotion involves a number of tools, such as newsletters, direct-mail, trade shows, seminars, and informational/capabilities brochures.

Newsletters

Newsletters can be wonderful self-promotion tools for any business that mails them on a regular basis to keep itself in front of prospects and customers. A newsletter should be, first and foremost, an *information* vehicle designed to help people in some way. Recyclers Jill and Jim Matlack of Matlack Environmental Services circulate a two-page newsletter to customers and prospects. The newsletter provides practical tips on recycling and cites the environmental activities of exemplary customers. Customers learn by reading about other companies and picking up helpful hints for living a greener life at home.

Annabelle Ship of The Green Planet retail store also makes good use of her newsletter to promote her store and educate her customers. She began by creating one-page information sheets about products she carries, designed to enlighten her customers and keep her own staff well informed. Later, she found that the information sheets provided a natural transition into the *Green Planet News*, a bigger publication covering a broad range of hands-on tips and information.

The more practical information the newsletter provides, the more you'll establish yourself as an industry leader and the vendor of choice. You might follow these suggestions for putting a newsletter to work in your ecobusiness:

- If you're an air-quality consultant, run feature articles about "sick-building syndrome" and what workers can do to remedy the problem. Perhaps each issue could feature a case study describing buildings that you've cured. The newsletter could also contain tips for reducing air pollution at home and on the job.

- If you're a green investment adviser, you could present feature articles explaining how you select environmentally responsible firms. Other parts of the newsletter could profile firms that have adopted a strong environmental conscience. In addition, you might offer a regular scoreboard of best and worst companies from an environmental perspective.

- A green product mail-order operation might issue a newsletter to supplement its regular mailings. The newsletter could explain some basic chemistry, along with do's and don'ts for consumers of environmentally sound products.

Any ecobusiness can inexpensively produce a newsletter. Keep in mind, however, that the more useful information you cram into each issue, the more you'll reaffirm your position as the expert in the field and the company of choice:

- Never accept advertising or put in your own; use a small, unobtrusive "What's New?" or "New Products and Developments" column instead.
- Never charge for the newsletter (unless you're in the newsletter business).
- Maintain a regular schedule.
- Don't start a newsletter unless you can afford to maintain it—if it appears irregularly, this will telegraph the message that you can't come through with projects.
- Solicit feedback from readers and print answers to questions, thus involving customers in the newsletter and demonstrating that you listen closely to what they have to say.

Once you've pulled your newsletter together, use it as a customer cultivation tool, making sure that everyone on your mailing list gets one, and that as prospects drop by your store or request literature about your products or services by mail, you send them your newsletter and place their names on your subscription list. If your newsletter creates interest, people will not only look forward to reading the next issue, they'll contact you the next time they need to buy.

Direct Mail

Do not confuse this form of direct mail with direct-mail solicitations aimed at overt selling. Rather, in this case, you inform prospects and customers about your business and what it does. If you've succeeded in getting yourself mentioned in the press or in publishing a bylined article, conduct a direct-mail campaign to everyone on your mailing list. This kind of self-promotion can only work if you keep a constant flow going out the door. Also, be sure to send such material to a specific name; otherwise, the recipient will quickly pitch it in the trash can.

Trade Shows

A trade show can provide an excellent opportunity for ecopreneurs to show their wares and cultivate potential distributors and customers. Be aware, though, that entrepreneurs constantly make the mistake at trade shows of trying to collar customers rather than educate them. You'll get better results, if, like Ed Jason of Squanto's Secret, you set up a booth at local mall events and garden shows designed to educate customers about the importance of your work. That's exactly how the founders of Squanto's Secret got into this book—they impressed a member of The Bennett Information Group with their informative display at the prestigious New England Flower Show, and, voilà, they achieved "promotion" in a book that no amount of money could buy.

Another company that has mastered the art of making itself the vendor of choice at exhibitions is Autumn Harp, makers of environmentally safe baby-care products. Autumn Harp relies on trade shows to locate distributors, any of whom may represent competing products. According to Bruce Gaylord, Autumn Harp's marketing director, the company uses trade shows as a vehicle to educate distributors about the field, the product, and the company. It also works hard to solicit valuable feedback from the distributors about how retailers are responding to its promotion, and what kinds of products retailers would like to receive in the future.

Seminars and Workshops

Financial-planning firms have refined the art of the "marketing seminar," where clients attend a free session that will teach them about a particular strategy for sheltering money, saving on taxes, and so forth. Ecopreneurs can emulate that practice by conveying information about their products or services at self-planned get-togethers with customers and prospects.

Sally Malanga's Ecco Bella, for example, once sponsored a local seminar on cruelty-to-animals–free cosmetics. In addition to a healthy turnout of potential customers, the seminar gained an unexpected benefit—it attracted a newspaper reporter who wrote a story on the company and its products.

Perhaps you're running a green investment service. You could sponsor a seminar in which you explain how you evaluate companies' environmental records. Rather than signing up clients on the spot, keep your focus on educating, establishing your expertise, and building credibility. In short, create a "magnetic situation" in which ecoinvesters will naturally think of you when they're ready to plunk their money into a fund or the stock market.

To conduct a successful marketing seminar you must maintain a sharp focus, yet offer an interesting mix of information. Also, make sure that you invite people with a personalized letter, rather than a generic "Dear Occupant" flyer or notice. Finally, carefully qualify the people you invite. There's no point in asking people to take up space and consume your tea and crumpets if they can barely afford the bus fare to attend the session (or purchase your wares).

Trade Associations

Every industry has formed a trade association. If you supply goods or services other companies will buy, try to get yourself on a convention program, either as a speaker or a panelist in a discussion group. Ben Benson, author of *Your Family Business*, does this with a number of trade associations, many of whose member firms are family-owned. Not only does he achieve status as a vendor of choice for consulting engagements, he often generates news coverage in major business periodicals, such as *The Wall Street Journal*. If you market alternative packaging materials, you might approach national associations of consumer products manufacturers or even grocery stores with ideas for presentations that will not only inform members about environmentally sound alternatives but will cement your credibility as a supplier of those materials.

Brochures

As John Graham points out in his book *Magnet Marketing*, brochures don't make sales, people do. This doesn't mean that a good brochure can't augment your sales effort—a good brochure can, in fact, create a positive impression that sets the stage for more intensive customer cultivation. Earth's Best, the nation's only maker of certified organic baby food, goes to great length to explain the need for baby food grown without the use of synthetic pesticides. The company's brochure features an inset with a well-known dietician and head of a prestigious children's hospital, who testifies to the important contribution that Earth's Best baby food makes. It also presents compelling facts from well-known organizations and experts regarding the impact of pesticides on child development. Only after setting up the educational framework does the brochure focus on "a better alternative"—Earth Best's own products. When you finish reading the brochure, you feel like you've been given a crash course in child nutrition and pesticides.

As the Earth's Best brochure demonstrates, you must convey the message that you satisfy customers by solving an important problem. Remember, people buy solutions to problems, not just products or services. Avoid abstract mood pieces that do nothing but show people that you know how to spend money on spiffy graphic design and printing.

Another company that produces baby products, Autumn Harp, also uses brochures effectively. One brochure, concerning its Talc-Free Baby Powder, provides hard-to-find information about the contamination of talc with asbestos. This brochure was reprinted by a number of diaper services that routinely provide the product information with their deliveries. Autumn Harp also gives the brochures, as well as other point-of-sale information, to distributors and brokers for dissemination at the retail level. One brochure, a "shelf talker," included a mail-in coupon for a free finger puppet to introduce a new baby-care product. According to Autumn Harp's Bruce Gaylord, distributors and retailers are always on the lookout for promotional material that will help them make a sale.

In addition to educating end users, distributors, and retailers, brochures can get your customers involved in an issue. Tell *their* story—they'll be flattered (of course, get their permission first). Show how you made their lives easier, made them money, or saved them time:

- If your recycling company has reduced a company's disposal costs or even brought in unexpected revenues, explain the situation and get a quote; customers trust other customers.

- If your environment-friendly cleaning solution is the only substance on earth that a particular person can use without an allergic reaction, get that person's story to prove how you solved a pressing problem.

- If your new erosion-barrier material made from otherwise unrecycled material helped a town during a major flood, tell the tale and get plenty of testimony. Success breeds success.

An effective brochure need not cost a fortune; what counts is the concepts and customer orientation, not the glitz. Done properly, the brochure will help position you in a prospective customer's mind as the company to have on his or her team.

This completes our tour of self-promotion. Now, let's look at advertising, the third and final component of a magnet marketing strategy.

Paid Advertising

Advertising may lack the credibility of publicity in unbiased publications, but it still forms the backbone of many marketing strategies. Though it can be expensive, you can find cost-efficient ways to do it.

Space Ads

Advertising poses a real challenge for any ecopreneur. Even seasoned marketers constantly experiment with it. It's a world of psychology and behavior, subject to fads and trends and the whims of the consuming public; and it often takes time, even months, to assess which ads and which publications get the best results.

As with all magnet marketing techniques, paid advertising—print and electronic promotion, and direct-mail solicitation—should focus on demonstrating why you're the vendor of choice. That means shunning gimmicks and getting down to the nitty-gritty facts, such as how your alternative energy product company genuinely helps people conserve energy by working with customers to satisfy their specific needs. This differs markedly from simply pushing the fact that your company is the biggest or the oldest and stocks more inventory than your competitors.

A good ad for an ecobusiness will give prospective customers a strong incentive to reach for their checkbooks or pick up the phone. Consider the copy for the following ad that appeared in an environmental publication.

Composting Toilet Systems:

- Nonpolluting
- Waterless
- Odorless

The ad then requests $2 for its brochure. Why should anyone spend two bucks for a brochure, let alone buy a product from this company?

The company should talk about how many gallons of water its products save, how quickly the products will pay for themselves, how long it takes to install the systems, how they benefit the environment, how they differ from competing products, and how the company will help customers pick the right product for the homes. And it shouldn't have charged for its brochure.

This principle applies to any product or service: you must create a compelling reason for the customer to pick up the phone, write a check, or send for your catalog. That means you must run ads with substance, on a repeated schedule. Sure, you'll hear stories about an entrepreneur who ran a single three-line classified ad and then retired with a fortune, but in the real world success rarely comes that way. You generally have to run an ad at least six times to get any results. People don't read ads the way they do news articles—they gloss over them. Repeated exposure eventually "burns" the ad into the reader's mind.

Direct Mail

The same rules apply to direct-mail solicitations. Most junk mail is just that—junk. To avoid wasting trees and insulting people, use direct mail as an opportunity to educate and establish a positive buying environment. As with ads, make sure that you sell solutions, not products and services. Explain how you will help customers alleviate a pressing environmental problem, save them time, save them money, and above all, provide after-sale service and information.

It is beyond the scope of this book to be a primer on direct mail; see "Basic Business Bibliography" on page 285 for a listing of several books that explain the art of direct mail. You should, however, bear the following two points in mind: pick your mailing lists carefully, and don't plan for an unlikely response. Just because someone has bought vitamins in the past doesn't mean that he or she will be interested in your recycling-bin system. When you rent lists, make sure that you understand the buyers' profiles. To rate lists for your ecobusiness, draw a target. At the center, include lists of people who have actually bought products or services like yours in the past. As you move out further from the center, isolate more abstract connections to your wares. Pour your money into the bull's eye, and allocate less or nothing on the peripheral bands of the target.

To sum up, advertising and direct-mail campaigns should complement the other, less costly marketing techniques of self-promotion and media relations. In all cases convey a clear and compelling message, and the world will eventually come to see your company as a leader in the field and the natural choice when it's time to place an order.

ᘔ

Even though you might not have amassed the funds to support all three components of a magnet marketing campaign in full, undertake as many complementary magnet marketing activities as you can handle and afford. Always recognize your goal of placing your company in front of prospects and existing customers as fully as possible. When you educate and create what John Graham calls the "right buying environment," you'll maximize your chances for ongoing success. Then you'll be ready to buckle down to managing your enterprise, the subject of the next chapter.

Chapter *Five*

The Ten Commandments of Ecopreneuring: *How to Manage an Ecobusiness*

So far, we've discussed how to dream up an idea for an ecobusiness, how to fund it, and how to market it. Now, you're ready to think about managing your business. Again, you can't rely on the fact that just because you're doing right, you'll automatically do well; the history of business is strewn with the skeletons of businesses that didn't survive because they ignored management fundamentals. Ecobusinesses may, in fact, be especially prone to premature death because their founders may be idealists who assume "right makes might." Before we delve into specific entrepreneuring opportunities, let's consider ten fundamental management "commandments," which constitute a crash MBA course.

1. Clarify Your Mission

Many entrepreneurs assume that they know exactly what their business does, when in fact they haven't formulated a clear mission. The mission statement of any company sets forth the core principle around which the entire enterprise revolves. It communicates a strong message to your customers, your employees and suppliers, and your competition. In a sense, a good mission statement serves as a flag around which all your "stakeholders" (everyone connected with your business) can rally.

Your mission statement should consist of one simple sentence that anyone can easily understand and remember. Before you try to write it, ask yourself:

- What am I trying to achieve?
- What distinctive competence do I bring to the endeavor?
- How will I solve my customers' needs?
- How will I differentiate myself from my competitors?

The resulting statement should answer these questions. For example, instead of

> "We're a paper-recycling business."
> try:
> "We teach medium-sized companies how to achieve greater profitability and become more environmentally fit by recycling paper goods."

The first could apply to any enterprise serving any segment of the vast paper-recycling market, from households to the Fortune 500. The second clarifies the fact that your company takes an educational approach, that it solves an economic as well as an environmental problem, and that it concentrates on a specific market segment. The statement can serve as an engine to drive marketing efforts and employee commitment, and it sends a strong signal to competitors that you have staked out a particular turf.

2. Plan, Plan, Plan

Many people assume that entrepreneurship means flying by the seat of your pants on your creative instincts. As an ecopreneur, your enterprise must certainly spring from your creativity, but unfortunately, that's not enough. Boring as it may seem, the successful ecobusiness depends on meticulous planning. The more time you spend thinking of every detail affecting your business, from the price of gasoline to pending legislation, the better you'll be prepared to withstand the fickle winds of the marketplace.

When planning an ecobusiness, you need to consider both best-case and worst-case scenarios. Take a cue from Cambridge-based environmental newsletter publisher Richard Golob, whose World Information Systems also sponsors hazardous waste business conferences. Golob has refined best-case/worst-case planning to a fine art. He says, "Once you've developed a product, service, or newsletter, you need to constantly adjust your marketing efforts to the marketplace. You have to know what you'll do if the bottom falls out unexpectedly, or the business takes off unexpectedly. Either outcome can strain a business if you're not prepared. Be sure that you have an 'angel in the wings' if you strike out; likewise, be sure that you have the staff and systems in place to service your customers—nothing is worse than seeing success go down the drain because you weren't prepared for an onslaught of orders."

Best-guess planning derives from positive assumptions about the marketplace, the economy, and your competitors. Ask yourself:

- How many people, ideally, will buy my products or service?

- What dollar results can I expect from my marketing efforts in three months? Six months? Twelve months?

- Who are my competitors and what strengths and weaknesses do they possess?

- Have I defined my market niche precisely?

- Why will customers buy from me instead of from my competitors?

- What new technologies will benefit my operation?

- What legislation can benefit my business?

- How will the overall economy affect my business?

Then ask the tough questions:

- What if my projected universe of customers turns out to be much smaller than I imagined?

- What if my projected response to marketing efforts is 10 percent, 20 percent, or even 50 percent below expectations?

- What if I miscalculated my competitors' strengths or failed to account for new competitors who have entered the field?

- What if traditional businesses with deep distribution and marketing channels begin offering my products and services—can I sustain my niche?
- What if a competitor offers lower prices, higher quality, and greater customer satisfaction?
- What if a new regulation prevents me from selling my products?
- What will I do if a new technology makes my current process or product obsolete?
- What if the economy takes a nosedive—will people consider my products or services too expensive or unnecessary?

Your ultimate success will probably fall somewhere between your most optimistic and pessimistic scenarios. Remember, you should plan for a bright future because optimism breeds self-fulfilling prophecies; but you should also plan for all these contingencies that can put a business in an early grave.

3. Be Ultrarealistic
The ability to cope with reality makes or breaks the ecopreneur. You should practice the art of multiplying and dividing expectations on the basis of your best-and worst-case scenarios. Doing so will help keep you in touch with reality. For example:

- If you assume a project will take two weeks to complete, allow four.
- If you think you'll sell 500 units a week, make sure the business can survive on 250.
- If you believe it will take three months to secure second-stage financing, make sure you can go for six months without it.
- If you calculate you'll need 12 hours of outside consulting help, budget for 24.
- If you project your company will grow at a rate of 7 percent a year, plan for a 3.5 percent growth rate.

Continue this list until you've covered every aspect of your business. Of course, some activities warrant even more caution then a 50 percent reduction: many marketers start off their direct-mail efforts assuming a 10, 20, or even higher percentage response rate, when in fact a response of 1 or 2 percent is more realistic. Likewise, if you're counting on a multiple of 10 sales return for your ads (e.g., you expect $5,000 worth of business for every $500 ad you place), then you might want to revise your reality factor by 80 percent to play it safe.

Many ecopreneurs base their initial assumptions on a highly unrealistic expectation. When Sally Malanga of Ecco Bella sent out 3,000 pieces of direct mail, she expected a 50 percent response but actually got 10 percent (in itself remarkable). But in terms of her planning, she thought it was a disaster. Nonetheless, it did garner some loyal customers and has enabled her to build up a business grossing more than a million dollars in annual sales.

Whether you're in the green products mail-order business or providing a consulting service, in most cases, it's easier to cope with a bonanza than a shortfall. If you find that you're swimming in orders, things are taking less time than imagined, or your growth rate actually rises far above anticipations, you can adjust your planning and resources quite easily. But if you suffer a shortfall, you'll find yourself mired in a crisis mode that can consume all your time and energy.

4. Think Total Customer Satisfaction

A business only needs one thing: happy customers. Strangely, many business-people treat customers as the enemy, where time-honored slogans such as "The customer is number one" and "The customer is always right" mask hostile feelings about "those people who make our lives miserable with their demands and complaints."

Smart businesspeople, however, treat customers as well as they treat employees and think of them as key assets. Sure, some will be a pain in the neck. But if you strive to satisfy your customers totally, you'll find that their loyalty gives you an unbeatable competitive advantage—they'll simply turn deaf ears to the wooing pleas of your competitors. To achieve total loyalty, you must offer the highest possible quality and the highest possible level of customer service before, during, and after the sale.

Earth's Best, the premiere producer of organic baby food, has made total customer satisfaction a key operating principle. Consumers are encouraged to call the toll-free number to learn more about using the products effectively, and about the benefits of feeding their children certified organic baby food. Helpful operators will also provide tips such as to take care when microwaving refrigerated jars of Earth's Best (could get local "hot spots") and to avoid feeding baby directly from the jar (could introduce bacteria from the spoon, which may incubate over time). As a result of the helpful and free advice, consumers of Earth's Best feel as if they've bought more than jars of baby food—they've bought expertise that they can count on when they need it.

Here are some tips for generating high levels of loyalty among your customers:

Make Life Easy for the Customer

- Install an 800 number, supply postage-paid envelopes, response cards, and any other devices that eliminate hassles for the customer. The benefits of doing so far outstrip the costs.

- Offer money-back guarantees whenever possible. This eliminates any pain and risk in buying from you. Aside from the fact that most people don't take up such offers, if you really believe in your product or service, you should stand behind it 100 percent.

Add Value Whenever Possible

- See yourself as a consultant to the customer, not just a supplier. That means adopting a problem-solving mode. Encourage customers to give you wish lists that would help them live more environmentally responsible lives, save money, or operate more efficiently. If customers see you as a partner, they'll not likely dump you for a competitor who suddenly drops prices, but offers no added value.

- Serve your customers as a broker of free information. As a provider of goods and services, you will come in contact with many different kinds of people and you'll see first hand how different people creatively solve nagging problems or add a creative touch to their companies, goods, and services. Share that information with your other customers, while respecting confidential and proprietary information.

Seek Feedback

- See your customers as sources of suggestions rather than complaints. Some of the best ideas for modifying existing products or services or creating new ones will come from your customers. After all, they're the ones who "field-test" your wares every day. When customers know that their input may result in an improved or new product, they'll more likely stick with you through thick and thin.

Finally, educate your employees that customers play a leading role in your business, and that there's no such thing as a captive audience. Never let those working on the front line of your business fall into the trap of thinking that customers are merely impediments to getting work done.

5. Think Total Quality

This rule ties in closely with the preceding one—you'll never create total customer satisfaction unless you deliver total quality. While quality can be as hard to define as "truth" or "beauty," it does not lie solely in the eye of the beholder. On one level, quality is simply the absence of flaws.

On a deeper level, however, the Japanese pioneered the concept in the auto industry by defining quality as the elimination of anything that doesn't add value to the product. What doesn't add value? Defective parts, unnecessary paperwork, inefficient processes. (Many people believe that the Japanese can offer higher-quality cars than U.S. manufacturers because of cheaper labor. Wrong—they've simply eliminated costly mistakes.)

In your ecobusiness, look for ways to eliminate unnecessary things that merely increase the cost without adding anything of value to the product or service. Ask:

- What defects can I eliminate?

- What processes can I streamline to make it easier for customers to learn about and obtain our products or services?

- What pleases or displeases our customers about anything we do?

- How can we induce our suppliers or subcontractors to "do it right the first time"?

Quality in manufacturing means *continuous* improvement. If 97 percent of your products leave your operation defect-free, go for 98 percent tomorrow. Then go for 99 percent. Then 100 percent. Instill a sense of pride in your people to raise the high bar every day.

No business can afford to stand still, resting on its laurels while competitors plot to steal its customers away. Customers want to buy from companies that continue to offer cutting-edge products employing the best and safest technology. Total quality means a total commitment to giving customers the best possible solutions to their problems.

6. Study the Competition

For some ecopreneurs, "competition" is a four-letter word. They assume no one could possibly vilify or attack them because, after all, protecting the environment is too important to permit cut throat and calculating competition. Others believe that there's simply room for everybody to succeed. Actually, competition exists for every business, and it's healthy that it does. Competition forces businesses to be all they can be. As more and more ecobusinesses begin dotting the landscape, only those with a competitive advantage will survive the inevitable shakeout.

Yes, ecopreneurs are kinder and gentler people who don't approach the world with a "zero-sum game" attitude (an "I win, you lose" mentality). Some companies actually share their mailing lists, because they see more to gain from cooperation than head-to-head combat. After all, the environment should be a "win-win" marketplace. But as more business-people begin to view the environment as a source of income and profit, it will surely attract well-financed players who are only in it for the profit. These companies will force you to take competition very seriously.

Big companies often wait on the sidelines while they monitor trends to make sure they're real. But once they're convinced that a trend is here to stay, they'll jump into the fray. According to competitive-strategy expert Eileen Shapiro of the Cambridge-based Hillcrest Group and author of *How Corporate Truths Become Competitive Traps*, "Ecopreneurs take advantage of opportunities created by sleeping giants. But eventually, the giants wake up. When they do, they adjust their mental models of the marketplace and the real process of competing begins. Those ecopreneurs who can in turn shift their own mental models have a shot at growing and thriving. Those who don't may find themselves blindsided by forces that they could have predicted."

Shapiro also comments that some ecopreneurs think that because they're succeeding now, the same strategies will work indefinitely into the future. These are the people who tend to be the most inflexible and the most easily hurt when the game changes. (Which is why a lot of entrepreneurs do extremely well and then lose their fortunes.)

Already, large consumer-product manufacturers have begun rolling out their own brands of environment-friendly personal-care products. Paper makers are deploying more unbleached and undyed paper towels and napkins, and food processors are touting more organic ingredients. At the same time, supermarkets, drug stores, and department stores are stocking all sorts of green products from mass producers. In the service arena, traditional players, from travel agents to investment advisers, are already jumping on the environmental bandwagon, and it is only a matter of time before even the most traditional companies begin trumpeting their green capabilities.

Does the invasion of large companies onto the environmental turf spell doom for the ecopreneur? Not necessarily. Some customers will always prefer mail-order shopping, and others will always support the "underdog." Even so, smart ecopreneurs focus on ways of competing more effectively, preparing for the day when they might have to fight to keep their customers. Scrutinize your competitors, assess their strengths and weaknesses; even if you dislike doing battle, you can learn a lot from competitive intelligence, which can help shore up your weaknesses and sharpen your focus.

7. Develop Company Strengths

Amazingly, many entrepreneurs do not fully comprehend or develop their personal and company strengths, usually because small business people are so busy doing what they do that they don't make time to step back and review their performance. They also tend to spend so much time putting out fires that they become preoccupied with fixing weaknesses rather than honing skills. Those who pay more attention to weaknesses than strengths usually lose their strength, while those who focus on strengths keep getting stronger.

In their book *Creating Excellence*, Craig Hickman and Michael Silva cite capitalizing on company strengths as one of the three key components to successful business strategy. The first three we've already talked about: satisfying customer needs and sustaining a competitive advantage. As Hickman and Silva point out, a successful company develops a distinctive competence. For the ecopreneur, that competence may lie in a functional area, such as marketing and sales, or it may involve a skill, such as innovation or communication. Ask yourself what you do best, which usually springs from what you most love to do.

The Body Shop founder Anita Roddick realized that her special strength was teaching people by stimulating their minds. Like her classrooms earlier, The Body Shop stores are chock full of easily accessible information—product flyers and a tome called *The Product Information Manual*, which describes in detail everything that The Body Shop makes and sells. She told an *Inc.* magazine reporter (June 1990), "When I taught history, I would put brilliant graphics all around the room and play music of the period we were studying. Kids could just get up, walk around, and make notes from the presentation. It took me months to get it right, but it was stunning. Now I'm doing the same thing. There is education in the shops. There are anecdotes right on the products, and anecdotes adhere. So I've really gone back to what I know how to do well."

Finally, hard times visit every new enterprise, but if you are doing what you love, you'll do it better than anyone else and thus better satisfy customers and sustain your competitive edge. You might read Marsha Sinetar's book, *Do What You Love, the Money Will Follow* to gain insight into your own strengths.

8. Emphasize Positive Cash Flow

You can boil business down to one very simple equation: make more profit by spending less and selling more. That's what creates positive cash flow.

Spending less entails observing the simple maxim, "Don't spend a dime unless it will make a dime." Unfortunately, entrepreneurs can be blinded by the stars in their own eyes, assuming that profits will magically materialize. As Arnold

Goldstein, bankruptcy attorney and author of 22 small-business books explains, when he's called to consult with a troubled company, he can always spot his new client's car in the parking lot—the Mercedes, the BMW, or the Jaguar. As he strolls by open office doors, he can always tell the office of the new client—it's the one with the aircraft carrier-size desk and the proverbial teak credenza. According to Goldstein, that entrepreneur should have taken the bus to work, and used two orange crates and an old door for a desk.

The fact is, lush office appointments will never make you any money, nor will a fancy car. And about the only thing you can do with a teak credenza is send it to the Smithsonian as an artifact of rainforest destruction.

Ecopreneurs, like all entrepreneurs, must evaluate every purchase from the standpoint of whether it will generate incoming cash. No matter how trivial the item, ask yourself what would happen if you didn't buy it? How did you live without it in the past? What alternatives (bartering, leasing, buying used, time-sharing, etc.) can get you a necessary item most cheaply?

Of course, as an ecopreneur you'll want to practice what you preach. Every envelope that you reuse saves you a dime; every box of used printout paper you sell to a recycler puts cash back in your pocket and saves landfill space; every drop of water you conserve by educating employees or installing conservation devices preserves an invaluable resource and cuts your energy bills, and every watt of energy you save by using energy-efficient bulbs and adhering to conservation practices keeps the air cleaner and your electric bill down.

Startup cash is also a precious resource for the ecopreneur, and every nonessential expenditure robs you of the opportunity to make a better product and expand your marketing efforts. Marketing drives the other side of the cash-flow equation. The best product in the world won't generate profits if it languishes in your warehouse. The best service idea won't make you a nickel if you aren't selling it. Marketing makes it possible for sales to happen.

Sadly, too many entrepreneurs assume that once a company has built up a firm base, they can back off their marketing dollars—the sales will steadily maintain themselves. Nothing could be further from the truth. Marketing requires an ongoing effort to keep your name out in front of the world, to predispose customers to buy from you, and to keep customers coming back for more. In short, it's the only way to grow your company.

If you work on slashing costs and continually sell, sell, sell, you'll generate the profits you need to satisfy your lifestyle and spiritual needs. As stressed earlier, if you can't save your own business, you'll never save the planet.

9. Manage Your Growth

You want to grow and grow and grow, right? Not necessarily. Ecopreneurs should carefully manage growth for two reasons. First, as a business develops in size, it expands exponentially in complexity. And the bigger the business, the harder it becomes to maintain your clear mission. No matter how steadfastly you inculcate your mission in your employees, customers, and competitors, as your systems grow, they tend to take on a life of their own. And you can't simply inject your values into a sprawling system. Suddenly, the quality of the products and services you offer suffers. People begin spending less time serving customers because they get so caught up in maintaining the system or complying with its bureaucratic needs.

Secondly, by managing growth you ensure that vital controls—checks and balances—stay in place. When a company experiences "hypergrowth," money tends to flow in every direction like water, and budget overruns tend to become the norm rather than the exception; accountability becomes impossible; plans go out the window as the company changes every day; new products tend to come on-line without due consideration as to whether they fit into existing product lines, whether they can be manufactured profitably, or whether they fill a genuine niche in the marketplace; and people tend to operate in crisis mode, putting out fires rather than dealing with core issues that can generate positive cash flow. In that case, a company can plummet into bankruptcy soon after its meteoric rise.

Many ecopreneurs, such as Sally Malanga of Ecco Bella and Jill Matlack of Matlack Environmental Services, chose to fund their own businesses so they could contain their companies' growth rate and ensure that the business remained faithful to the initial vision. Regardless of how you fund your company, plan for orderly growth, which requires making conscious decisions about the size of the company three, five, even ten years downstream.

Every quarter check growth rates and look at the qualitative aspects of the company:

- Are we still making quality products or offering the quality services on which we founded the business?

- Do we still cultivate and serve customers totally?

- Are we still selling solutions to problems rather than pushing goods and services?

- Does everyone here understand the company's mission?

- Have we acquired layers of bureaucracy that thwart accountability?

- Would I want to work here?

If these questions bring troubling answers, it's time to reevaluate your situation and bring about the changes necessary to steer your ship back on course. One thing is certain—the longer you let it drift at sea, the more likely it will come up high and dry on the rocks of reality.

10. Recession-Proof Your Operation

During economic downturns, entrepreneurial businesses can flourish because they're more flexible than large, established companies. Whereas large companies typically react to negative changes in the economy by downsizing (a euphemism for massive layoffs), small entrepreneurial companies can react by finding new niches or by "rightsizing"—readjusting the work to match the existing work force.

Entrepreneurs live and die in the niches during any period, but especially in tough times. No matter how difficult the times, people and businesses will always need certain goods and services, and the ecopreneur sits in an ideal position to provide them with an environmentally sound twist.

When times get tough, the ecopreneur needs to look for niches that the large company cannot fill or can't fill effectively. Go back to Chapter 2 and look at the universal ecothemes. Then ask how, in a changing economy, you can apply those themes in new ways.

Another aspect of recession-proofing your business has to do with "exporting." While this may seem to run counter to the First Law of Environmentalism, "Act locally, think globally," it may be a life-saving strategy in recessionary times. When the economy in your town takes a beating, do business in the next town; if the whole city falls on hard times, extend your marketing efforts to the next city. Or the next state. Or the next country. People around the world are craving environmentally responsible goods and services. When the going gets tough, the tough make their motto: "Act locally, sell globally."

Part II

Taking Care of the Planet

Overview

Curing Environmental Ills

Imagine a November morning in the year 2018. You've just made your coffee with $30-per-gallon bottled water because your tap water is too foul to drink. You're coughing like an asthmatic because periodic brownouts have forced you to stop running your house's air-filtering system. It's 98 outside, for the fifth day in a row, but you have to wear a long-sleeved shirt and a hat because of the increased risk of sunburn since the ozone layer has been severely depleted. You fight your way past a mound of trash—no pickups for two weeks because the ships that carry it to other countries for burial have been turned back again—and board a bus because you can't afford the $28-per-gallon gasoline for your 2012 Chevrolet.

Sound pleasant? No, but that's what life could be like in the not-too-distant future if a number of unfortunate environmental trends are not checked soon. Let's consider the environmental problems associated with the preceding scenario.

Solid Waste

Every day, each American throws out an estimated 3.5 pounds of solid waste, a total of 160 million tons per year—enough to fill a convoy of garbage trucks stretching halfway to the moon. That total has increased by 80 percent since 1960, and will probably grow by another 20 percent by the year 2000. An estimated 10 percent of this trash is recycled and between 5 and 10 percent is burned or incinerated. But the vast bulk of it, more than 80 percent, simply goes into landfills.

According to the Environmental Protection Agency (EPA), by far the largest segment of the solid-waste stream is paper, an estimated 37.1 percent by weight. Yard wastes account for 17.9 percent, metals 9.6 percent, food wastes 8.1 percent, glass 8.6 percent, plastics 7.2 percent, and miscellaneous materials 10.4 percent. When you consider the volume, however, the percentages change. Newspapers account for 14.1 percent; paper packaging 16.2 percent; and magazines, cardboard, and other paper a total of 14.1 percent. Plastic leaps to 16.3 percent, while yard wastes slip to 5.1 percent and glass shrinks to .9 percent. Diapers account for a full 2 percent and fast-food packaging .3 percent, while food wastes, metal, rubber, wood, and textiles account for the rest.

The basic question is this: Where will we put it all? In 1979, about 18,500 landfills were accepting trash for burial. By the beginning of 1990, about two thirds of them had been filled to capacity. Within five years, according to the EPA, one third of those remaining will be full, with only 4,800 left functioning. The United States must open about 500 new landfills each year simply to keep pace with trash production. Clearly, the country is running out of space.

Air Pollution

The thin blanket of air that surrounds the earth is the site of four of the most serious environmental issues of our time: depletion of ozone in the upper layer of the atmosphere; air pollution in the dense, life-sustaining portion of the atmosphere immediately adjacent to the earth's surface; acid rain, which causes the death of marine life and forests over wide areas; and global warming, caused by the accumulation of so-called greenhouse gases, such as carbon dioxide, throughout the atmosphere. The first two are related primarily to the unnecessary release of air pollutants. The last two are both related directly to energy production.

The ozone layer is a wispy blanket of gas that screens out virtually all of the sun's damaging ultraviolet radiation. But it is slowly being destroyed by a family of chemicals called chlorofluorocarbons, widely used as refrigerants, solvents, and for making foam insulation. As the ozone is destroyed, more ultraviolet light will reach the earth's surface. One major effect will be a sharp increase in the incidence of skin cancer. Other effects will be reductions in agricultural productivity, decreases in marine life, and changes in global weather patterns.

Six out of every 10 Americans, more than 146 million, live in areas that do not meet federal standards for clean air. The EPA has identified at least 320 toxic chemicals in air, at least 60 of which are known to cause cancer. Many of these chemicals come from industry: according to a 1985 congressional survey, 230 facilities in 36 states emit 62 million pounds of toxic chemicals annually. But the bulk of the 2.4 billion pounds of toxins released every year come from more mundane sources, including cars and trucks, solvents from dry cleaners, power mowers, oil-based paints and varnishes, charcoal lighters, and a multitude of other products used around the home.

You don't have to be a Ph.D. in chemistry or a physician to figure out that the situation is unhealthy for the environment and the people who inhabit it.

Pollution from Energy Production and Use

Although energy production causes some water pollution, its most profound effects are on the atmosphere. Global warming is caused by the buildup of certain gases, most notably carbon dioxide, throughout the atmosphere, producing what is known as the greenhouse effect. The gases permit the sun's radiation to reach the earth, but prevent that heat from being radiated back into space. Carbon dioxide is produced during the burning of fossil fuels, primarily by electric power plants, but also by cars and trucks; researchers believe that the amount of carbon dioxide in the atmosphere has increased by more than 25 percent since the beginning of the Industrial Era in the late 1700's and that it will more than double by early in the next century.

Scientists believe that the earth's average temperature has risen by about one degree Fahrenheit since the 1850's and that it could climb another eight degrees by the middle of the next century. Most researchers agree that global warming will cause at least a partial melting of the polar ice caps, leading to sharp rises in sea level that will inundate coastal regions and some island nations. Prime agricultural regions will shift poleward, and global weather patterns will change significantly, with rainfall decreasing in the United States and monsoons becoming more powerful.

Acid rain is an air pollution problem that stretches far beyond its source. Sulfur dioxide (produced by burning sulfur-containing petroleum and coal) and nitrogen oxides (produced by all types of combustion) combine with water vapor in the air to produce particulates of sulfuric and nitric acids, which are spread hundreds of miles by winds. When these particulates are ultimately washed from the air, the resultant rainfall can be as much as 10,000 times more acidic than ordinary rainfall.

Acid rain corrodes metals and eats away granite and other stone building materials, causing billions of dollars of damage each year in the United States. It also weakens trees, making them highly susceptible to bacterial, viral, and fungal infections; vast stretches of trees in the eastern United States, Canada, and Germany have been decimated by acid rain. Finally, acidification of streams and lakes kills off the microscopic life that is at the bottom of the food chain, interferes with the reproduction of fish, and ultimately kills the fish directly.

Somehow, we must find a way to generate cleaner energy and use it more efficiently for the sake of all living things on the planet.

Water Pollution

Americans dump 16 tons of sewage sludge into rivers, streams, and the ocean every minute, a total of 8.5 million tons per year. Industry adds another 9.5 million tons of wastes. Both of these totals, however, are dramatically lower than they were a decade ago, largely as a result of stringent federal regulations. Today, a greater source of concern is "non-point-source" pollution—pesticides and fertilizers from lawns and farms, as well as gas, oil, lead, deicing salts, animal waste, and other materials from city streets. Non-point-source pollution accounts for as much pollution as sewage and industrial wastes combined.

We take it for granted that there will always be safe water to drink, but unless we begin acting now, that fundamental assumption may prove to be painfully false.

௸

If all this sounds ominous, be assured that it is. The good news, though, is that as an ecopreneur, you can attack many of these problems directly and make a small but important contribution to their resolution. The problems of solid waste can be alleviated by ecobusinesses that promote the recycling of paper, aluminum, glass, and a variety of other materials. While large-scale air pollution control is the province of government and major corporations, the ecopreneur can help in important ways such as recycling CFC's and by helping companies and individuals cure dangerous "sick-building syndrome." The environmental problems associated with energy production can also be addressed by ecopreneurs who sell alternative energy technologies, high-efficiency appliances, and high-efficiency light bulbs and other devices designed to consume less energy. Finally, ecopreneurs can tackle water pollution problems by marketing technologies that clean up fouled rivers and streams.

These are but a few of the ways that ecopreneurs can help heal the planet; the opportunities for businesses that will allow you to do well for yourself and well for the earth are virtually endless. Each chapter gives you an overview of a specific business branch, along with technical considerations, marketing advice, and a glimpse of strategic issues. You'll also get inside advice from people who have tried it already. Guided by their insights and experience, you'll maximize your chances of success.

Chapter *Six*

Paper Recycling:
Making a Living from Yesterday's News

In Angelus Androutsopolous's native Greece, paper recycling is a way of life. His country has virtually no forests, so all virgin pulp must be imported, and most paper made there is recycled. Also, almost all companies routinely recycle their office paper. "The companies just do it, it's not a big deal," says his wife, Valerie Smith-Androutsopolous. Androutsopolous had worked in his family's recycling business for 12 years before the couple moved to the United States in 1988 to start their own firm, and he was not prepared for the more cavalier attitude with which U.S. offices viewed their paper wastes. "We needed to package the [recycling] idea and make it more attractive," she says. Their Vangel Paper Co. in Baltimore, Maryland, provides a textbook example of how to begin a recycling business from the ground up.

Since their first task was to learn something about the local recycling market—prices, buyers, needs, and so forth—Angelus took a job with another recycling company in the area. His new boss, who occupied a somewhat different niche in the recycling market, knew about his plans, helped him make contacts, and, when Angelus left four months later, even gave Vangel its first piece of business—a subcontract to strip the insides from books for recycling. Vangel obtains old textbooks from school systems, discarded books from government agencies, remainders from publishers, and books thrown out by libraries and other institutions after they have been microfilmed. The company then cuts off the bindings, extracts the paper, and bales it for shipment to recycling mills. Currently, book recycling accounts for about half of Vangel Paper Co.'s business, but Valerie expects that portion to decline as their office-paper recycling programs expand. Even so, it played a key role in helping them get through the difficult early stages of organization.

The pair began with a nest egg of $25,000, and during the first year of operation they borrowed an additional $10,000. "It definitely was not enough," she said. "We didn't know enough about the recycling business and we underestimated the costs. Inevitably, costs are higher than you expect. That's true of any small business."

Their first acquisition was a paper cutter, used for removing book bindings, followed by a suitable truck for hauling their stock, a forklift, a scale, and an appropriate warehouse.

Advertising proved to be of limited value to Vangel, because most of the calls they received concerned newspapers, magazines, and telephone books, none of which the company recycled. Initially, Vangel acquired many small customers through Valerie's contacts in the local environmental groups to which she belongs. Though these small-office customers were not profitable at first, Valerie says that contacts made through them led to some of Vangel's larger accounts.

Once the couple had a business plan in hand, Valerie began visiting potential customers to explain their services. Among their initial targets were companies that did a lot of data processing and thus produced large quantities of computer printouts. But many of these companies were already recycling their paper, so she was forced to focus more on other types of companies, as well as universities and hospitals.

When Valerie and Angelus started in November 1988, they were the only staffers, and they did not draw salaries. Valerie's mother would also come over occasionally to answer the phone and help out. "It got to be kind of an addiction for her," Valerie said. "My grandfather, who is eighty-two and retired, is also here every day. He cuts off covers and does small jobs around the shop, like attaching the pencil sharpener to the wall. But it took a long time before we got to the point where we could hire people to move [paper] out faster."

After two years, Vangel is self-sustaining, and servicing seventeen larger companies and three universities. Valerie constantly seeks more corporate customers, and would like to expand into other areas, such as newspapers and aluminum.

What is the biggest complaint of these ecopreneurs? The belief that trash means cash, regardless of the content. "People are under the impression that we are getting something for nothing," says Valerie with a sigh. "That's certainly not the case when I have to pick it up myself in the car or go around in a twenty-foot truck." Trash *can* mean cash. But like anything else in life, only when you work at it.

৫১

The United States uses an estimated 67 million tons of paper annually, the equivalent of a forest containing about 850 million trees. Sunday newspapers alone consume 500,000 trees every week. About 25 percent of all U.S. paper is recycled at nine plants scattered throughout the country, representing a savings of about 200 million trees. Producing one ton of paper from wastepaper uses 64 percent less energy and 58 percent less water than producing it from trees; it also produces 74 percent less air pollution and 35 percent less water pollution. Cardboard is the most commonly recycled form of paper, with newspapers a close second. Other types of paper with potential for recycling include junk mail and high-quality paper used in offices.

Technical Considerations

The first step in recycling is to moisten and shred the paper in a machine that works like a gigantic kitchen blender. The pulp, which consists primarily of long cellulose fibers, then passes through a series of filters of decreasing size to remove contaminants and globules of glue. It is then rinsed to remove inks and bleached with either chlorine or peroxides to improve whiteness. At this point, it is sometimes mixed with virgin pulp from wood, but increased supplies of paper from recycling facilities have decreased the need for such mixing. In some modern recycling plants, the pulp also goes through a machine called a refiner that roughens the surface of the smooth cellulose fibers so that they will bind together more tightly—much like strips of Velcro—thereby strengthening the paper. The pulp finally progresses into paper-making machines that press it flat and remove all the water.

Paper can be recycled only a finite number of times. Virgin paper made from wood is composed of very long cellulose fibers, which provide its strength. Each time paper is recycled, these fibers are broken down into shorter fibers, which provide less strength. It also generally cannot be made as white as virgin paper. Still, it has many applications, ranging from book publishing to product packaging.

Market Overview

The current status of paper recycling is double-edged. The good news: recycling of paper is increasing dramatically, thereby reducing the load on landfills. The bad news: these increases are being mandated by local governments and are being achieved in ways that will reduce the opportunities for ecopreneurs to make a profit from them. Even so, ecopreneurs can still fill many niches, particularly in collecting high-quality papers from businesses and marketing recycled paper products.

Recycling paper creates very definite environmental benefits. According to *Garbage* magazine, if one ton of paper were to be made entirely from wastepaper rather than from virgin wood pulp, it would save 17 trees, 4,100 kilowatt-hours of electricity (enough to power an average home for six months), 7,000 gallons of water, 60 pounds of air-polluting effluents, 3 cubic yards of landfill space, and tax-payer dollars that would have been used for waste-disposal costs. Of course, new paper is never made entirely from recycled wastes, but the principle holds nonetheless. Every increase in the percentage of recycled wastepaper in new paper contributes to solving environmental problems.

Paper recycling has been growing slowly over the last two decades. According to the American Paper Institute, in 1970 about 13 million tons of paper were recycled, approximately 22.5 percent of all the paper used that year. By 1988, the most recent year for which figures are available, about 26 million tons were recycled, or approximately 31 percent of all paper. That slow growth rate will most likely accelerate during the coming decade, according to a survey conducted for the American Paper Institute by Franklin Associates of Prairie Village, Kansas. Researchers there predict that about 40 million tons of U.S. paper could be recycled by 1995, accounting for an estimated 40 percent of U.S. production.

It is important to remember, however, that not all paper is the same. The length of fibers in the paper, the amount of ink used for printing, and the amount of processing performed (such as during the manufacture of high-gloss papers) all play a role in the recycling of wastepaper. In general, high-quality recyclable papers such as stationery and computer paper can be used to make lower-quality stationery or paper towels; old newspapers cannot be used to make new stationery, and old cardboard containers cannot be used to make new computer paper.

Understandably, different types of paper have different recycling rates. The statistics below were compiled by *Fibre Market News* for 1988:

- Virtually 100 percent of preconsumer waste, which is primarily scrap material produced by the paper industry itself, is recycled. This material, which includes such things as leftover paper from the manufacture of envelopes and paper strips trimmed from books, amounted to 3.6 million tons in 1988. These so-called pulp substitutes, when baled, are worth as much as $200 per ton on the East Coast but as little as $30 per ton on the West Coast.

- About 50 percent of all cardboard boxes were recycled, accounting for 12.4 million tons. This material is worth $25 per ton on the East Coast and $60 per ton on the West Coast.

- About 37 percent of all high-quality office papers and computer printouts—so-called deinking papers—were recycled, accounting for 2.5 million tons. Office grades of paper were worth $50 to $60 per ton in the East, $100 to $120 per ton in the West.

- About 34.8 percent of old newspapers were recycled, accounting for 4.8 million tons. These papers have a value of as much as $40 in the West and less than zero in the East, meaning that brokers have to pay to have them hauled away.

- Only about 13 percent of mixed papers, which includes all uncontaminated wastepapers not classified elsewhere, such as unsorted office papers, magazines, envelopes, direct-mail items, and other household papers, were recycled, accounting for about 2.9 million tons. These have a value of perhaps $5 in the East, as much as $25 in the West.

Wastepapers are used in 500 of the 600 U.S. paper mills. About 200 mills, most of them relatively small, depend virtually entirely on wastepaper for their raw material. Another 300 use between 10 and 50 percent wastepaper in their manufacturing process. According to Franklin Associates, the U.S. paper industry is rapidly increasing its recycling capacity, which spells "unprecedented growth in wastepaper demand by domestic mills."

Supplies of Recycled Paper

The greatest increase in recycling during this decade will involve newspapers. Communities throughout the country are beginning to mandate curbside recycling for newspapers, where the home owner must separate newspapers from trash and leave them on the curb for pickup by the regular trash collector. This mandated recycling is occurring because it represents the simplest way to make significant reductions in the volume of trash buried in landfills, but it has had an adverse impact on the recycling industry. Supplies of old newspapers now exceed demand, and the price paid for them has dropped substantially, often by more than half. In some areas of the East, old newspapers are being stored in warehouses because no market for them currently exists.

But that situation will change over the decade, albeit slowly. The prime mover in the change will be state laws that require newspapers to use a higher proportion of recycled paper in their printing plants. California and Connecticut have already passed such laws and other states are expected to follow suit. In response to these laws, mills are increasing their capacity to use old newspaper, investing more than $1.1 billion by 1995, primarily to increase their ability to wash ink out of old papers.

Some ecopreneurs are also finding new uses for old newspapers that do not involve recycling. Old newspapers can be shredded and used to make animal bedding (for more details, see page 116) or as a hydromulch in gardening. In the latter application, the shredded newspaper inhibits the growth of weeds and helps the soil hold moisture. Old newspapers can also be used to make molded pulp products, such as egg cartons or the fiber drink holders used at fast-food restaurants for carrying several milkshakes and sodas.

The combination of all these factors, according to Franklin Associates, leads to a projected 1995 recovery of 8 million tons of old newspapers, equivalent to 51.6 percent of the new supply of newsprint.

Unfortunately, this increase will be of little benefit to the small ecopreneur. Traditionally, newspapers have been collected by service organizations such as the Boy Scouts and community groups, and are gathered and shipped by small "mom and pop" operators. But the growth of curbside collection is "squeezing the Boy Scouts and the community groups out," according to Peter Bunton of the American Paper Institute. Increasingly, collection and shipping of the papers is being handled by refuse companies. Except in isolated circumstances, newspaper recycling does not offer a good option for the potential ecopreneur.

Cardboard is probably also not a good option. Although Franklin Associates projects that recycling of cardboard will increase to about 65 percent by 1995—essentially the maximum amount of recycling technically feasible—that recycling will be carried out primarily by the same groups that are doing it now. Finally, preconsumer waste is also not a viable option for the ecopreneur, since that paper is already in the hands of the paper companies.

That leaves only mixed wastepaper and high-grade deinking papers as potential niches for the budding ecopreneur. Historically, the demand for mixed wastepapers has been limited because of two factors: first, the demand for products for which mixed papers are most suitable has either declined or, at best, not grown; and second, the technical problems involved in using mixed papers in other products are great. There is some reason for optimism in the future, however. Use of mixed papers in paperboard manufacturing will probably increase, as will exports. Furthermore, newsprint producers who have installed the newest systems for deinking wastepaper will be able to use magazines for a significant proportion of their wastepaper needs.

Opportunities also exist for technological innovation with respect to mixed papers. The potential problems that do not yet have solutions include devising ways to upgrade the paper so that it can be used for stationery and other forms of high-grade deinking paper; developing new ways to use the mixed paper to produce such products as telephone books and catalogs; and discovering ways to burn nonrecyclable paper in existing industrial boilers to recover its energy content.

By far the best opportunities in the short term, then, involve collection of high-grade deinking papers, such as those produced by offices. These papers are—and for the foreseeable future are likely to remain—in short supply and high demand. The potential also exists to upgrade mixed wastepaper to deinking grades by sorting manually or by machine. Franklin Associates projects that by 1995 the collection of deinking papers will nearly double, to 4.4 million tons, or about 50 percent of the total available.

Collecting Paper from Offices

A wide variety of models for collecting office papers exist, and these are driven by a variety of economic factors in a particular region. It can be much less expensive to set up shop in a city where mandatory reductions in the volume of business waste are in effect than in one where they are not. Such considerations will also determine whether the ecopreneur can sell or rent collection bins to the business or must provide them for free, and whether the fledgling company will have to pay for the wastepaper or will be able to obtain it in return for hauling it away.

The extremes are represented by two examples, the Undaunted Recycler in Eugene, Oregon, and Newhallville Recycling, Inc. in New Haven, Connecticut. Dan Hayden began his business in Eugene with just $2,000. The three partners who started Newhallville invested "a couple of hundred thousand dollars," according to manager Suzanne Angier. Hayden's low startup cost probably represents an exception that other ecopreneurs cannot easily duplicate. Newhallville more accurately reflects the investment required to run a cutting-edge organization.

Other companies have generally incurred startup costs somewhere between these two extremes, although in general closer to Hayden's than to the Connecticut operation's. Matlack Environmental Resources, Inc., of Durham, North Carolina got started on a stake of $100,000, and coowner Jill Matlack estimated that they could have started on only $50,000 if they had restricted their efforts to collecting only paper. Their startup costs were also increased because the company serves as an intermediate processing center (IPC), performing some steps in the recycling process such as crushing and drying cans and crushing and baling plastic bottles before shipping the processed materials out.

Getting Started

A paper recycler essentially performs three tasks: acquiring clients and arranging for them to save paper and, perhaps, other recyclables, such as aluminum cans and glass bottles; picking up the collected paper on a regular schedule; and storing the paper and preparing it for shipment to a paper mill. In addition, a recycler might offer related services, such as shredding confidential documents.

For his $2,000, Dan Hayden bought an old truck, a telephone line, some advertising, and some cardboard barrels to give to his customers. He then went out and started soliciting for clients. To his chagrin, he found that most of the large-volume generators of office and computer paper were already working with recycling groups with more resources than he had. "But no one was doing it on such a small scale as I was planning . . . and I had a much lower overhead," he says. Those factors offered him a ready niche.

His most profitable clients are small print and copy shops, which account for a large percentage of his volume, even though they represent fewer than 20 of his 375 clients. "They often have to waste a lot of stuff to get it right," he says. This means he is able to acquire a lot of used paper from them. Most of the rest of his clients are offices with 10 to 20 employees, although some are even smaller.

Hayden provides cardboard barrels for his clients, who call him when the barrels are full. The barrels become filled at sporadic intervals—some don't need to be picked up for six months, although, Hayden says, "It doesn't matter how long it takes as long as they are willing to provide the space to store the barrel." Others he must pick up daily or every other day.

Once he collects the barrels, he sells the paper to a local mill operated by Weyerhauser, which pays him a small premium above normal rates because of the high quality of the paper he provides. Recently, however, the prices for all types of paper he carts to Weyerhauser have gone down by as much as 20 percent, and he expects further price decreases because of oversupply in the area.

In late 1990, Hayden was collecting about 20 tons of paper per month, about four times the volume he had been achieving at the beginning of the year, and his monthly revenues were more than $4,000.

Newhallville, in contrast, started off more ambitiously, with a truck, scales, paper shredder, baler, and a warehouse. It also offered a broader selection of services, picking up not only office paper, but also newspapers, cardboard, bottles, and cans. The company does not particularly want to pick up all those items, Angier says, but a Connecticut law that comes into effect in January 1991 requires that offices recycle them. "Because of the law, people want one vendor to handle everything," she says.

Newhallville sells or rents collection and storage bins to clients. A desktop box for paper, for example, costs $2.20, and comes with a variety of educational and promotional material. Stackable central storage bins for all types of recyclables cost $10 to $18 apiece. For $15 per month, the client company can also rent large storage containers that are kept at a site accessible to Newhallville's trucks; there is no charge for these containers if the client produces more than four tons of paper per month, but only the very largest customers produce that much. Clients can purchase most of the containers elsewhere if they desire, but they have to purchase the desktop boxes if they want to get their people trained in the recycling procedures. "And we don't want to pick up from people who haven't been trained," Angier stresses, because different items get mixed together, which necessitates manual sorting.

Like Hayden and other recyclers, Angier found that most of the companies that produced large amounts of papers, including large offices and print shops, were already recycling. Newhallville has thus concentrated on smaller offices and print shops, as well as copy shops. After about a year in operation, the company had approximately 60 clients. Recently, however, Newhallville secured a contract for all the state offices in New Haven, which covers about 5,000 employees.

Also like Hayden, Newhallville gets the paper for free, but not every ecopreneur in the business is as lucky. Vangel Paper Co. in Baltimore pays its clients as much as $50 per ton for high-grade deinking paper. Matlack Environmental Resources also pays for the goods it collects, offering large customers a small rebate on the profits it makes. But because of the soft market for many of the papers the company sells, it is considering imposing a fee for removal of materials from small companies.

Selling Your Product

Perhaps the greatest potential for finding a niche in recycling paper lies in selling goods manufactured from it. This field has been tapped only to a very limited extent so far, and seems likely to grow dramatically as the volume of recycled paper expands during the coming decade. Much of that potential will be absorbed by main-line paper goods suppliers who will incorporate recycled goods into their normal product mix. But a good opportunity should remain for specialty operations—in effect, boutiques—that sell *only* recycled products. Dealing with such businesses will definitely appeal to the environmentally committed.

Tapping this market is as crucial to the success of paper recycling as is collecting wastepaper. Unless a market develops for products made from recycled paper, paper mills cannot afford to pay a sufficient price for wastes to encourage recycling, a problem that could hurt the whole paper recycling industry. "If you are not buying recycled paper," say the editors of *Garbage* magazine, "then you are not recycling."

In most ways, starting a business that sells recycled paper products does not differ from establishing any other type of business, be it mail order or retail. The only real difference lies in the selection of products and in lining up potential suppliers. Beyond that, the business practices look identical.

The cost of starting up a business can vary dramatically, however, depending on the type of operation. A mail-order operation requires enough capital to print an initial catalog, to advertise in selected locations, to acquire appropriate licenses, to install a telephone, and to purchase a small amount of product. Daniel Jerrems started Atlantic Recycled Paper Co. in Baltimore with only $16,000 in cash and credit. Once initial orders begin to come in, you can buy more product to fill the orders, and your enterprise can quickly become self-sustaining.

Establishing a retail store can be much more expensive. The ecopreneur will need to have funds for a deposit on the retail space and for several months' rent. It will also be necessary to purchase enough product to have the store well stocked. For a small store in an older area of town, and with a modest inventory—the most likely conditions for a newcomer—the required capital would probably be in the tens of thousands of dollars. For a store in a trendy mall, where a somewhat larger inventory would be advisable, the requirement will be substantially larger.

The profit margin in selling recycled paper goods is likely to be smaller than that for many other retail products. Recycled paper goods cost more to manufacture than those made from virgin paper, primarily because most of the paper is made by smaller mills that do not benefit from the economies of scale. That higher price will be passed on to the retailer in the form of higher wholesale prices. But the retailer will have to absorb much of the increase in order to keep prices competitive with those for virgin paper products. A few dedicated environmentalists may be willing to pay a premium to purchase recycled goods, but the companies that should make up the profitable core of the retailer's business will not. This price differential may decrease in the future, however, as small paper mills expand their operations and begin to benefit from large-volume production as makers of virgin paper now do.

Marketing Considerations

Advertising is of only minimal benefit for paper collectors. Advertisements in the Yellow Pages, for example, mostly bring calls about newspapers, telephone books, and other types of papers that most small recyclers do not handle, says Valerie Smith-Androutsopolous of Vangel. The best way to find clients, she says, is to solicit them face to face.

For mail-order businesses, the best places to start are publications directed at environmentally concerned individuals (see page 296). These are much more likely to reach potential clients who are already inclined to purchase environmentally acceptable products, and they are typically cheaper to boot. Paper recycler Daniel Jerrems says that although you will probably advertise in national publications, you may find that the costs of shipping products to distant locations is prohibitively expensive.

Free advertising is even better. Be on the alert for special issues of consumer magazines that are dedicated to environmental topics and television programs with a similar focus. A brief mention there can be much more effective than an expensive advertisement. Jerrems noted that a one-inch segment of text in a listing of environmentally conscious purchasing sources in *Better Homes and Gardens* doubled his business in that month. An 80-second spot on MTV brought in 400 phone calls. Also be alert to environmental writers for the local newspaper, who may be able to benefit from your insights.

Participation in environmental groups also represents a valuable source of goodwill. For the recycler, such effort may provide entrée into companies that are interested in beginning recycling programs. For the retailer, members of such groups can provide a core of motivated customers. Recyclers will also find that marginally profitable work with small companies and offices may result in contracts with larger organizations. In addition, the recycler should maintain good relationships with other recycling groups. Dan Hayden notes that many of his clients were referred to him by larger paper recyclers who did not want to service small accounts.

Strategic Issues

Competition

As discussed above, the primary competition for the retailer on the local level will be conventional paper goods dealers. In that case, matching prices is probably the most effective way to compete. On a national basis, the primary competitors will be other ecopreneurs, and the competition will be keen, particularly for the newcomer bucking an established company. In those cases, strong media relations and self-promotion campaigns may be the deciding factors in becoming fully competitive.

For the recycled-paper collector, the primary competition comes from large refuse contractors who provide curbside service to home owners and who may decide to diversify. Other competitors may be service organizations and community groups that work without pay to provide funds for their causes. Such competition can be particularly difficult to counter. Jill Matlack notes that her city is also serviced by a larger recycling company that has contracts with the city and has consequently received far more publicity. Furthermore, that company is organized as a nonprofit corporation and is thus perceived as a charity. "They are getting paid lots of money to do the work, but people still think of them as a charity and eighty-five percent of their work force is composed of volunteers," she said. "It is difficult to compete against such a group, but we just have to keep plugging away."

Impact of Government Activities

Legislation can have a powerful impact on the ecopreneur, both positive and negative. Since 1983, 30 states have passed laws granting tax breaks and even loans to recycling operations, or mandating curbside recycling or overall waste reduction. As mentioned above, for the ecopreneur in the paper-hauling business, this can cut into business. On the positive side, recent federal laws require government agencies to purchase recycled paper whenever practical.

Diversification

Most of the opportunities for diversification are rather obvious. For paper haulers, the opportunities arise primarily in collecting other types of materials, including aluminum cans, glass and plastic bottles, and newspapers. While Vangel Paper's primary interest is high-quality, recyclable office papers, the company also picks up aluminum cans and, for a few clients, glass bottles. "The market for glass in our area is weak now, but we do it for some companies as a favor," cofounder Valerie Smith-Androutsopolous says.

Collecting cans is also another added service that Vangel provides for its customers. Vangel pays clients between 27 and 30 cents per pound for the cans and receives only 40 cents from recycling companies, barely enough to cover its costs. The company also has to do hand sorting to remove bimetal cans from the aluminum ones (see Chapter 9, "Aluminum Recycling," page 146 for details). If the volume of cans were larger, Vangel could potentially receive as much as 73 cents per pound. But that would probably also require investing in a can-crushing machine and perhaps also a sorter.

Yet another option for paper recyclers is to do business with the general public. The Matlacks have recently opened a "buy-back center" where they purchase recyclables from individual consumers. They also have begun to sell certain types of environmentally related products, such as can crushers and garbage bags made from recycled plastic. A similar expansion of product lines would also be appropriate for retailers of recycled paper goods.

Alternative Uses for Paper

Recycling is not the only way to reuse old paper. Several entrepreneurs have found alternative applications, particularly for types of paper that are not now in high demand for recycling. Anthony Conigliaro sells kits for turning old paper—such as wallpaper, calendars, and giftwrap—into envelopes and bags. Vince and Dawn Hundt (Coon Valley, Wisconsin) convert old newspapers into bacteria-resistant bedding for cows and other farm animals and sell the machinery to others.

Conigliaro is vice president, engineering, for one of the large high-tech companies on Route 128 near Boston. He has a number of patents and inventions that have been quite valuable to his company, but few seem to make him as happy as the Envy-Lopes and Freeby-Bags that he invented in his spare time. The Envy-Lopes are a package of plastic templates that allow the user to create envelopes of all sizes from virtually any sort of paper, although Conigliaro favors old calendars, old wallpaper books, and used giftwrap. The Freeby-Bags are similar templates that can be used to make lunch bags, gift bags, and other containers from the same materials, as well as from cloth.

Conigliaro made a number of prototypes at home in his garage and tested them on his friends and relatives. "There was absolutely no question that they worked," he said. "There's no gimmickry, and within fifteen seconds you can make an envelope of any size. Gift bags take a couple of minutes." Eventually, for about $3,000, he purchased steel-ruled dies for making the templates, but he still makes the kits in his garage. He sells them ($5.95 for Envy-Lope, $8.95 for the Freeby-Bag) by mail and at craft shows. His biggest cost is advertising in magazines such as *Sierra*, *Garbage*, and *Buzzworm*, although he also uses newspaper ads. Much of his business comes from people who have received Envy-Lopes in the mail from friends. "We get a lot of referrals from customers. It's a real pyramid effect." He is also now planning to do direct-mail marketing.

Conigliaro plans to continue operating Anthony's Originals (Natick, Massachusetts) in his spare time until he retires, considering it a hobby, like golf for someone else. He also has a number of other ideas he is working on and hopes eventually to have a full line of products that are his own inventions. "I enjoy selling my own items," he says. His latest, called No-Fuss Foam, is a sponge container in which the remnants of bars of soap are converted into shaving cream. "You use up the rest of your soap, and you minimize aerosol pollutants," he says.

The Hundts are veteran dairy farmers who encountered a shortage of animal bedding during the drought of 1988. Vince Hundt took an old piece of machinery he had lying around, a heavy-duty wood chopper, and modified it so that it proved to be "a very successful newspaper shredding machine. It chopped it into the correct particle size for animal bedding." He found out that local recyclers were happy to get rid of their newspapers and the farmers were happy to get the bedding.

"Shredded paper is hands down the best bedding because it is practically sterile. It's ground up from thoroughly dried wood and doesn't have any sugars to make it palatable to pathogens. It doesn't harbor disease and flies," he says. The only problem is that "it looks like garbage, like somebody didn't clean up after a party. It wasn't easy to introduce it to Norwegian bachelor farmers." The shredded paper typically sells for $60 to $80 per ton during the winter, and has gone as high as $100. Straw, in comparison, is about $80 per ton.

Although the Hundts continue to sell bedding and raise animals, they are now concentrating primarily on marketing an improved version of the wood chopper, which shreds plastic and other materials as well as newspapers. The cost ranges from $7,000 to $30,000, depending on the number of accessories chosen and whether or not it has its own power source. The device has been purchased by other recyclers, as well as by many Midwestern communities. Some communities began shredding newspaper and giving it away, but they started selling it when they discovered its worth, according to the Hundts. They market it through various recycling magazines, and word of mouth has also proved valuable.

Vince Hundt is now designing a mobile shredding machine that a waste handler "could drive through suburbs, tossing in bags of compostable yard waste and food waste. They could haul it to a composting site and then go back for more." Their initial investment was low. "The most critical ingredient was to have a good idea, and then you have to know what the market is. I happened to be a farmer who needed bedding. I had access to a chipper, and my wife said to throw newspaper into it. Everything just grew from there."

Recycling in Action: Atlantic Recycled Paper Company

Daniel Jerrems was the voluntary chairman of a Baltimore environmental center in the summer of 1989 when he began looking for recycled paper for printing the center's newsletter. "I realized it wasn't available at the corner office-supply store, that it was pretty hard to get." He also realized that, for recycling to continue to grow, there had to be uses for its end products. "Having been an environmental activist, I knew of a lot of [recycling] programs that had been started only to be halted for lack of a market." He launched Atlantic Recycled Paper Co. in an effort to help solve that problem.

Atlantic sells anything that can be made from recycled paper: copy paper, printing paper, computer paper, mailing labels, legal pads, paper towels, toilet paper. In its first year of operation, Atlantic was strictly a mail-order catalog operation, but in September 1990 Jerrems opened a retail store in Baltimore as well. The company ships its products throughout the country, as far away as Alaska and Hawaii.

"People come to us because they know we sell true recycled products," he says. Generally, recycled paper is thought of as paper that has been used once, thrown out, and then made up into new paper and used again. This is called post-consumer wastepaper. But there also exists a second category of recycled paper called preconsumer waste that is comprised of envelope cuttings, strips trimmed from the edges of books, and all types of other paper scraps produced during the manufacturing process. "Companies have always used this without telling the consumer about it," Jerrems says. "But with the new environmental consciousness, some companies are relabeling this same product as recycled and increasing the price, even though they're doing very little for the environment. We are probably the source for the widest variety of true recycled papers, papers with the highest amount of postconsumer waste content. We are also trying to market papers that are not bleached with chlorine, but only with hydrogen peroxide."

Jerrems began Atlantic with $2,000 of his own savings and two $5,000 credit lines, "the type you get advertisements for in the mail all the time." He subsequently put in an additional $4,000. For most of 1990 the operation was internally financed. The first thing he did was track down as many recycled paper goods manufacturers as he could and put together a small, four-page catalog. He then began placing small ads in environment-related magazines and mailing out the catalogs. "We went right to national advertising, but as it turns out, most of the business is local because of the shipping costs." But they do get some large orders: the University of Oregon, for example, just purchased 400 cases of recycled copy paper, "and they paid the shipping charges."

As orders came in, he would purchase products from the manufacturers, break them down into smaller lots for retail sale, and store the rest in his garage. He mostly shipped by United Parcel Service, which stopped by his house every day. Slowly, he has also developed some larger business accounts, whose purchases are shipped by commercial trucking concerns. Salesmen in Baltimore, Philadelphia, and Washington—working on commission—have provided much of the commercial business. "Businesses have been very receptive, as long as our products don't cost more than virgin paper," he said, although some will tolerate a slightly higher price for the cachet of using recycled materials.

Although he relies largely on his own ads and catalog—which has now grown to eight pages and "is straightforward, no hype, just basically a listing of the products"—Jerrems has gotten some help from publicity. "An inch of text in a tiny section of *Better Homes and Gardens*" doubled his business in that month. "The business has continually grown, and each month has been better than the last," he said. In the fall of 1990, business was improving to as much as $40,000 per month.

Jerrem's biggest problem is the small profit margin. "Most mail-order companies work on a 50 to 200 percent markup, but we can't do that because we could never sell the product. We don't want it to be a specialty item that only the affluent environmentalist can afford. Our purpose is to replace virgin paper with recycled, and in order to get anywhere with the business, we have to be competitively priced with virgin paper. It costs us more to buy it, so our markup has to be low."

Initially, Jerrems handled everything himself. He shortly had to quit his full-time job, but he continues to work some evenings and weekends as a physician's assistant at a local hospital. "That pays the mortgage while I do this," he says. He also performs volunteer work, focusing on citizen advocacy, and is chairman of the Baltimore Recycling Coalition.

Atlantic now employs two full-time people, who handle the order-taking, billing, and other office duties. But the company contracts out warehousing, packaging, and shipping to a local workshop for the handicapped. "We're doing something for the environment, but we're also providing jobs for people who have trouble in the [conventional] workplace because of their handicaps. That makes the business even more worthwhile."

~

At this point, you've gotten a pretty good idea about the basics of paper recycling. If you're sure that paper recyling is the business for you, you might want to browse back through the beginning chapters and think about ways of launching your ecobusiness. Or perhaps you'd like to explore other "earth-healing" ideas first, in which case, read on.

Chapter *Seven*

Plastics Recycling: *Turning Containers into Profits*

Iowa Falls, Iowa, a sleepy agricultural community in the heart of the rural Midwest, hardly seems a likely site for one of the most successful plastics recycling operations in the country. But a combination of fortuitous circumstances and a salesman who wanted to please his customers has produced just that—a plastics company that grossed more than $4 million dollars from two plants in 1989 and that, as 1990 closed, was scaling up to a total of 18 plants around the country.

Hammer's Inc. opened its doors near the turn of the century as a rather typical agricultural business, selling hog waterers, pig nursers, drip irrigation systems, and the normal mechanical contrivances necessary for running a thriving farm. In the 1960's, Hammer's expanded with a line of plastic stock boards, one-by-twelve-inch planks imported from Germany and used to make hog pens and fences. After the founder's son, Floyd, came into the business in the 1970's and began making calls on old accounts, he found that customers loved the plastic boards, but were having maintenance problems because the wooden two-by-fours used to provide a framework for the stock boards were rotting and falling apart. "They wanted to know why they couldn't get plastic two-by-fours that would have the same durability as the stock board," says Dennis Kuhfus, the company's materials manager.

Hammer went to Germany to see if his source could provide the two-by-fours. "They couldn't," he says, "but they knew about an Englishman who was doing a lot of experimenting." So he went to England and met with chemist Brian Harper who developed a way to manufacture the two-by-fours. "Now, Hammer's Plastic Recycling Corp. dwarfs Hammer's Inc."

The plastic two-by-fours made an immediate hit with the farmers. They could nail and saw the stuff just like wood, but they would never have to worry about rot. Hammer knew, however, that he needed a much broader client base to be successful. Wouldn't the materials be ideal, he reasoned, for park benches, picnic tables, and piers, to minimize maintenance costs? Among his first customers was the Chicago Park District, which has already purchased more than 40,000 plastic timbers for benches and landscaping. Now a truck from the Chicago district will show up with a load of used milk jugs and other plastics and go back with a load of lumber. Hammer's has also sold its products to the Bureau of Land Management, the U.S. Department of Agriculture, the Forestry Service, and about two-thirds of the country's state parks and recreation services. The company has also begun producing plastic car stops and speed bumps for parking lots.

Hammer's has been so successful that it recently opened a second plant in Florida and plans to open an additional 16 over the next five years, eight of them as joint ventures with the chemical giant, Research Cotrell. The company's biggest problem now, Kuhfus says, is not finding customers but finding new sources of supply. The company currently purchases plastics from municipalities in virtually all the states surrounding Iowa, as well as from other ecopreneurs. Iowa itself does not mandate curbside recycling, but many cities there are gearing up for it. "We're getting more and more [sources] within the state. It should make a big difference by next summer. I won't have to make a lot of long-distance calls to get material."

ଏଓ

One of the great ironies of modern society is that we use materials with the greatest endurance for the most transient purposes. Plastics are virtually impervious to sunlight and weathering and indigestible to bacteria and other microorganisms that serve as nature's scavengers. Plastic products will remain intact and virtually unblemished long after a tin can has rusted away or an aluminum can has corroded to nothingness. Yet we use plastics primarily for throwaways and disposables with useful lifetimes of days, hours, or even minutes. A polyurethane foam cup that will hold coffee for perhaps 10 to 15 minutes will survive in a landfill for hundreds, perhaps even thousands of years. A foam hamburger container might serve its purpose for all of two minutes before it sails into the trash can. A plastic coffee stirrer may see five seconds of use.

Although plastics still account for only a small proportion of the wastes in landfills—about 7 percent by weight, perhaps 15 percent by volume—burying them represents a severe waste of natural resources. Virtually all plastics are now made from petroleum and natural gas, unrenewable raw materials that are becoming increasingly scarce. Fortunately, governments and ecopreneurs around the country are finding a variety of new ways to encourage recycling of plastics and to find new uses for them. Overall, the strategic and competitive issues involved in recycling plastics parallel those that apply to paper. Increasingly, furthermore, the two businesses overlap on the collection end, as paper recyclers begin to accept plastic, and vice versa. There are, however, some unique characteristics to the plastics industry.

Technical Considerations

One of the prime considerations in recycling plastics is that virtually each type of plastic (and there are many) has unique chemical and physical properties. Substantial quantities of polyurethane mixed into a batch of polyethylene terephthalate (PET), for example, can greatly reduce the strength of the PET and render it unsuitable for many applications. In most cases, that means that recyclers must separate the different types of plastics before doing anything else with it. Sometimes separation occurs during the collection process, such as in machines that will accept only PET beverage bottles. In other cases, the collecting group does it manually. This is the least desirable alternative because of the high cost of manual labor. In the most highly automated systems, the separation can be accomplished automatically at a later stage in the recycling process.

At the processor, the bottles are washed and delabeled, then shredded into small chips. In automated systems, residual aluminum (from the neck rings that hold on caps) can be separated electrostatically, by applying an electric field. Another process is used for automatic separation of different types of plastics. Because varying plastics have different densities, chips of varying composition can be separated by flotation in water. The dried chips can then be melted and used directly to make some types of products or combined with virgin material to make other types. Because of concerns about potential contamination, recycled plastics have not been used to make containers for food or beverage products, but both Pepsi-Cola and Coca-Cola have announced plans to begin using recycled plastics in 1991. Plastics can be recycled an indefinite number of times, with the only limits being losses during processing.

Market Overview

In 1987, more than 57 billion pounds of plastics were sold in the United States. Polyethylene was by far the most important single type, accounting for about 30 percent of the total or more than 17 billion pounds. Polyesters, which are most highly recyclable, accounted for about 9.2 percent of the total, two thirds of that being used for textiles. Only about 1.8 billion pounds of polyesters were used for nontextile purposes.

Although plastics have been recycled for about 12 years, it is still an industry in its infancy with plenty of room for growth. Consider PET, for example, the primary material in beverage containers and the most widely recycled plastic. In 1979, one year after the PET bottle's introduction, 8 million pounds of bottles were recycled. By 1989, 190 million pounds were recycled, according to the National Association for Plastic

Container Recovery (NAPCOR). But that still accounted for only 28 percent of all PET beverage containers and only about 20 percent of other PET containers, such as bottles for oil and peanut butter.

In 1990, plastics processors were paying 10 to 12 cents per pound (about $240 per ton) for separated and baled PET bottles, and recyclers are paying as much as $1,000 per ton for PET chips, making the annual volume about $23 million at the level of bottle collectors and $95 million per year at the level of the recycler. By 1993, according to Caroline Spielmann of NAPCOR, the demand will reach 640 million pounds "and the big problem is going to be collecting enough to meet demand." About 22 companies are currently recycling PET into finished products.

Recycled PET can be made into a variety of products, including geotextiles (such as the liners used in landfills), foam for insulation, and recreational products, such as skis, surfboards, and sailboat hulls. Other industrial uses include the production of fiberfill (the stuffing in pillows and quilted jackets), carpeting, fence posts, paintbrushes, and strapping (to replace metal straps for industrial packaging).

High-density polyethylene (HDPE), the material our familiar milk bottles are made from, is the other important plastic that is currently being recycled in significant quantities. In 1987, only 72 million pounds of HDPE were recycled out of a total of 7.8 billion pounds sold. According to a report by the Plastics Recycling Foundation, however, demand for recycled HDPE could grow to 440 million pounds by 1993. Prices for HDPE are about the same as for PET.

HDPE has a slightly broader range of uses than PET. It is ideal for pipes, for example, and makes excellent lumber, signs, traffic cones, and curb stops. It can also be used in some children's toys, flower pots, garden furniture, and golf bag liners. In the home, it often appears in the base cups for beverage bottles, drums and pails, kitchen drain boards, matting, and trash cans.

One of the largest potential markets in the future involves products made from mixed plastics. Most promising are items such as lumber and industrial pallets, that don't require the same strength as beverage containers, geotextiles, or pipes. Recycled mixed plastics also have a wide range of other potential uses in agriculture, marine engineering (where it resists corrosion by saltwater), civil engineering, and recreational products. Europe and Japan have been particularly active in recycling mixed plastics, and it is just now catching on in the United States. No current estimates are available, but the Plastics Recycling Foundation predicts that as much as 870 million pounds could be used by the mid-1990's. Prices for mixed plastic waste are lower than those for other types of plastic.

Supplies of Recyclable Plastics

Plastic beverage bottles have traditionally been the most difficult item to get consumers to recycle because of the low price collectors have paid for them—a function of their extremely light weight and high volume. But that situation is changing rapidly because of two different types of increasingly popular legislation: bottle deposit laws and mandatory curbside recycling.

In the first case, consumers pay a deposit, generally on the order of two to five cents per container, when they purchase beverages. That deposit is large enough to significantly increase the number who will return the containers to an authorized collection center. In the latter case, residents are forced to separate their recyclables from other trash, and municipalities or franchised trash haulers collect them, typically at the same time that trash is collected.

Neither situation favors the ecopreneur. Mandatory curbside recycling is heavily biased toward large trash haulers who are already making rounds in expensive trucks and are thereby able to pick up plastics without a significant increase in overhead. Opportunities may exist in smaller towns, but special circumstances may be required to make it profitable, and a large investment for trucks and employees may be required.

Bottle bills also tend to favor larger companies, which are able to make large-scale investments, for example in "reverse vending machines," which collect and crush bottles and dispense refunds. But there is still opportunity for ecopreneurs in both collecting containers and serving as drop-off sites. And there is one strong potential advantage to the bottle bills. In many cases, the recyclers simply return the consumer's original deposit. Where once recyclers were paying cash for recyclable plastics, they are now getting it for free.

New Products for Old

The greatest opportunity for innovation in recycling involves plastics. Ecopreneurs have discovered a broad variety of items that can be made from recycled bottles. Usually these products are cheaper than those that would be made from virgin plastics. And generally they are more durable than those made from alternative materials. Unfortunately, making new products from old plastic is expensive. Many of the obvious applications in the future will thus be dominated by large companies such as Rubbermaid Commercial Products, Inc., and E. I. du Pont de Nemours & Co., both of which have become actively involved in recycling.

But there are many opportunities available to a person with a good idea and access to a certain amount of capital. According to Kurt H. Ruppman, president of Western Environmental Plastics, Inc., in Lewisville, Texas, the minimum investment is probably on the order of $300,000 for equipment, assuming that a source of properly cleaned plastic chips is available. That includes roughly $200,000 for the machinery for injection or blow molding, $50,000 for molds, and another $50,000 for support equipment. "To get a system like ours to recycle two thousand pounds of containers per hour, you would spend $750,000 just for capital equipment and installation," he says. "But that's not expensive, compared to the costs of using virgin resins."

Polyester fiberfill, plastic bottles for laundry detergents, and similar items are most likely to be successfully produced by large manufacturers like Du Pont. The niche for ecopreneurs is in the more offbeat type of product, perhaps where there is not a large enough market—at least initially—to interest a large company. Hammer's Plastic Recycling Corp. started off making artificial lumber for farmers, then found other uses for the lumber, such as for park benches and picnic tables. Eventually, they diversified into speed bumps and curb stops as well. Other companies are also making speed bumps and curb stops, and that is a market that is likely to be saturated relatively quickly. Lumber, however, has a much larger growth potential. Port-A-Pier of Manitowoc, Wisconsin, is another company that specializes in producing artificial lumber, in this case for making long-lasting, maintenance- and splinter-free piers. Plastic Pilings, Inc., of Rancho Cucamonga, California, and Trimax Lumber of Lincoln Park, New Jersey, are other producers of plastic lumber.

Aqua Glass of Adamsville, Tennessee, manufactures fiberglass bathtubs, shower stalls, sinks, and portable spas from PET. Aqua was already manufacturing the products from virgin PET when it was approached by processor George Sutch of Alpha Resins in Collierville, Tennessee. Sutch was able to convince the company that their processed PET was chemically equivalent to virgin plastic, but could be obtained less expensively. The products are now distributed in 38 states.

M.A. Industries of Peachtree City, Georgia, recycles base cups from plastic soft drink bottles to make new base cups, which provide added strength to the thin bottles. The base cups are made of HDPE, while the bottles themselves are PET, and the two components must be separated during recycling. M.A. Industries buys HDPE chips from a processor and converts them into base cups, which it supplies to bottle manufacturer Owens-Illinois.

Cyklop, of Downingtown, Pennsylvania, is the world's largest manufacturer of strapping. It has recycled PET beverage bottles to make new strapping since 1981. Household Recycling Products of Andover, Massachusetts, manufactures recycling bins from HDPE bottles. Custom Pak of Clinton, Iowa, converts HDPE bottles into portable toolboxes and other long-lasting products.

Finally, Montville Plastics & Rubber, Inc. of Parkman, Ohio, produces two-inch square fuel pellets from mixed plastic waste by melting and compressing it. Plastic has a high energy content, about 10,000 to 12,000 Btu per pound, which makes it a useful source of energy in steel mills and other furnaces. The company is working on new equipment with which manufacturers could use their own plastic scrap as fuel pellets. "Large companies could reprocess their own contaminated plastics plant scrap into a fuel more economical than coal," says Montville president Don Hofstetter.

Collecting Plastics

The most likely place for a small ecopreneur to enter the plastic recycling business is either collecting plastic bottles or serving as a broker or intermediary between collectors and recyclers. This section of the industry is dominated by large trash collection companies, such as Waste Management, Inc., and Browning Ferris Industries (BFI), but plenty of opportunities remain in niches that are too small for such mammoths. The potential ecopreneur also can enjoy a major advantage in that the plastics recyclers and their trade organizations are actively promoting recycling in order to maintain a steady supply of bottles. These groups will provide helpful hints and advice to the ecopreneur and help her find outlets for her materials. Among these groups are the Council for Solid Waste Solutions, the Plastics Recycling Foundation, and the National Association for Plastic Container Recovery (see Part IV).

Before starting a collection operation, you should determine where the markets are, according to Bailey Condrey of the Council for Solid Waste Solutions. The Council and other groups will help communities and individuals get into contact with potential purchasers of the plastic bottles. Condrey will also encourage them to collect other items as well, such as aluminum and steel cans. "The more things of value you add to the program, the lower the operating costs," he says.

The very low weight-to-volume ratio of plastic presents a major problem in any collection operation. Several truckloads of plastic bottles may be required to match the weight of one truckload of aluminum, for example, thereby increasing costs. One partial solution to the problem is to have consumers crush the bottles before collection. A Philadelphia community group successfully decreased its costs by means of television and radio advertising that featured a memorable jingle, called the "Philly Stomp," that encouraged crushing. Some groups have relied on trucks with built-in compactors; others have hung nets on the outside of trucks to increase storage space.

The weight-to-volume ratio also governs the type of neighborhood that can effectively be served. The ideal situation would be rowhouses or condominiums in a city, where the truckdriver would have to move forward only a few feet between stops. The least desirable might be in a rural area, where the truck would have to travel several minutes between stops. In the latter case, a drop-in recycling center may be the most cost-effective alternative, but the problem then becomes getting consumers to bring in their plastics. The trade groups have designed educational programs to help in this process, but some local ingenuity is probably also necessary.

Having one or two large clients may provide the foundation that allows the ecopreneur time to develop other, smaller sources. Waco, Inc., of Sioux City, Iowa, is a plastics recycling center that incorporates a workshop for the handicapped. The bulk of the plastic bottles is provided by local beverage and milk producers, says Miles Patton. "Iowa is a bottle-bill state, which means that used containers go through grocery stores back to the bottling company," Patton says. "They can't be put in a landfill and can't be used over, so they give them to us." The milk company has bottles that are returned to it when milk on the store shelves passes its pull date and can no longer be sold. "These provide a backbone on which to let our business grow," Patton said.

"We've also established drop boxes at supermarkets and encouraged the public to deposit plastic in these, which they have done. We accept any container that holds liquids that you can buy in a grocery store—everything except cottage cheese, yogurt, and so forth. We also pick up from restaurants and from a local Tupperware dealer, who sometimes has products returned because of their guarantee." In 1990, Waco will recycle about 500 tons of HDPE and PET, employing 30 handicapped people to do sorting, baling, and other tasks.

All in all, the future looks very bright for collectors and processors, says Dennis Kuhfus of Hammer's. "I often get calls from guys who are thinking about getting into the business," he says. "They ask, 'What happens if, after I invest in equipment, the market gets so swamped with trash plastic that it is not going to be worth anything?' I just have to cluck my tongue. For everybody that's out there getting into the gathering business, there's somebody else finding new ideas as an end-user. As the volume of raw materials increases, we're seeing the diversity of the industry increase along with it."

Strategic Issues

Competition

The amount of future competition in plastics recycling depends on which aspect of the business you enter. The most highly competitive area will be the manufacturing of new products from recycled plastics. Several major chemical companies, such as E. I. du Pont de Nemours, Dow Chemical, and Mobil Chemical have recently established new divisions or subsidiaries to produce such products, and they seem likely to dominate the market in the foreseeable future. A smaller recycler may have trouble competing with these industrial giants for the (relatively) small amount of recyclable plastics that will be collected.

By the same token, the increased demand for recycled plastics will be beneficial to collectors and processors, who will be virtually guaranteed a market and reasonable prices for the material they collect. Plastics are currently the least recycled of the major waste materials—only a little over 1 percent is now recycled—and the opportunities should be virtually boundless. The primary competition will arise from mandated city-operated or contracted curbside recycling and from other recyclers. That should not present a severe problem because the ecopreneur can effectively compete by purchasing the plastic bottles from the consumer. That advantage can be even greater in bottle-bill states, where the consumers will presumably be eager to have their mandatory deposits returned.

Impact of Government Activities

Governments have taken or are considering taking several actions that can affect plastics recycling. Perhaps the most draconian are those that would ban certain types of plastics outright. One target of such laws is polystyrene, the foamed, insulating plastic that is most often used for coffee cups and fast-food packaging. Some areas, such as Suffolk County, New York, have flatly banned polystyrene fast-food packaging. Others, such as Berkeley, California, have banned polystyrene foams made with chlorofluorocarbons as a blowing agent. Berkeley has also required that all fast-food packaging be biodegradable, effectively eliminating plastics from use.

The impact of beverage deposit bills is still the subject of controversy. Proponents argue that the deposits provide an incentive for consumers to return the plastic, aluminum, and glass bottles to a recycler in order to get their deposits back. Critics, however, say that consumers are cheated by the bills because they get only their deposit back, and are not paid for the value of their containers. Critics also charge that the recycling rate for many types of containers is just as high in some states that do not require deposits as it is in those that do. That argument is likely to continue for some time; meanwhile, more states are enacting such bills.

A minor legislative problem is federal laws that prevent the use of recycled plastics in food containers for fear that they would be contaminated by disease-causing bacteria. Although several large companies are developing techniques to ensure that the recycled plastics are effectively sterilized, it may be several years before this law is withdrawn. For the moment, at least, there are enough other uses for recycled plastics that the law is not an excessive hindrance.

The U.S. Congress has been considering measures that would encourage recycling by placing a tax on the use of virgin materials, thereby creating or increasing a price differential that would make use of recycled materials more profitable. The fast-food and soft-drink industries have supported such a tax because they fear that more severe restrictions on use of plastics and other materials might be enacted if such a law is not passed.

Diversification

The opportunities for diversification in plastics recycling are similar to those in other recycling industries. The most important is simple diversification into collecting other types of materials, including paper, glass, and aluminum. The plastics collector could also diversify and increase profits by expanding into processing as well. By cleaning plastics, removing labels, and shredding the bottles, recyclers can substantially increase the monies they will receive from the manufacturer using the material. As demonstrated by the experience of Klark Hagan, below, the ecopreneur can also expand into waste collection.

Dropping Off Profits

Klark Hagan is one of Hammer's Plastic Recycling Corp.'s smaller suppliers of plastic for recycling, but he has visions of growing a much larger company. The Monticello, Iowa, landscaper has been carving out his unique recycling niche in rural Jones County and hopes to parlay that into contracts that would make his VIP Industries the largest refuse collector in the area.

Recycling may be "a big item" on the two coasts, Hagan says, but it has come more slowly to the conservative Midwest. Nonetheless, he says, "We're seeing recycling become more and more a part of everyday life," in large part because local landfills are filling up or being ordered closed by EPA because of their poor original construction, which allows potentially toxic materials to leach into local groundwater. The state is also encouraging communities to shut down such landfills. "So," Hagan continues, "the local communities are looking for alternatives to deal with their solid-waste situation. I was looking for an opportunity, and I saw that as a need that was going to have to be filled."

Iowa is a bottle-bill state, so aluminum and plastic beverage containers were already being recycled through local grocery stores. Hagan decided to focus on everything that was left over, especially plastic milk and food containers. He also collects glass bottles, tin cans, newspapers, and scrap metal. "At this point, plastics are our biggest moneymaker, but it's not that big. Prices are ten to twelve cents per pound, and let me tell you, it takes a tremendous amount of milk jugs to make a pound of plastic." Glass sells for about two cents per pound and tin cans for about a penny. "We've been having problems getting rid of paper, but we're beginning to develop a market with local farmers for livestock bedding."

To get started, Hagan purchased a used trailer from a beer distributor and refurbished it in his own shop. Total investment: only $500, because he already had a truck to pull it with. He then went looking for a high-visibility location where he could park the trailer, something like a grocery store. The first two stores he approached were not particularly cooperative. "The first wanted a big statement full of insurance. Another wanted us to cement our own pad and put a fence around it. The third was smaller and locally owned, and they said go ahead. It's worked out well for both of us. They've noticed an increase of sales. People come to drop off stuff and go in and pick up a gallon of milk or something."

Hagan has not spent any money on advertising. The local newspaper ran a couple of stories about the company, which have helped. But his business has been promoted primarily by word of mouth, and collections are increasing. By the fall of 1990, a little over a year after he started out, he was collecting 1,500 pounds of glass every two weeks, 1,000 pounds of tin, about 1,000 pounds of paper, mostly newspaper, and 30 to 40 pounds of plastics, mostly milk jugs.

Because Hagan already had a building he could use, his only other costs were for inexpensive bins to store the collectibles and about $550 for a cutter to chop the plastic into pieces. Commercially available cutters for plastic are quite expensive, but he made do by purchasing and modifying a $350 used "recutter" designed to chop up corn from a silo. He also plans to purchase a baler for the plastic at a cost of about $2,000. Hagan and his father—a farmer who is the public works director for Monticello—do all the physical work themselves, so there is no cost for labor.

Hagan envisions taking over the trash-collection business for the two largest cities in Jones County—Monticello, population 5,000, and Cascade, population 3,000—as well as for some of the smaller communities. "We basically want to take over the entire sanitation project for them, to recycle what we can and get rid of the rest." The cities currently do their own trash collection, and computerized bills are sent out along with water and gas bills. "We want to bill them so much per year to collect the entire city's sanitation and have them send us a check every month . . . We're very close to getting at least one contract."

Hagan would purchase compactor trucks for his own use from each of the two larger communities, since both vehicles are in good shape. "Once I get the contracts, I'll have no trouble arranging the financing," he says. His employees would run the regular trash route with the compactor truck to collect everything that cannot be recycled, then go back over the route with a second truck to collect recyclables. The primary holdup so far is that Hagan has told the communities they would have to mandate recycling to make it work. "The cities are getting interested, but they don't want to force it on anybody. They don't like the idea until their budget starts getting squeezed. Then they finally decide that's what they are going to have to do." Hagan plans to be positioned to take advantage when they finally decide to mandate recycling. "The first person up and running in the community is going to be the one to stand to benefit."

೮೨

For the ecopreneur deeply committed to cleaning up the environment, plastics recycling can an ideal business for "getting even." Plastics are symbolic of the disposable world and are an environmental nightmare. But as you've learned in this chapter, an ecopreneur can do something about the fantastic plastic trap and make a living at the same time. The next chapter covers another ecobusiness designed to heal the planet, glass recycling.

Chapter *Eight*

Glass Recycling:
Grinding Glass into Greenbacks

George Henebury got into recycling long before the green revolution of the late eighties. Beginning with a $3,000 investment in 1971, when empty glass bottles were practically worthless and before overflowing landfills had made the news, Henebury built Circo Glass Company of San Francisco into the largest glass recycler in California, with gross sales of about $8 million in 1989. That same year, he merged Circo with Allwaste Inc. of Houston, Texas, and the company now runs 20 operations throughout the country, making it the largest glass recycler in the United States.

Henebury was working for a rubbish company in the Bay Area when he recognized the need for recycling, particularly of glass bottles, virtually the only beverage containers in use at that time. He quit his job and, with $3,000 in personal savings, began buying glass bottles and selling them to glass manufacturers after collecting them in his pickup. His most important sources at the time were small drop-off recycling programs and the bottling industry itself, from which he bought bottles broken during the filling and capping process. He also purchased bottles from a woman who had set up a curbside recycling service in Berkeley. He would clean the bottles, remove labels and caps, sort them by color, and crush them into an appropriate density before selling the cullet, as crushed glass is called, to manufacturers.

With the first profits, Henebury began buying equipment for the company. Among the first purchases were large roll-off containers, some about the size of conventional rubbish bins, which he would install at various sites, such as the many universities in the area. Henebury provided the containers and helped the schools develop educational materials to encourage students and staff to "pitch in." He then paid the universities a token fee for the bottles, typically $10 to $20 per ton. Initially, he hired local rubbish companies to place the containers for him and to pick up the bottles, but as volume grew he was able to purchase his own trucks. He also won a grant from the State of California that helped him purchase some of the equipment he needed, including washing machinery, crushing devices, and scales.

As his volume grew, local bottle manufacturers were not able to use everything he collected, so he began seeking alternative markets. Those to whom he eventually began selling included manufacturers of glass fibers (for insulation), roofing, acoustical tiles, and reflective markers for highways. Previously all of those manufacturers had used only virgin materials. "It took many years of testing and development to break into those industries," says Henebury. "We had to learn how to crush the glass to the proper size and build up a reputation as a reliable supply source so that they could be sure they would have a steady source of materials. That's a difficult thing. We're still growing and developing."

About seven years ago, Circo needed more raw materials. "I asked myself, 'Where's a lot of glass being generated?' The obvious answer was bars, restaurants, and hotels." Henebury began visiting such establishments and getting commitments. "They were interested both in reducing waste and getting some money for it." As with the universities, he would provide a container, the customer would fill it, and he would collect the bottles, giving them a token payment. "Some are really diligent and their volume is large, so the payments are fifteen hundred to two thousand dollars per year. Plus, they were paying to have it taken away before, so they are actually making four to five thousand per year." Henebury works with large hotels, such as the Sheraton, Hyatt, and Hilton, as well as many restaurants and bars—a total of around 1,500 establishments throughout California. With the materials from these sources, as well as others, Circo now processes about 7,000 tons of glass per month.

In 1989, Circo merged with Allwaste via a stock swap, becoming part of the latter company's resource recovery division. Henebury now works as an executive vice president of Allwaste, but his roots remain firmly embedded in glass recycling. "I've always really liked what I do," he says. "I'm a recycler, and I believe in it."

$$\infty$$

Americans throw away an estimated 28 billion glass bottles and jars every year, enough to fill the 1,350-foot-tall twin towers of the World Trade Center in New York City every two weeks. That glass accounts for a little more than 8 percent of the total trash that now goes into landfills. Consider also that less than 10 percent of glass containers are now recycled. Although national figures for recycling are not available, in California, which has one of the most active glass recycling programs in the country, 350,000 tons were recycled in 1989 out of 2 million tons manufactured—only about 17 percent. "There's a tremendous amount of material left in the waste stream that could be recovered and could be a profitable item for a recycler to handle," says Lee Wiegandt of the California Glass Recycling Corp., the West Coast arm of the Glass Packaging Institute.

Supplies of the raw materials for glass manufacturing, primarily sand and soda ash, are cheap and virtually inexhaustible, but the use of recycled glass can still produce substantial savings in energy and pollution. Because the cullet melts at lower temperatures than the materials used to make virgin glass, recycling requires about 32 percent less energy and produces about 20 percent less air pollution and 50 percent less water pollution. Of course, bottles such as refillable soda bottles can be reused simply by washing and sterilizing them, producing a much higher savings in energy and pollution.

Technical Considerations

Recycling glass is a straightforward process. The bottles and jars are washed to remove food residues and labels, and aluminum rings from caps are removed. In automated operations, the metal can be removed at a later stage of the process, along with other contaminants, by sorting with air. The light aluminum pieces fly out of the waste stream, while heavy glass particles continue through. If the bottles have not already been sorted by color during the collection process, they must be sorted at this point or earlier in the processing. The bottles are finally crushed into cullet, which is then mixed with virgin materials during the manufacturing process. Glass can be recycled an indefinite number of times. The only limiting factor is the small loss that occurs during the manufacturing process. There is also no limit to the amount of cullet that can go into new bottles. Some plants operate using 100 percent recycled cullet.

It is crucial for manufacturers to have a steady supply of cullet. The amount of cullet used in a manufacturing process can vary by only 5 percent from one day to the next, Wiegandt says. Larger changes will interfere with the process and ruin that batch of glass. They can't simply stop using cullet because their supply dried up," he says. That need for an uninterrupted supply has discouraged some manufacturers from using cullet.

Some types of glass are not readily recyclable. Most recycling centers will not accept dishes, light bulbs, ceramic glass, or plate glass because the chemical composition of these products is different than that of glass bottles and the two different types cannot be mixed.

Market Overview

Glass bottles typically come in three colors: clear, brown, and green. Clear is the most valuable because it can be used to produce any type of glass. It can be sold for as much as $90 per ton in most locations. The colored glass is more of a problem for manufacturers. As recently as a couple of years ago, says Barry Love of Anaheim Disposal CVT in California, the percentage of glass used in recycling was so small that the pigments in the colored glass would simply be diluted to near invisibility. As the percentage of recycled glass has increased, dilution is no longer possible and the recycled bottles can only be used to make colored bottles. As a consequence, its value is lower than that of clear glass, sometimes as low as $60 per ton.

Crushed glass that has not been sorted by color has the least value of all, often much less than $60 per ton, because it has fewer potential uses. Typically, it is used in the manufacture of products other than bottles, including ceiling tiles, roofing, and glass fibers. The recycling industry is looking to find other applications for mixed-color cullet, as well as for cullet that has been contaminated by small debris. One possible application is as a substitute for gravel in road bases. Glass Aggregate Corporation of Grand Rapids, Michigan, is selling bags of cullet for erosion control in landscaping and to provide drainage under roads.

In the last year, there have been many reports that large amounts of recyclable bottles have been dumped into landfills because there was no market for them. Experts agree there have been some problems, but that they have been exaggerated. According to Wiegandt, most bottle manufacturing plants were built many years ago, a majority before 1940, when "nobody ever dreamed of using recycled materials." Furthermore, most were built in rural areas that have now become congested urban sites with very little room for storing cullet. "They choke sometimes on the volume that comes through," Wiegandt says. "That has frustrated many recyclers who have been sending cullet to plants, only to find waiting lines of trucks and plant locations filled to the brim and having trouble accepting more loads."

Furthermore, recyclers have had "to go through a learning curve. The more cullet you use in manufacturing, the more critical the specifications [of the cullet] become. You have to learn how to clean and sort for maximum value." In short, some loads have been dumped in landfills because they did not meet the manufacturer's criteria for acceptance for such reasons as being contaminated or improperly sorted. But recyclers say that now there is no problem. "Manufacturers can use as much clean, sorted material as you can give them," says Barry Love, director of operations for Anaheim Disposal.

Getting Started

A glass recycler typically performs four tasks very similar to those of the paper recycler:

- Acquiring clients and arranging for them to save bottles, jars, and perhaps broken bottles.
- Picking the glass up on a regular schedule.
- Cleaning, sorting, and crushing the bottles into an appropriate-sized cullet.
- Storing the cullet and shipping it to a manufacturer.

Many glass recyclers also collect a variety of other materials, most often aluminum and plastic beverage containers.

As with other types of recycling, startup costs can run the gamut from very low to very high. Henebury's $3,000 start up cost probably represents the absolute low end, and he began nearly 20 years ago, when that amount would stretch much further. By contrast, New England Container Recovery, Inc. (CRInc.) of North Billerica, Massachusetts, began in 1982 with a multi-million-dollar investment—but beer and soda bottlers banded together to provide the funds for CRInc. in response to a newly enacted state bottle bill. The startup costs were high because the company had to establish a recycling network throughout the state in a short period of time, and it accepted all types of beverage containers. CRInc. services about 5,000 retail accounts across the state, according to vice president Matthew Cox.

For the individual just starting out, smaller is better. The initial investment must go toward recycling bins to be provided to clients, as well as for purchase of the glass. Initially, it may be possible to make collections with a car or pickup, or to hire someone with a truck to do it, but eventually it will be necessary to purchase a truck. Similarly, washing equipment, a crushing machine, and a forklift will soon prove essential.

When you are starting out, local bottling and packaging companies are a good place to make contact. Their breakage can provide a steady source of material. Bars, hotels, and restaurants are another ideal source. An average bar or restaurant can generate a ton of glass per week, according to Wiegandt. All you have to do is place a bin behind the building and ask the manager to put glass in it. The recycler typically pays the owner $10 to $20 per ton, and the owner "reduces his garbage charges and looks like a hero in his community." Another possibility is to work with charitable organizations that can use glass recycling as a fund-raising tool. The recycler provides containers for the glass and the charity does the promotion, asking its members and others to save glass and put it in the containers. The entrepreneur might then give the charity a percentage of the proceeds and keep the rest for costs and profit. And finally, there is the traditional method of simply opening a recycling yard for many different materials, with glass being one of them.

Marketing Considerations

Advertising is of relatively small benefit for the glass recycler; most of the product comes from companies, restaurants, bars, and so forth, and personal contact is much more likely to bring results. One potential exception to that rule is for recycling done in conjunction with a charitable group. In that case, direct advertisement to both members of the group and outsiders can be useful, but such advertising may best be done by the group itself through its internal communication channels. As is the case with paper recycling, free advertising in newspaper and magazine articles is also beneficial. So is participation in environmental groups, which will bring you into contact with dedicated recyclers.

Strategic Issues

Competition

The amount of competition a potential glass bottle recycler will face depends on location. In a bottle-bill state, you may be facing an already established network of recyclers with direct links to both beverage bottlers and bottle manufacturers. In such a situation, the budding ecopreneur may be able to compete only by offering higher prices and greater convenience. Many recycling stations also keep "bankers' hours," making it difficult for the two-job family to bring in their containers. In some states, such as

California, consumers have responded poorly to the recycling networks because of the inconvenience of using them, and the recyclers have had to seek state subsidies to keep the centers in operation. If mandatory curbside recycling is in effect in your community, then the rubbish companies themselves are also major competitors. Again, your primary advantage is paying consumers to bring their bottles: the refuse companies are not doing so.

Finally, even if a recycling network has been established, it may not be collecting from bars and restaurants. Check them out before you get started and learn what the prospects are.

Impact of Government Activities

Two types of laws affecting recycling of glass bottles are generally passed by states. The most common is the bottle deposit law, which requires that customers pay a deposit when they purchase beverages, then get it back when they return the bottles to a recycling center. Reaction to this type of bill has been mixed. The glass bottle industry has generally been opposed to such bills, according to California Glass's Wiegandt. In California, he says, the law required the establishment of a network of recycling centers "that are not very well used by consumers because they are not convenient. Only 10 percent of [recycled glass] is coming back through the centers. The large bulk is coming back through curbside recyclers and old-line recyclers." Many consumers also dislike the recycling centers because they get nothing for their containers except their deposits. Before the bottle bills were passed, they were getting paid for the value of the containers.

More productive is the second type of bill, which requires a higher content of cullet in new bottles. These so-called market-development bills stimulate the recycling market by, in effect, requiring bottle manufacturers to purchase cullet. California passed a bill in 1990 requiring all glass bottles to contain at least 15 percent recycled materials by 1992 and 65 percent by the year 2005. Virtually everyone agrees that this type of bill will sharply stimulate glass recycling.

Also beneficial are laws in many states that require cities and towns to reduce the volume of their trash by a set amount, often 20 to 25 percent, in the near future. Such laws will stimulate recycling of glass and other materials as a simple way to reduce trash volume.

New Uses for Glass: Glass Aggregate Corporation

Recycled glass has very few uses beyond making new glass. Researchers have used it in place of gravel as a base for new roadways, and some have used it as a component of asphalt, but neither of those potential applications consumes significant amounts of material yet. It is particularly important to find new applications for cullet that has not been color separated before being crushed, and thus has little value for making new glass, or that contains various types of contaminants. Felicia Frizzell, a cofounder of Glass Aggregate Corporation in Grand Rapids, Michigan, believes she has found an important new use for such cullet in landscaping and roadbuilding.

Frizzell is a civil engineering technician whose family spent 30 years in the waste-hauling business before selling the company to Browning Ferris Industries. In 1988, she was looking for a way to get involved in recycling. "I thought there were already a lot of uses for newspapers, and plastics were doing fine, but there really wasn't much use for glass. The only market [in Michigan] is one plant in midstate, and they would buy only clear glass. And the glass is pretty heavy, so it costs a lot to get rid of it in landfills."

In her work for a civil engineering company that specializes in land development, Frizzell saw two possible items that could be replaced by a product made from crushed glass: sand bags that are used for erosion control, and 6-inch plastic perforated pipes that are used to provide drainage under roads and parking lots. Both could be replaced by the product that Frizzell and her partner, William Kozak, developed: a 6-inch-diameter, 40-inch-long geotextile bag filled with 40 to 45 pounds of crushed glass.

Frizzell sees the greatest value for the bags in replacing the plastic pipe, whose perforations allow water to seep into the interior and be carried away, preventing deterioration of the pavement. The glass-filled bags do exactly the same thing. Water seeps in through the porous bag and then flows away through the glass at about 90 percent of the flow rate of hollow pipe. The bags are stronger than the pipe because they won't crush, are more durable, and, at 65 cents per linear foot, are cheaper. They also save money because they don't require the fittings necessary for connecting the plastic pipe. "As long as they are placed in contact, they will conduct water," Frizzell says.

In building highways, the pipe is typically buried along each edge of the roadway about three feet beneath the pavement. The bags would be used in exactly the same way, and each mile of highway would use 71 tons of glass that would have otherwise clogged landfills. Under a parking lot, the bags would be laid out in a regular pattern to drain the water away.

Identical bags manufactured using a slightly different geotextile for the bag itself can also be used for landscaping, Frizzell says. Water passes readily through the bags, she says, while mud and soil are blocked and held in place. The glass-filled bags can be used for any application where sandbags are now used, such as for controlling erosion when soil has been denuded of grass during construction. The bags have also been used as weirs in stream beds where too much soil and sand are being carried away. Such applications not only provide a way to get rid of the glass without burdening landfills, but also allow conservation of sand and gravel so that it can be used for other purposes.

Frizzell and Kozak spent about $30,000 developing the bag and patenting it. After announcing the availability of the product in the summer of 1989, they began putting together the first bags by hand. "We spent the dog days of July and August 1989 filling the sleeves before we were really set up to be fully operational," she says. That problem eased when they built a pilot plant in her garage out of scrap metal. That plant, since installed in a 20- by 40-foot garage stall in an industrial park, now produces four bags per minute. They have also purchased pallets for the bags and plastic sheeting to hold them on the pallets, as well as a forkloader to move the pallets around. The firm is currently buying glass already crushed, but they would like to buy their own crusher.

Although Frizzell and Kozak usually buy glass to put in the bags, they have received some free loads as well because it is cheaper for companies to give it to them than to haul it to the nearest landfill. Unfortunately, they have had to turn down some glass because they don't have much storage space at their small pilot plant. Frizzell notes that they are able to use virtually any type of crushed glass: unsorted, contaminated, even plate glass that cannot be used for recycling.

The company is now selling the bags through a local building supply company, and a part-time salesman they have hired is attempting to sell it to state and local agencies. Those agencies, Frizzell says, "think it's a good idea, but they won't buy it yet. The municipalities want to sell us their glass, but they haven't got the procurement program in place to buy what we're producing with it." But they eventually will buy it because they are "running out of choices" for disposing of their wastes. Sales to private companies have been better because of the savings from using the bags instead of pipe.

The pilot plant still produces all the product that the firm needs, and Frizzell is not really interested in expanding production. "We'd really like to sell the technology and license people to [manufacture the products] themselves. The equipment is so simple you can set it up anywhere, and it makes more sense to make the bags where the glass is than to haul the glass to the manufacturing plant. That's our real goal, but we have to sell it here and prove that it works." Overall, Frizzell sees bright prospects for her products. "With the expansion of recycling in this country, we can only see a strong future for our product and process."

⋐⋑

At first blush, glass recycling seems like a marginal line of work. But as you can see from this chapter, it's quite possible to make a living at it, and there are numerous opportunities for creative innovation. If you want to get into recycling, but you're not convinced that paper, plastics, or glass is the right area for you, then consider aluminum, which is described in the next chapter.

Chapter *Nine*

Aluminum Recycling:
Squeezing Cash from Cans

Mike Harvey, who owned a small gas station and check-cashing business in a predominantly Hispanic section of Los Angeles, was looking for a way to expand without having to invest a large chunk of cash. He already owned some empty land on the same corner as his other businesses that he reasoned might make an ideal location for a low-overhead operation such as recycling. Because several other scrap yards already operated in the area, Harvey decided to focus primarily on aluminum cans and glass bottles when he opened Alameda Aluminum Can Recycling in 1982.

After erecting a small building, Harvey purchased scales and bins to hold the cans and bottles, hired an employee to run the store, and hung out his shingle. The operation runs very simply. The employee weighs the material and writes out a ticket the person can redeem for cash at Harvey's gas station. "That keeps overhead low, and we don't have to have a separate cashier, which is a big factor in this area." Harvey also advises potential recyclers to squirrel away a reserve of money when they begin a business. "Some of the companies [I sell to] don't pay right away, so there's a little bit of 'float' there. Some of the companies pay cash on delivery, but they usually pay a couple of cents per pound less," so it is worth it to wait for the delayed payment.

Initially, the glass bottles provided the largest volume. Within a couple of years after opening, Alameda was handling 200 tons of glass per month. But it got to be a big storage, health (from the residues of beverages and food in the bottles), and transportation problem." It was also not very profitable. "We were paying out forty dollars per ton for the glass and getting only fifty." He stopped accepting glass in 1985.

After opening, Harvey advertised in the local Spanish-language newspaper. "It got all the scrap dealers on the street excited when people started bringing ads in to them," he says. That's when Harvey decided to quit advertising and keep a lower profile. The other scrap dealers "could easily put us out of business by raising can prices higher." Instead of advertising, he now occasionally gives out coupons that give customers a bonus of three to five cents per pound the next time they visit.

Harvey attributes much of his success to location. "Low-income areas are usually good recycling areas," he says. Convenience also plays a part, since the center sits next to Harvey's gas station and an adjacent liquor store. "They feed off each other." Harvey also takes pains to keep the lot tidy. "A lot of people don't want to go into junkyards, but will come to us because it is clean." He notes, "It is very critical that my employees speak Spanish to converse with customers." Because of these factors, Alameda now handles 20 to 25 tons of aluminum every month.

When California enacted a bottle deposit bill in 1989, Alameda began purchasing glass and plastic beverage bottles as well as aluminum. "But we just handle beverage containers," he says. "We don't take any other kinds of bottles like we used to." He notes that the mandatory deposits on the bottles and cans did not increase his business volume. "We didn't see much effect at all."

༄

Aluminum is one of the most expensive and polluting metals to produce. It is made from the mineral bauxite, which is normally mined in open pits, often in tropical rain forest areas. Producing aluminum from the bauxite is also very energy-intensive and generates large amounts of pollution. Despite these costs, Americans throw out enough aluminum every three months to rebuild our entire commercial air fleet. Fortunately, aluminum recycling has been promoted extensively since aluminum beverage cans were first introduced in the early 1960's. In 1989, 49.4 billion aluminum cans were recycled in the United States, nearly 61 percent of the 81.25 billion cans sold, according to the Aluminum Association. Currently, says the association's Frank Rathbun, there are an estimated 10,000 aluminum can buy-back centers in the United States.

But beverage cans are not the only type of aluminum that is recycled. In the United States, 35 companies operate 46 plants that recycle other types of aluminum, according to Richard Cooperman of the Aluminum Recycling Association. Four or five of those companies are owned by conglomerates, but the rest are family-owned businesses that have been passed down for three or four generations. In 1990 these companies will recycle about 2.1 billion pounds of aluminum, representing as much as 25 percent of the aluminum that is used in the country. This type of recycled aluminum is not used in beverage containers. Typically, between 50 and 60 percent of it ends up in automobile parts.

Technical Considerations

Recycling aluminum cans is by far the simplest of all recycling processes. There are no labels to remove and no bottle caps that must be separated. The cans are simply melted and recast into new cans. Ink on the cans is burned away during the melting process. The process uses only 5 percent of the energy required for making cans from bauxite and produces only 5 percent as much pollution. The process is also very speedy: recycled cans can be filled with beverages and returned to store shelves within six weeks of reaching a recycling center. Beverage cans can be recycled indefinitely, the only losses being the small amount of aluminum that vaporizes during the melting process.

Recycling other types of aluminum is somewhat more difficult because other metals have typically been added to it to change its properties, most often to make it harder. Also, this scrap generally comes in with some contaminants, says Cooperman. The recycler first burns off the contaminants, then places the aluminum in a furnace and melts it. After the metal has been mixed thoroughly, the foundry pours off a disk about 3/8 inch in thickness and 2.5 inches in diameter, allows it to cool, and then determines its chemical content. Other metals are then added to the molten aluminum to reach the specifications the recycler needs for his customer, and the testing process is repeated. Once the precise composition is attained, the metal is cast into ingots or the desired form. Because of the contamination, recycled aluminum cannot be used interchangeably with virgin aluminum. But the savings in energy and pollution is nearly as great as that for aluminum beverage cans.

Market Overview

Of all types of recycling, aluminum may be the most difficult area in which to start a new business. The 10,000 buy-back locations already in existence are recycling more than 60 percent of beverage cans, and many experts believe that the percentage recycled cannot go higher than 75 to 80 percent. The Aluminum Association's Rathbun notes that recycling rates are low in high population density areas because of lack of storage space. In New York, recycling rates are significantly higher in rural upstate areas than they are in New York City, despite the presence of a 5-cent-per-can deposit. Also, in many areas recycling centers are zoned into industrial areas that are inconvenient for consumers, and these areas also have low recycling rates. Furthermore, "Some people don't participate and never will."

The opportunities are probably somewhat better for recycling other types of aluminum, but establishing a recycling center for them requires considerable knowledge of materials in order to identify different aluminum alloys and price them accordingly. Most aluminum is recycled through multimaterial recycling centers that handle a variety of metals. Some such centers, such as Tri-R Systems in Denver, Colorado, are expanding through franchising, and such franchises offer a good way to enter the field.

Getting Started

By now, the pattern should be obvious. If you want to recycle aluminum cans, you are most likely going to have to establish a buy-back center in an area that has not yet been tapped. Finding such an area may be difficult, but there are probably some left. If your area is already serviced by buy-back centers, it may be possible to find a niche by offering greater convenience to consumers, such as by being open in the evenings and on weekends. Because of the inherent value of aluminum, a simple drop-off site is almost certainly not feasible. Consumers will expect to be paid for their cans, so you will need to have a staffed center, so you will most likely have to have a store or other building, although it may be possible to work out of a truck trailer if your weather is normally good. You will also need scales, and money to purchase the cans, as well as a sufficient amount for advertising to make your presence known. Figure on at least $5,000 to $10,000 initially.

If you are planning to open a multimaterial center to handle scrap aluminum and other materials, your investment will have to be larger because you will need a permanent location as well as adequate space to store the metals you purchase. Tri-R Systems estimates the initial investment in a multimaterial recycling center at $38,000 to $48,000, including a $20,000 franchise fee. That price does not include the cost of a truck and a baler.

Marketing Considerations

Advertising is crucial for the aluminum recycler—to let people know you are in business, to tell them your hours, and to indicate that you are competitive in your pricing policies. The need for advertising can be minimized, however, if you are located in a high-traffic area and your business is readily visible to passersby. Take advantage of all the free advertising you can get, either through news stories or by working with environmental groups. Working with charitable groups might also be a useful way to generate business: they can provide advertising and a "captive" source of clients for a percentage of your volume. Coupons represent another way to build repeat volume: offer return customers a slightly higher price for their cans.

Strategic Considerations

Competition

Your primary competition will be established buy-back centers that already deal in aluminum cans. Aluminum can recyclers have been in business since the cans first appeared on the market in the 1960's, and many have already built up a large clientele. Your primary ways to compete with them will be through a better location, more convenient hours, and higher prices for the cans. You may also be able to compete more effectively by expanding the number of items that you will purchase, including glass bottles, plastic bottles, paper, scrap metals, and a variety of other materials. If you do become a multimaterial center, you will probably do best by creating a store that entices consumers who might otherwise simply throw their cans and other recyclable items away.

Impact of Government Activities

Aluminum can recycling is probably the least susceptible of all recycling businesses to government stimulation. Although many states have passed mandatory deposit bills for beverage cans, those laws have never been shown to effectively stimulate recycling. Relatively high recycling rates occur in those states, but equally high—and even higher—rates occur in many states that do not have them, such as Arizona, Florida, and Washington. Market-development laws that require can manufacturers to use recycled materials are also ineffective. The manufacturers are already using all the cans they can purchase because of the cost-saving involved, and they will purchase even more if increased supplies become available.

A Franchise on Success

David Powelson liked Denver when his New York City metal fabricating and lighting company sent him there to run a company that, unfortunately, was subsequently closed. Rather than return to New York, he quit his job and joined a Denver-based wastepaper company that had been operated by one family for three generations. After two years at that company, he was fired in 1977, leaving him once more at loose ends. He took the opportunity presented by that firing to form Tri-R Systems Corp., which has subsequently become one of the largest multi-commodity recycling firms in the western United States.

"One of the things I looked at was the structure of the existing scrap business," he says. "It was all commodity-oriented: there were people in scrap metal, people in scrap paper, people recycling beverage containers, and so forth. The public had to go to a beverage-recycling plant with their cans, to a wastepaper dealer with their newspapers, to a scrap metal yard with their aluminum yard chair. Our goal was to be a one-stop recycling center that would buy everything we could from the household. We wanted to be customer-oriented, not commodity-oriented." The company now buys 35 types of items, including not only the commonly recycled materials, but also such unusual things as aluminum storm doors, window frames, siding, lawn mower housings, wire, pots and pans, and foil; copper wire, coils, tubing, pots and kitchen materials; brass fittings, valves, pumps, faucets, furniture, and shell cases; photographic film (for the silver content); gutters and downspouts; heater cores; stainless-steel sinks, countertops and containers; and automobile catalytic converters.

Powelson was convinced that he needed to differentiate himself from conventional scrap dealers. He began by having a logo designed "that presented a highly professional image," and decided on locations that would be different from those normally associated with the scrap business. " Then I went to the library and found out I needed a good business plan," which he subsequently developed. Finally, he went to "a lawyer that I understood was the best in town at organizing small businesses, and asked him to do our incorporation papers and to advise me how to raise money so that I didn't violate any laws." Instead, the attorney put him in contact with two people who read the business plan and agreed to raise the necessary capital if the business could be structured as a limited partnership and as a tax loss for at least the first year. "And so, about three months after I was fired, I started with about two hundred thousand dollars and a game plan that approached the market in this unique way."

Tri-R began with one location in a heavy industrial area. Powelson characterizes the first six years of operation as "a struggle-for-survival period," but he spent that time developing and refining the business techniques that have since proved highly successful. Among the primary ingredients of the company's success are close control of inventory and careful attention to pricing. Because Tri-R's recycling centers are indoors, or in 45-foot semi-trailers, space is at a premium and collected materials cannot be kept on site for long periods. Often, materials are moved out to a processor the same day they are collected. Similarly, purchase prices are adjusted daily to reflect the prices that Tri-R can sell the materials for. Trying to predict where the market will go can lead to disaster, Powelson says.

Operation of each Tri-R center is straightforward. A customer drives to the recycling center, where the materials are unloaded and weighed. The type of material and its weight are entered into the computer system, which calculates the purchase price. The customer receives a computer-generated receipt detailing each commodity, its weight, the purchase price, and the total for all items recycled. The customer is paid in cash and leaves. The material is then sorted, loaded, and shipped to a processing plant. On the basis of this simple procedure, Tri-R's sales have grown from $1.5 million in 1983 to $5.3 million in 1988. In Colorado alone, Tri-R now deals with an estimated 350,000 customers per year.

By the end of 1990, Tri-R expected to have 20 recycling centers in operation in Colorado, Wyoming, and Arizona. Sixteen of those are franchise operations licensed by Tri-R. For a $20,000 franchise fee, the company helps a prospective recycler find an appropriate location and get established in business. Tri-R also provides training in how to conduct the business, daily price updates, and recommended purchase prices to the operators. In addition to the franchise fee, Tri-R estimates that startup costs will range from $20,000 to $30,000. The company has developed proprietary methods for determining the size of the recycling market in a given geographical area, and has also created highly computerized marketing techniques that are shared with franchisees. But their most effective marketing tool, Powelson says, is simply having a highly visible and convenient location.

Tri-R also services businesses and government agencies with a fleet of 10 van-type trucks that collect scrap at designated locations, as well as four tractor-trailer trucks and 40 semi-trailers that are used to make scheduled or requested pickups at the businesses. The company now services approximately 1,500 commercial accounts in Colorado. Between the commercial and residential businesses, Tri-R now processes 400,000 to 500,000 pounds of recyclable material daily through its main warehouse in Denver. The most profitable items include aluminum cans, other scrap aluminum, copper and brass, computer printouts, and white office papers.

The company has recently been diversifying its operations. In 1985, it created a new division, DataGuard Systems, that specializes in destroying confidential documents and business records. Instead of paying customers for their paper, DataGuard charges a fee to shred and bail it so that competitors and others cannot obtain confidential information from it.

Tri-R's most ambitious effort has been a curbside recycling program begun in April 1990 in the Ken-Caryl Ranch section of Littleton, a Denver suburb. Residents of the 2,700 homes in the community are able to recycle all of the 35 items that Tri-R normally purchases simply by placing them in a bin that is collected once a week by the company that also collects trash in the subdivision. The trash company delivers the material to Tri-R, whose employees sort the materials and forward them to the processors.

Instead of paying home owners for the recyclable materials, Tri-R returns between 25 cents and 40 cents per month per household to the community for municipal projects. In the first two months of operation, the Ken-Caryl residents recycled 253,000 pounds of material, about half of that newspapers, for an average of about 50 pounds per household. Nancy Larson, director of Recycle Now!, says this is much higher than the national average of 25 to 30 pounds per household for conventional curbside recycling programs.

In the future, Tri-R hopes to add a variety of other materials to the recycling program, including tin cans, junk mail, and polystyrene. One item that is not on the recycling list and unlikely to be in the future is telephone books, even though they have been singled out by environmentalists as prime culprits in needlessly filling up scarce landfill space. The problem, Powelson says, is that there is only a small overseas market for the used books: some countries use the pages to wrap fruit.

⁊ა

Aluminum recycling provides yet another means for the eco-preneur to help solve the solid-waste problem. While the competitive issues must be watched carefully, the field has good potential for people wanting to start ecobusinesses. The next chapter covers opportunities for making a living by improving the air quality and safety in commercial buildings and private homes.

Chapter *Ten*

Atmospheric Business:
Silver Linings in Dark Clouds

It's rare to find a doctor these days who will make house calls. But Dr. Peter Sierck is an exception: he has to make house calls because his patients are the houses themselves, as well as stores and office buildings. Sierck is one of a small but growing number of environmental-medicine specialists, who cure their human patients by treating their homes and offices, removing air-borne volatile organic chemicals, mold, fungi, and bacteria that make the occupants ill. By restoring a healthful environment, he has been able to cure a large number of patients whose more conventional physicians had given up on them, writing off their complaints as psychosomatic.

Sierck reached his current profession in a straightforward manner, even though he ended up half a world away from his native Germany, where he graduated from medical school in 1980. In five years of practice there, he saw many patients with allergies and asthma, which drew his inquiring mind to the "biology" of houses, and how their structural environments contribute to health problems. When he immigrated to the San Diego suburb of Encinitas in 1985, he began looking for a job with a company that diagnosed and treated building-related illness, but he couldn't find one, so he decided to start a firm of his own, Environmental Testing & Technology, Inc. Friends back home in Germany thought he was crazy but he told them that Americans hadn't yet caught on to indoor pollution. But like those of other doctors who treat environmental illness, his business has begun to grow.

The most common symptoms of sick-building syndrome are nose, throat, and ear irritations; headaches; fatigue; general malaise; and skin problems. Often when an individual has such symptoms, the problem can be traced to either the home or the office. Sierck's job is to track down the source of the problem and suggest ways to remedy it.

Sierck follows guidelines established by the EPA and the National Institute of Occupational Safety and Health (NIOSH) to track down problems. He will go into an office and interview employees with health complaints and perhaps have them fill out a health questionnaire in order to assure himself that he is dealing with a pollution-related complaint. He will then perform a walk-through, visually inspecting the interior environment and recording its layout. Among other items he studies are materials in the rooms, the nature of room dividers, equipment in the various rooms, number of people in the office, location and size of air vents, and visible damage from water or mold. Next he performs a thorough inspection of the heating, ventilation, and air-conditioning (HVAC) system. "In ten years studying five hundred twenty-nine sick office buildings, NIOSH found that in fifty-five percent of the cases the HVAC was the culprit," Sierck says. "Buildings can have insufficient air intake, contaminated filters, bacterial growth, and contaminated air ducts. Nobody ever cleans air ducts."

If necessary, Sierck analyzes air samples from the building, searching for organic chemicals, carbon monoxide, ozone, bacteria, and other contaminants. Some of these he can analyze on site, while others require capturing an air sample and sending it to a lab. Finally, he prepares a written report with recommendations for improvement.

For homes, Sierck uses an inspection procedure that pays special attention to the attic and crawl spaces. "It's a different approach, but a similar way of looking at it," he says. An inspection of a home can take as little as two hours. An office building can take one or more days, depending on size. "We want to get away with as little testing as possible in order to save the client money." He typically charges $80 to $400, but the price can increase for larger buildings or more difficult problems.

Sierck has criss-crossed the West making his house calls. In the affluent Los Angeles suburb of Bel Air, he demonstrated that a leaky pool had dampened soil beneath one client's home, causing an outbreak of mold and bacteria that made a family member severely ill. In the Santa Fe Opera House, he showed that poor ventilation in a costume room had stimulated the growth of bacteria and mold, sending one seamstress to the hospital in serious condition. In Reno, Nevada, he showed that a dentist's wife had become sick from an intense magnetic field generated by a faulty electric motor in a thermal heating system. Back in San Diego, he demonstrated that a leaky gas stove had caused an otherwise healthy woman in her early thirties to become sickly and bedridden.

Sierck began operating his company out of his home, and he still does. "I have to go to the client's premises to give a proper estimate," he says. "I like to get in contact with the company or the home owner, develop a rapport, and get information on what is actually happening because that's an indication of the testing needed." He notes that someone entering the business can easily spend $100,000 to $200,000 on testing equipment, but "through much trial and error, I found out which instruments are essential and which are an adjunct. You can get the essential equipment for ten thousand dollars." He also frequently uses off-the-shelf test kits for detecting pesticides, mold and bacteria, formaldehyde, animal dander, dust mites, etc.

Originally, Sierck began advertising in national magazines like *Garbage*, *East-West*, *Environment*, and *Sierra*, but soon stopped because 90 percent of the inquiries were coming from the East Coast. "The expense of flying there was just not feasible." Now, he advertises in local magazines and newspapers to drum up business. In additon, he runs various workshops and delivers numerous lectures, arguing that public education is an important aspect of the business. "Employers have to understand that it is better to solve the problem now than to wait because it will cost them money in absenteeism, loss of productivity, and perhaps even in lawsuits. It's more cost-efficient to remediate than to let it slide by."

For a fee, Sierck will also teach others how to begin a sick-building consulting business. Does he worry about competition? Not at all. "This is a fairly new field," he says, "and it will have a lot of potential in the future. There are an unbelievable number of office buildings that need to be improved."

℗

Concerns about the atmosphere fall into three broad categories. Two of these, ozone depletion and global warming, have global impact. The third category includes air pollution, indoor air pollution, and radon—all of which have a more immediate impact on humans. Global warming is addressed primarily through technologies that conserve energy, thereby minimizing production of carbon dioxide, the primary gas responsible for global warming, and other greenhouse gases. Those technologies are discussed in Chapter 11, which covers energy alternatives.

To a large extent, the problems of ozone depletion and global warming are best addressed by major corporations that can afford to work toward technological solutions. Despite the broad-based role that large companies can and should play in cleaning up the air, there are still a number of small niches for the ecopreneur. Many of the opportunities lie in detecting air pollutants or radon and remedying the problems they cause. Others involve production of specialized products that can minimize an individual's exposure to harmful substances.

Indoor Air Pollution

Technical Considerations

Indoor air pollution is a growing problem, especially for houses and commercial buildings that have been tightly sealed to boost energy efficiency. People can be exposed to levels of air pollution indoors that are as much as 100 times higher than those outdoors, even in heavily industrialized cities. Indoor air pollution has been linked primarily to short-term health effects, including symptoms such as headache, depression, irritation, fatigue, dry throat, sinus congestion, dizziness, and nausea. But many of the chemicals that contribute to indoor air pollution are also known to be carcinogenic, and the Environmental Protection Agency estimates that each year as many as 11,400 deaths in the United States are caused by indoor air pollution. Some researchers place the estimate much higher.

Indoor pollution typically arises from two different sources, microorganisms and toxic chemicals. Mold, bacteria, fungi, and dust mites growing in heating, ventilation, and air-conditioning systems in commercial buildings and houses cause a variety of allergic and toxic reactions. One of the best-known examples is the bacterium that causes Legionnaire's disease. It grows in the cooling water of air-conditioning systems and then spreads through the air.

Toxic chemicals are probably a more severe source of indoor air pollution. Cleaning solvents, photocopying machine chemicals, and pesticides are typical sources of chemicals, but many also come from unexpected sources, including carpets, furniture, plywood, wallboard, latex caulk, adhesives, latex and enamel paint, telephone cable, and particle board. All contain a variety of volatile organic chemicals that evaporate and contaminate the air, particularly in the first few months after installation.

Market Overview

Two different ecopreneuring markets are related to indoor air pollution: identifying the pollution as a source of illness and correcting it. The former is a narrow discipline that requires at least some knowledge of medicine and chemistry, while the latter is a more general area that may not require a specialized education.

Poor indoor air quality may affect as many as 1.2 million commercial buildings in the United States, according to David Bierman of Safe Environments, a consulting firm in San Leandro, California. Others put the number even higher. No estimates are available for the number of homes with contaminated air, but it is probably at least as large as the number of office buildings, and perhaps much larger. Many sick people live with polluted air for years without realizing the source of their symptoms. Currently, only a few companies are diagnosing such buildings, but

Bierman is convinced that every major city will soon have such professionals available.

Many of the remedies, such as providing more fresh air intake and improving circulation of air, can be handled by conventional tradespeople. But some are more specialized and provide a good opportunity for ecopreneurs. Two such opportunities involve cleaning carpets in an environmentally sound way and cleaning the air ducts in houses and office buildings. Many of the detergents and other agents normally used for cleaning carpets are themselves toxic or irritating, particularly to people who suffer from asthma and allergies. To make matters worse, residues of these chemicals are left behind on the carpet because the vast majority of carpet cleaners do not rinse the carpet with clear water.

Heating and air-conditioning ducts represent another problem, because under normal conditions, they're rarely cleaned. As a result, they build up years', if not decades', worth of dust and dirt, as well as a large variety of other materials. Gray Robertson, president of ACVA Atlantic, a company that cleans up sick buildings, has found dead birds, snakes, rats, and insects in ducts, as well as hundreds of pounds of beer cans, food wrappings, and other filth that serve as a breeding ground for bacteria and viruses that can subsequently be carried throughout the building.

Getting Started

If you set out to diagnose indoor air pollution problems, you should probably have a scientific background, ideally in chemistry or medicine. Both types of knowledge are essential; the medical background for diagnosing illnesses that may be related to indoor air pollution, and the chemical background for performing correct analyses on the air. Many of the analyses can be subcontracted to commercial laboratories, but an individual with no knowledge of chemistry is at a distinct disadvantage in interpreting results. Even with such a background, however, you will also need to acquire the specific skills involved in diagnosing indoor air pollution problems. These are best picked up by working for someone who is already in business. Some environmental consultants also conduct courses for prospective diagnosticians.

As a sick-air diagnostician, you will probably need at least $10,000 worth of analytical equipment, and perhaps more, depending on the scope of the potential work. Most of the equipment will most likely be mounted in a truck for mobility. You won't need an office, because most of your work will be conducted at your client's home or building.

The field of remediation services is somewhat easier to enter, and may depend simply on your having a good idea. Robb Bucklin's Organic Carpet Care in St. Paul, Minnesota is one of the few carpet-cleaning companies that specializes in environmentally sound cleaning techniques. Bucklin has developed his own detergents and cleaning agents that are themselves nontoxic. In addition, he makes it a point to rinse with clear water to ensure that chemical residues are removed to the greatest extent possible.

Bucklin does not dress or act like a conventional carpet cleaner. For one thing, he always wears a white shirt and a suit and tie when he goes to do a job, and he always makes sure that he is wearing his certification tag. "I want people to know that I have passed a very rigorous training program," he told *In Business*. "When I charge one hundred eighty-five dollars for what another cleaner would charge only seventy-five to a hundred for, I want customers to know that they are getting what they pay for from me. When I tell them the facts about chemical residues left by conventional cleaning, I sound believable and professional."

Some ecopreneurs are also creating a niche for themselves by cleaning ducts, in a sense making a living as the latter-day descendant of the chimney sweep. In fact, many duct cleaners got their start as chimney sweeps. Duane Krissin, owner of Clean Air in the Los Angeles suburb of Laguna Niguel, used to work for a chimney sweep who also operated a vacuum truck for cleaning ducts. "I was embarrassed to drive the truck," he says. "It was old and beat up and it leaked oil all over the customers' driveways. But I saw how well he was doing with it and I thought that if a person had the right equipment, he could make a good living." Krissin contacted a friend of his who teaches automotive mechanics at the local high school and asked if he could build a custom truck. "A couple of weeks later, he called back and said he could, but that it would take sixty thousand dollars." Krissin managed to obtain that amount, plus another $40,000 for other expenses, through a bank loan.

The truck is essentially a huge vacuum cleaner on wheels. A powerful diesel engine allows it to create a vacuum that moves 20,000 cubic feet of air per minute. The truck also carries 500 feet of 8-inch vacuum hose, 400 feet of compressed-air hose, and portable equipment for cleaning higher stories of buildings that cannot be reached by the hoses, as well as chimney-cleaning equipment.

When Krissin and his technicians service a house, they open the furnace, remove the fan, and install the vacuum hose. While the vacuum is running, they cover each register with plastic or newspaper to improve suction. Then they go to one register at a time and use the compressed-air line to clean the duct leading to it. After they have cleaned the ducts and the return, they clean the furnace, the heat exchanger, and the fan. Next, they reassemble and sanitize the equipment and perform a safety check. For a normal house, the whole procedure takes about one and a half hours and costs $150 to $250. The average house they service is about 20 years old and produces 5 to 10 pounds of dust. Some older houses have produced 15 to 20 pounds. A similar procedure is followed in offices, but it takes longer and costs more.

Krissin says the duct cleaning is particularly valuable where the individuals in the house have allergies, asthma, sinus problems, or other types of environmentally induced illness, or when water damage has allowed mold or fungi to grow in the ducts. But it is also useful in other circumstances. Among the conditions that a duct cleaning will cure are black streaks on the walls and odors when the furnace is started. He recommends that the ducts be cleaned every three years.

Marketing Considerations

Advertising is important for the environmental diagnostician, but other ways of getting your name known can also be important. Make an effort to meet asthma specialists, for example, and tell them about your programs and services. While some traditional doctors do not want to recommend their patients to an environmental diagnostician, because they believe only in a traditional medicine–oriented approach, other, more progressive members of the medical community are excellent sources of referrals. Also, get to know doctors who specialize in treating environmental illnesses—they're much more likely to recommend clients.

Most diagnosticians also present a variety of lectures and speeches to community groups, environmental organizations, and other groups. Some also organize one-day conferences for architects, contractors, developers, realtors, and home owners. Participation in home shows is another way to build credibility and attract clients.

The same general marketing principles apply to the remediators as well. Most often, however, clients will be referred to them by the diagnosticians rather than doctors. Referrals from satisfied customers are also an important source of new clients.

When Krissin opened his business, he sent out press releases to newspapers and radio and television stations. One local television station was coincidentally airing a feature on indoor air pollution, and devoted five minutes to his busines. "I picked up three months' worth of work off that five-minute segment," he says. Krissin notes that his truck itself is a good selling tool. When he turns it on, 12 large dust-collection bags pop out, giving it a very unusual appearance. Neighbors and passersby see it and often stop to inquire about his services. The truck is also an attention-getter at trade shows.

Strategic Considerations

Competition

Although telephone books in major cities are full of environmental consultants, few of them are specialists in indoor air pollution, according to Sierck. Only about 500 doctors throughout the United States are interested in environmental medicine, and the number of diagnosticians is smaller still. But expanding the field will require substantial education of the public.

Environmentally sound carpet cleaning is a very new field with very few practitioners and, at present, a small client base. Pioneer Bucklin believes the field is ripe for expansion. "Just recently, one of the trade journals that serves our business pointed out that one way to avoid sick-building syndrome was to use a freshwater rinse when cleaning the carpets," he told an *In Business* reporter. "That's the first time I've seen that in print. This business is going to explode and the scope is going to be big."

Duct cleaning is a rapidly expanding area, but it still holds great potential for the future. Krissin notes that when he started Clean Air two years ago, there were only about a dozen similar businesses in the metropolitan Los Angeles area. Today 25 are in operation. Despite the competition business is good. He now has two trucks and is getting ready to build a third, and the company has a three-week backlog of clients.

Impact of Government Activities

Except for regulation of diagnosticians, government activities do not now have significant impact in this area. Government agencies are unlikely to pass any laws that would affect the treatment of indoor air pollution in homes, but it is entirely possible that the government will require testing for air pollution in office buildings and other commercial sites in the future. Such requirements would be a major benefit to practitioners, but so far, none have been passed or are under consideration.

Diversification

The most likely area of diversification for the diagnostician is in radon monitoring, although this does require the development of new expertise, as well as the purchase of a significant amount of new equipment. Nonetheless, it would be logical to test for radon while testing for other pollutants. Testing for radon, furthermore, gives the diagnostician an entrée into houses and offices where he or she might spot other problems and thus be able to offer the client additional services.

The logical extension of the carpet-cleaning business would be to expand into cleaning draperies and furniture. In many houses where contaminants have been introduced through the air, cleaning the carpets will not be effective unless the contaminants are removed from other sites as well. Of course, for any of the remediators, another route to expansion would involve teaming up with other professionals to extend services to other types of remediation, such as repairing or restoring air vents, repairing water damage, and so forth.

Ancillary Businesses Related to Air Pollution

Air Filtration

E. L. Foust was a steelmaker whose wife developed an environmental illness more than 15 years ago. He attempted to find some air filters that would alleviate her problems by removing most of the noxious materials from the air, but no one was selling them. Eventually, he located a researcher in Oklahoma who was producing a small quantity of high-efficiency air filters. He bought the rights to the filters, patented them, and began selling them by mail from his garage. Today, under a different owner, E. L. Foust Co., Inc. (Elmhurst, Illinois), has 12 employees, a 5,200-square-foot building, and does $750,000 worth of business every year, making it one of the largest specialty sources of high-efficiency air-cleaning devices in the country.

The core of Foust's business is air filtration equipment. The company sells a variety of different filtes for diffrent purposes, ranging from face masks to activated-carbon filters, which remove organic chemicals from the air, to electrostatic filters that will trap materials as small as bacteria and viruses. The company designs most of its own filters and either contracts for their manufacture or manufactures them itself. Compared to a normal filter in a home furnace that can trap perhaps 5 percent of the material that passes through it, Foust's best filters can trap more than 99 percent of the material.

The company has subsequently expanded to other products, selling activated charcoal and other types of water filters to remove environmental toxins. It also sells a special foil vapor barrier that can be installed on walls to prevent formaldehyde released by insulation from entering the house, and special tape for sealing the edges of sheets of vapor barrier.

Many of Foust's customers are referred by doctors and environmental diagnosticians, but the company also advertises in newsletters and environmental magazines. At one time, the company had a number of dealers in the United States who sold its products. It stopped selling through this route because, says Joe Muchow, Foust's research and development director, "The dealers weren't as picky about products as we are" and often attempted to sell lower grade products to customers. Foust does have dealers in Canada, however, because it's an easier way to get products into that country.

The vast majority of the company's customers suffer from environmental illness, but company officials are trying to tap a larger market of individuals who want to remove tobacco smoke from air or who are just interested in cleaner air.

Automobile Air Filters

Highways are filthy places. Soil and dust particles, industrial and automotive emissions, pavement abrasions, tire abrasions, fuel ash, chemicals, plant matter, and seasonal pollen, spores, and bacteria are mixed together into a potent brew that is often as much as 100 times more dense than it is in air just a few feet away from the side of the road. Most vehicles use what is known as "positive-flow ventilation," bringing fresh air in through vents and circulating it through the passenger compartment, where dust and pollutants settle out. "A cynic might compare the inside of a middle-aged and older car to riding inside the dustbag of a vacuum cleaner," says Frank Keresztes-Fischer of Filtrona Co. in Plymouth, Michigan, a Detroit suburb.

Some luxury European automobiles, such as Mercedes-Benz and BMW, install air filters to remove such pollutants from the air stream before it enters the passenger compartment. Such filters are generally the "pass-through" type in which the air is forced through paper, fleece, woven fabric, or charcoal mats. Holes in the filters are smaller than the polluting particles and the pollutants cannot get through. Unfortunately, Keresztes-Fischer says, because the filters work by trapping pollutants they clog up and must be changed frequently. Furthermore, they are very sensitive to high humidity and low temperatures and their efficiency drops significantly under such conditions. But those are precisely the conditions when high air flow is often needed, such as for defrosting windows.

Started in 1988 by retired auto executive Lynn W. Ledford, Filtrona produces filters specifically for automobiles. At first the company tried to interest Detroit manufacturers in using filters from Europe, but the companies did not bite because of the previously mentioned problems. Filtrona then decided to develop a new filter that would work by a different technology.

The result of Filtrona's R&D effort was a centrifugal or "cyclone" filter that does not have the clogging problems of a conventional filter. In the Filtrona Elixaire filter, the intake air passes through a series of curved passageways. As the air stream is forced around the curves, particles in it tend to continue traveling in a straight line and therefore impact on the porous sides of the filter. A wetting agent on the sides traps the particles, making the filter insensitive to low temperatures or to high humidity. The filter never becomes clogged or impedes air flow, but it can become ineffective when the sides become completely covered. Nonetheless, Filtrona says it has three times the useful life of a conventional filter. The filter has been successfully tested under a variety of environmental conditions, and two European auto companies and a German university have evaluated it favorably. At the time of this writing, the company was attempting to market the new filter to U.S. and overseas automakers.

Radon

Technical Considerations

Radon is a colorless, odorless gas formed during the decay of uranium. Although it undergoes radioactive decay itself, emitting alpha particles that can damage cells, radon is not generally considered hazardous because it is expelled from the lungs nearly as quickly as it is inhaled. But the elements produced during its decay—primarily radioactive isotopes of polonium, lead, and bismuth—are dangerous because they react chemically with airborne dust and smoke particles. These can then lodge in the lung for long periods of time and produce cancer. The EPA estimates that at least 10,000 people, and perhaps as many as 43,000, die from lung cancer each year as a result of exposure to the products of radon decay.

Most soils contain small amounts of uranium and thus release radon continually. Granite contains larger amounts. Outdoors, the radon is dispersed quickly, but it seeps into homes through dirt floors, cracks in walls and floors, floor drains, and sumps. It can build up to high levels, particularly in winter when the house is closed up. Houses that have been well insulated and highly weatherized often have the most severe problems. Radon can also enter houses via water, particularly well water. Houses containing high levels of radon have been found in every state, but the highest levels have been found in Iowa, North Dakota, Minnesota, Colorado, and Pennsylvania. The EPA estimates that one in every 10 houses in the United States has levels of radon above its acceptable limit of four picocuries per liter.

There are two primary methods to test for radon. In the most accurate, a piece of special film is left in an unobtrusive location in the house for as long as a year. It is then sent to a special laboratory, where technicians measure the number of spots where the film has been exposed due to radiation released by radioactive decay, and thereby calculate an average annual concentration. In a simpler test, a canister of activated charcoal is placed in the house for two to six days. The charcoal absorbs radon from the air. The canister is then taken to a laboratory, where the amount of radon is measured and the average amount in the air calculated.

If levels of radon above four picocuries per liter are detected, remedial measures are generally recommended. In some cases, sealing cracks in the floors and walls in the basement and installing ventilating fans may be sufficient. In more severe cases, it may be necessary to install special exhaust pipes to collect radon and vent it back outdoors.

Market Overview

By most estimates, only about five to eight percent of houses in the United States have been tested for radon. The EPA has recommended that virtually every house in the country be tested for radon, but many experts suggest that testing a far smaller percentage would suffice. In either case, it is clear that a large potential market exists.

Getting Started

Bart Ecksel had been in the pest control business in Southampton, Pennsylvania, for 15 years when he decided to add radon testing as a sideline. By 1989 his testing business had grown so rapidly that he sold the pest control business and concentrated full time on radon testing and remediation. In late

1990, he began selling franchises to help other people enter the business.

Like many other environmentally related businesses, radon monitoring and mitigation requires a significant amount of technical proficiency. Unlike most other ecopreneuring businesses, however, to enter this field, you must now demonstrate proficiency to state and even federal licensing agencies—a far different situation than when Ecksel began. In those days, radon monitoring and remediation were more free-form and had minimal governmental supervision. Since then, however, the EPA and state agencies have developed detailed protocols that must be followed in carrying out both inspections and remediations, sometimes called mitigations.

Before obtaining a business license, you will be required to pass the EPA Radon Measurement Proficiency Exam. To prepare, you might consider apprenticing with an existing company or purchasing a franchise from a company such as Ecksel's Advantage Radon Control Centers (ARCC). The University of Michigan also offers an intensive two-day course on radon measurement developed in cooperation with the EPA.

ARCC charges a franchise fee of $17,500. For that fee, Ecksel will help the franchisee select an appropriate area to establish the business, help establish an office, help select appropriate equipment, and provide training and technical support. "We'll give them the complete know-how to run the business," Ecksel says. That includes two weeks of training at ARCC's headquarters in Southampton and another week at the franchise location. "All during the first year, we'll be visiting them and holding their hand. We want them to be successful." In addition to the franchise fee, Ecksel estimates that a new franchise will require $15,000 to $30,000 for analytical equipment, plus an additional sum for the normal accoutrements of an office.

Marketing Considerations

Ecksel advertises in all of the conventional local media, including the Yellow Pages and local newspapers. For the franchising end of the business, he advertises in national media, including *Entrepreneur* magazine, *Franchising Yearbook*, and *The Wall Street Journal*. He also delivers a large number of lectures and speeches every year, addressing community groups, real estate groups, schools, PTA's, nonprofit organizations, and businesses. A substantial proportion of his clients are first contacted through such speeches, he says.

Strategic Issues

Competition

Currently, there is little direct competition for the ecopreneur who monitors radon or carries out remediation, except in the few states, such as Pennsylvania, where radon has been recognized as a problem for many years. Most hardware stores around the country now sell film packages or other devices for measuring radon that can be placed in the home for the requisite amount of time, then mailed off to a laboratory for analysis. Such devices have limited accuracy, however, so you should be able to compete effectively by offering a much more complete analysis, along with personal consultation.

The primary competition for the remediator is the home owner. When low to moderate concentrations of radon are detected, home owners themselves can often take most of the necessary steps to correct the problem, such as sealing cracks and installing fans. "We'll consult with them for free and tell them what needs to be done if they're a customer," Ecksel says. More complicated problems, such as installing subslab air pipes, must normally be handled by a licensed remediator. The average cost for a remediation is about $1,400. Some home owners attempt to use a regular contractor instead of one licensed by the state or federal government, but many states are cracking down on the practice.

Impact of Government Activities

The most obvious impact of the government is in licensing radon inspectors and remediators. Most states now require such licensing, and it is likely that eventually the rest will follow suit. Some states are also considering making a radon test a required part of selling a house, as termite inspections now are mandated. Such an action will obviously increase business for the ecopreneur. But some states that do not yet require radon testing before a house is sold do require that the results of any previous radon testing be revealed to a prospective purchaser. Some home owners are thus reluctant to have radon testing for fear of potential liability if the remediation is not conducted properly.

Diversification

The most obvious way for a radon tester to diversify is to begin monitoring other types of indoor air pollution. Presumably, such an individual will have a sufficiently technical background that learning the new technologies will not be difficult. This kind of expansion will require purchasing a broad variety of new equipment, however, since that used for monitoring radon is not appropriate for monitoring other forms of pollution.

Chlorofluorocarbons (CFC's)

Because of their threat to the ozone layer, the manufacture of CFC's will be sharply curtailed in the near future, and eventually eliminated. Large chemical companies are developing alternatives to CFC-containing gases such as Freon, as well as new equipment to use the replacements. That type of research and development is extremely expensive, however, and does not really offer any opportunities for the individual ecopreneur. Some opportunities are available in capturing CFC's from used refrigeration equipment and purifying it for reuse, but these opportunities are also dominated by large companies. Perhaps the most likely opportunity for an ecopreneur interested in CFC recycling is as an adjunct to an existing business, such as refrigerator repair or automobile air-conditioning repair.

Recycling CFC's is important for two reasons. One is that every CFC molecule released into the atmosphere contributes to the destruction of the ozone layer. Recycling CFC's rather than releasing them will delay the time when the gases are inevitably released into the air—perhaps to a time when they are no longer manufactured and the impact will thus be smaller. Second, used CFC's are going to become much more valuable. As CFC production is curtailed and eventually eliminated, recyclers will be able to charge substantially higher prices.

At least a dozen manufacturing companies in the United States now produce equipment for capturing and reusing CFC's. These machines, called "vampires," suck CFC's out of a refrigerator, freezer, or air conditioner before repairs begin. Some machines filter and dry the CFC's before they are injected back into the cooling coils after the repairs are completed. Others store it in compressed-gas containers so that it can be sent to a large company, such as Du Pont, for purification and reuse. Vampires typically sell for as little as $2,500 for a stripped-down, basic model, to more than $7,000 for a state-of-the-art system.

The vampires are typically used by existing repair services that hope to expand their clientele—by appealing to their environmental instincts. The assumption is that someone who is interested in the environment is more likely to, say, have his or her automobile air conditioner repaired at a shop that recycles CFC's than at a shop that simply vents them into the atmosphere. As the cost of replacement CFC's becomes higher, such shops will be able to reduce their own costs by reusing CFC's, perhaps offering a small competitive advantage. As more and more service organizations begin to use vampires, however, that competitive advantage is likely to disappear and everyone will be back on the same footing.

Another potential opportunity is in removing CFC's from appliances before they are discarded. In general, this operation is best accomplished as part of an overall effort to recycle the metals and plastics in the appliances. A comparable market does not exist for junked cars, however, experts say. By the time a car is considered ready for the junkyard, all of the CFC's have normally leaked out of the air conditioner.

Freeing Up CFC's

These days, the only figures former accountant Jack Cameron thinks much about are his growing revenues and the increasing number of operations he is establishing around the country. In 1976, Cameron, who had previously abandoned accounting to sell computers, abandoned that occupation as well and opened a modest appliance collecting and recycling service. As environmental concerns have burgeoned during the last decade, Cameron's Appliance Recycling Centers of America, Inc. (ARCA), in Minneapolis, has diversified into CFC recycling and PCB (polychlorinated biphenyls) disposal, in the process opening new branches in four other states and becoming the largest appliance recycler in the country.

When you buy a new refrigerator or air conditioner, one of your biggest problems often is finding a way to get rid of the old one. The company that sold you the new one doesn't want it because they can't do anything with it. Landfill operators don't want it because it is too bulky, using up too much valuable space. In fact, many states now ban the disposal of appliances in landfills. And junkyard operators don't want them because many appliances contain potentially toxic chemicals.

Enter Cameron. In 1976, he bought a small truck and secured a contract with Sears to begin disposing of the used appliances that the company took in when it sold new ones. He separated out and rebuilt the ones that were still in good condition—about one in every 20—and sold them at an outlet store. He then sold the rest to junkyards for scrap.

ARCA grew rapidly, entering into contracts with other appliance dealers, nearby communities, and even rubbish collectors to dispose of appliances. In 1987 the company also landed a contract with the Wisconsin Electric Power Co. when the latter launched its Smart Money Energy Program. In that program, consumers were given either a $50 or $100 U.S. Savings Bond for turning in old but working refrigerators, freezers, and room air conditioners. The idea was to remove these inefficient appliances from homes to conserve energy and thereby minimize the need to build new power plants. In the first three years of the program, 154,000 units were turned in, saving the utility 42 megawatts of power. Cameron recycled the appliances.

But in June 1987, Cameron ran into a major roadblock when junkyard operators told him they would no longer purchase the appliances from him. Their primary concern was the PCB-containing electrical capacitors in the appliances. They feared that the highly toxic PCB's would contaminate their yards and equipment, as well as the "fluff" produced when the appliances were shredded, endangering their employees and subjecting the junkyards to substantial liability. "I had a real problem," Cameron says. "We were handling a thousand appliances a week and, if I couldn't get rid of them, we were out of business."

After some thought, Cameron reasoned that the only way to continue operating was to remove the PCB-containing capacitors himself. Once he did so, the scrap dealers were more than willing to take the metal from the appliances, and Cameron had the glimmerings of a larger notion. "I started looking at the environmental issues surrounding disposal of appliances. There was not only the PCB problem, but also that of CFC's escaping into the air and mercury escaping from electrical switches. So in 1987, we changed direction to become more of a recycler and reprocessor in an environmentally sound manner."

Once Cameron began collecting capacitors, he needed to be licensed by the EPA to handle hazardous materials. Because his volumes were small, he was designated a "small quantity generator." (The licensing procedure enables the EPA to "track" hazardous materials.) The licensing process can open the door to other problems, says Cameron. "The inspectors don't just look at the PCB issue. They look at how you dispose of your used motor oil and everything else. That's why many scrap yards don't like to get licensed. You open the door to an unknown." ARCA, however, has not had a problem with the EPA. The PCB's are loaded into approved 55-gallon drums and shipped to a hazardous waste facility in Kansas for incineration.

CFC's are removed from appliances using specially built equipment designed by ARCA. They are cleaned, filtered, and distilled to bring them back to the same purity level required for new materials, then bottled and sold. ARCA uses some recycled CFC's to recharge the appliances that it rebuilds. Cameron says the firm scrapped 54,000 refrigerators, freezers, and air conditioners in 1989 and recovered an average of seven to eight ounces of CFC's from each, for a total of nearly 25,000 pounds. In the summer of 1990, Freon was selling for about $1.60 per pound, but many experts predict prices will rise as high as $5 per pound within the next couple of years as government-mandated cutbacks in production become effective and the materials become more scarce. "The market hasn't developed as much as it is going to," he says.

At any one time, ARCA's subsidiary, Major Appliance Pickup Service, has 20 trucks traveling the streets of Minneapolis to collect discarded appliances. When the trucks return, the appliances are unloaded and technicians select those fit for repair and resale. Technicians then remove CFC's from the other units, as well as mercury-containing switches (which are not yet recycled, but are simply collected in a hazardous waste bin) and valuable copper coils. The appliances are then shredded and the metal sent to scrap yards. "We're also looking at ways to recycle the plastics in them," Cameron said. "The only thing that is now sent to landfills is shredded insulating foam, and we're looking at ways to get the [CFC's] out of that as well."

In recent years, the company has expanded its operations to Milwaukee; Hartford, Connecticut; and Jacksonville, Florida, and Cameron is eyeing other locations. "Every community needs an appliance recycling service," he says.

Ecobusinesses that help improve the quality of air in businesses and houses will have strong potential in the nineties given the growing concern with global warming and related problems. Also, as "sick-building syndrome" becomes better understood and more recognized as an environmental and health threat, the opportunities for the ecopreneur will surely increase. Therefore, consider getting into the field while the window of opportunity is still open. If work in the air pollution field doesn't strike a responsive chord with you, consider the niches in the water pollution field, which are described in Chapter 12.

Chapter *Eleven*

Fuel for the Planet:
Generating Profits from Energy Conservation

In the picturesque little town of Ukiah, California, two hours north of San Francisco on the fringes of redwood country, sits the largest alternative energy mail-order company in the world, an outlet with the unlikely name of Real Goods Trading Company. Originally started in 1978 as a small store to serve the needs of "retro-hippies" attempting to "get back to nature" in Northern California, the company drastically shifted focus in the early 1980's and began serving farmers, seasonal residents, and others who often built homes far from the nearest power lines. That change in focus transformed Real Goods into a $6-million-per-year company in 1990.

When John Schaeffer and his friends graduated from the University of California, Berkeley, in 1978, they moved to a 290-acre spread in Mendocino County, just outside Ukiah. The house that Schaeffer subsequently built had no electricity, so the group had to make do with candles and kerosene lamps. Then, one of the commune members came back with the news that a hardware store in town sold 12-volt light bulbs that could be connected to a car battery. Soon they had what Schaeffer calls "a real crude power system." Later, they obtained a 12-volt television as well. "One thing led to another and I decided to open a store to sell the stuff," Schaeffer says. "We were catering to urban refugees from the sixties who wanted basic creature comforts." A year after Schaeffer and his partner opened their Willits, California, store, solar panels became commercially available, and the business blossomed. The two ecopreneurs opened a second store in Ukiah in 1980 and a third store in Santa Rosa in 1982.

In 1985, after a falling out with his partner, Schaeffer sold out his share in Real Goods. According to the terms of the deal, Schaeffer would receive a down payment on the buyout amount, followed by monthly payments over a five-year period. If, for any reason, the monthly payments stopped flowing, Schaeffer had the right to take over the company. Once the ink was dry, Schaeffer took off for an extended vacation, and his ex-partner brought in a troupe of Tibetan Buddhists from Boulder, Colorado, to help run the business. Within nine months Real Goods was in real trouble; Schaeffer's ex-partner declared personal bankruptcy, the Buddhists went back to Boulder, and the creditors took the inventory, along with the proceeds from an auction of the desks, chairs, and miscellaneous equipment. "My family and I had been going around the world, thinking we had a steady source of income for five years, when we ran out of funds," Schaeffer says. "I came back to the country and tried to sue, but there was nothing left."

In fact, there *was* one thing left—the store's mailing list of 2,000 customers. After trying unsuccessfully to sell the list to competitors for $500, Schaeffer decided to take one last shot at making the list work for himself. In the fall of 1986, he managed to scrape together $3,000 for a 16-page catalog, and mailed the piece to all of the old Real Goods customers. "The catalog was miserably produced," he says with a laugh. "And at the time we were operating out of a six-by-six office with no inventory—we shipped directly from manufacturers. Despite our low level of operation, the business took off right away." The initial mailing brought in $30,000 worth of orders, and sales reached $80,000 by the end of the 1986, effectively tripling each year thereafter.

To meet growing inventory and overhead needs, Schaeffer adopted a unique method of raising cash. Instead of turning to banks or venture capitalists, he turned to his customers, mentioning the need for loans in his catalogs. Each time he has solicited funds in this manner, he has been oversubscribed within a few days after the catalogs have been mailed. The arrangement works well for both sides. The company borrows at 10 percent interest, which is substantially less than a bank would charge the company, but the investor earns more than he would on a certificate of deposit. (See page 51 for more details.)

Schaeffer notes that his sales very much reflect events in the world. Sales boomed after the first Earth Day and have shown sharp upward spikes after environmental crises such as the Chernobyl nuclear disaster, the Exxon oil spill, and the Iraqi invasion of Kuwait. "Whenever there is a recession or some kind of fear," he adds, "the business just takes off."

Real Goods has expanded its product line substantially since Schaeffer took it over. While the main focus remains on alternative energy hardware like solar electric apparatus (Schaeffer claims to have electrified more than 10,000 houses, using solar panels), his company now sells items like recycling bins, recycled products such as toilet paper and paper towels, solar battery rechargers for nickel-cadmium batteries, energy-saving light bulbs, and Sunfrost refrigerators that, according to Schaeffer, are "ten times as efficient as most American products. If everyone had one, we could shut down eighteen large nuclear power plants immediately." The company also sells a variety of water-related products, including low-flow showerheads, water conservation kits, and flow-through or "instantaneous" water heaters (which have no storage tank; the burner comes on when the tap is turned on). Real Goods even sells some novelties, like a solar iced-tea jar that has a paddle turned by a photovoltaic cell on the lid, and a solar-powered device that repels mosquitos in a 12-foot radius by mimicking the sound of the dragon fly, a natural predator.

Real Goods' Ukiah showroom displays one of every item that the company sells. "It was set up as a kind of 'exploratorium,' where people could come in and play with various devices, like low-flow showerheads," Schaeffer says with pride. The whole showroom, including telephones and computers, is powered by solar energy. They don't do much advertising to get people to come into the showroom. "It mainly generates a lot of curiosity seekers who take our people off the phones where we get most of our sales." In fact, 95 percent of sales are mail order, and Real Goods does spend a lot of money on advertising for mail orders; about 10 percent of sales is spent for producing the catalogs and advertising them in environmentally related magazines.

Schaeffer plans to mail out one million catalogs in 1991 in an effort to continue the company's tremendous growth rate. Looking back, he sees his rescue of Real Goods as the ultimate act of recycling. "It was a matter of taking something with a perceived value of zero and proving that it had life, that it could grow and turn a profit. That to me is the most satisfying aspect of this whole thing . . . that's real business."

੭৯

Energy conservation addresses a broad variety of environmental problems, including air pollution, acid rain, and global warming, as well as the depletion of natural resources. Coal-fired power plants emit sulfates and nitrogen oxides that can contribute to local air pollution as well as to acid rain, and they emit carbon dioxide that contributes to global warming. Automobiles emit the same pollutants, although they make no contribution to acid rain. In contrast, alternative energy sources such as photovoltaic cells and wind-powered generators emit no pollutants and no carbon dioxide and their use preserves scarce natural resources. Furthermore, using solar panels at remote locations prevents the environmental degradation associated with construction of power lines.

Beyond environmental concerns, energy conservation makes exceptionally good economic sense because it saves money. Although most energy-efficient light bulbs and appliances have higher purchase prices than their conventional counterparts, their lower cost of operation offsets the higher initial cost and leads to net savings. When consumers and businesses cut their energy use, they save money. Surprisingly, however, such conservation also generates profits for utility companies.

That was not the case in the past. Only a few years ago, when a utility's customers cut their energy use, the utility company's net revenues went down accordingly. Consequently, it was in their best interest to promote energy use and increase both their revenues and their profits. Utility companies, in effect, rewarded high energy use by using a sliding rate scale that charged the lowest rates to the largest users.

But as the cost of building new power plants escalated during the 1970's and 1980's and environmental concerns came to the fore, utility companies began to rethink their position. Promoting energy conservation could, they realized, minimize the need for the massive investments—as well as expensive fights with conservationists—associated with new construction. The breakthrough came in the late 1980's when state regulatory agencies began to allow the utility companies to profit from their conservation efforts at roughly the same rate as they profit from selling power. New England Electric Co. spent $66 million on energy conservation programs in 1990. The state utility commission allowed the company to raise its rates sufficiently to recoup the $66 million plus an additional $7.4 million in profit, for an 11.2 percent return. Despite the rate increase, the program will save the company's customers $154 million.

Utility companies have taken a variety of measures to reduce energy use. Some of them have been directed at large commercial customers, but more have been aimed at the consumer. In some cases, utility companies have paid cash fees ranging from $50 to $100 to consumers for discarding old, inefficient freezers, refrigerators, and air conditioners. In other cases, they have provided similar rebates to customers who purchased new appliances with the highest efficiency ratings. They also encourage customers to use high-efficiency light bulbs, often by selling them at reduced prices or even by giving them away. In 1990 Southern California Edison launched a $250-million program to give high-efficiency compact fluorescent light bulbs to its customers; the utility even hired a new staff to go to the consumers' homes and install the bulbs. This increased activity of the utility companies is of great benefit to the potential ecopreneur, because the large companies are stimulating the purchase of energy-efficient appliances and because they are raising the energy awareness of their customers.

Technical Considerations

According to the Electric Power Research Institute (EPRI) in Palo Alto, California, replacing existing appliances and light bulbs with their energy-saving counterparts could save 24 to 44 percent of the nation's total demand for electricity by the year 2000, enough to meet the entire power needs of the 11 Western states. EPRI also calculates that 26.4 percent of the savings could come from more efficient industrial motors, 24.6 percent from commercial cooling and lighting, 17.4 percent from home heating, lighting, and water heating, 10.3 percent from more efficient home appliances, and 21.2 percent from other sources.

Light Bulbs

Conventional incandescent light bulbs operate by passing an electrical current through a tungsten filament in an inert atmosphere. The filament's resistance to the passage of the electric current causes it to glow brightly, emitting light and a great deal of heat. A typical incandescent light bulb lasts for about 750 hours of use. Long-life incandescent bulbs operate at a lower filament temperature, so that the filament doesn't evaporate as quickly. But they operate less efficiently, producing more heat and less light per watt of electricity.

Fluorescent lights operate by a completely different principle. In fluorescent bulbs, the flow of electricity causes an arc to form at the lamp's electrodes, much like the short-lived arc that forms when you attach the second jumper cable to a car's battery. Electrons are given off by the arc, and they collide with gaseous mercury atoms in the interior of the bulb, causing the atoms to emit ultraviolet radiation. The ultraviolet radiation, in turn, excites the lamp's phosphors—the white powder on the inside of the glass—causing it to fluoresce and emit light at visible wavelengths.

Fluorescent lights produce much less heat than incandescent bulbs and thus operate much more efficiently. In fact, a fluorescent bulb uses only about a quarter of the electricity that an incandescent bulb uses to produce the same amount of light. Moreover, most operate for 9,000 to 10,000 hours before they fail. The new "compact fluorescents" can be screwed into a regular bulb socket, and are extremely energy-efficient. Each 75-watt compact fluorescent light bulb prevents the release of a ton of carbon dioxide and 20 pounds of sulfur oxides over its lifetime. According to John Schaeffer, if every American had just one compact fluorescent bulb, we could shut down one nuclear power plant. If everyone had five, he adds, the United States could be an energy-exporting country in five years.

Solar Electric Power

Engineers have made great progress in developing and refining photovoltaic cells, also called solar cells, for converting sunlight into DC (direct current) electricity. The most common solar cells are small crystals or ribbons of silicon; other materials are also used, but they are much more expensive. One side of the silicon has a positive charge on it and the other a negative. When sunlight strikes the positive side, it forces electrons to the other side and produces an electric current. The silicon is normally encapsulated under glass for protection, and large numbers of such capsules are connected together into flat panels.

A typical solar installation normally requires other devices as well. These include a charge controller and safety disconnect system, a metering panel, batteries for storage of electricity during the night, and a converter to convert the DC into AC (alternating current) for the operation of conventional appliances.

A decade ago, solar electrical power cost about $1.50 per kilowatt-hour, making it a very expensive option for most uses. Today, it costs about 30 cents per kilowatt-hour, a much more reasonable price but still substantially more expensive than electricity from gas, oil, coal, and nuclear power, which averages between 3 and 7 cents per kilowatt-hour. Engineers hope that the price of solar electric power will be competitive with that of conventional electricity within the next decade.

Solar Thermal Power

Solar thermal power makes use of the heat in sunlight rather than the light. It is most commonly used for heating water, either in place of a conventional water heater or for heating pools, buildings, and so forth. Solar thermal technology for such applications has changed very little since it was first developed before the turn of the century. A typical solar collector is a black box with a glass window in the front. The black finish collects as much heat from the sunlight as possible and the glass keeps it from being radiated back into the air. Water pumped through the box is heated, often to quite high temperatures. That water can be used directly or, in more expensive applications, stored for heating during the night, when it radiates back the heat.

The price of solar thermal heaters too has gone down recently. Two or three years ago, a system might have cost about $4,500. Some of the newest now cost as little as $2,300 installed for a comparable system. The systems can thus pay for themselves in reduced energy costs within five to eight years. "In New England, a solar boiler can provide two thirds of a home's hot water needs," says Leigh Seddon of Solar Works Inc. in Montpelier, Vermont. "In California, it can supply ninety percent or more. This is a tremendous opportunity to avoid new power plant construction."

Energy-Saving Appliances

The refrigerator is the most energy-consuming appliance in a house, other than central air conditioning. Even the best currently available energy-saving commercial refrigerator, in a 17-cubic-foot size, uses about 3,000 to 5,000 watt-hours of electricity per day. In comparison, energy-saving refrigerators of the same size made by specialty manufacturers can use as little as 550 watt-hours per day. These units typically use highly efficient compressors, which are normally placed on top of the refrigerator; most conventional manufacturers place the compressor beneath the refrigerator so that the heat it produces rises into the interior. The energy-saving refrigerators also have more insulation.

Water heaters also use substantial amounts of energy, much of it to maintain a large tank full of hot water ready for use. Energy leaks out from the tank, and is lost in the long water lines by which the tank is connected to faucets throughout the house. One solution to this problem is the instantaneous, or flow-through, water heater, which has been used almost exclusively for the past 30 years in Japan and Europe. In the instantaneous heater, the natural gas burner is ignited when the water is turned on. The water flows through a copper coil and is heated exceptionally quickly. Depending on the size of the unit, it can heat any volume of water; the desired temperature is set by the user. Instantaneous water heaters cost $100 to $150 per year less to operate than conventional gas water heaters, and $400 to $500 per year less than electric water heaters.

Getting Started

The primary opportunities for you in the alternative energy field lie in selling and installing energy-conserving products and solar-powered systems, although a few individuals have succeeded in developing and manufacturing specialized equipment, such as solar-powered ovens and stoves. A half dozen or so mail-order houses now dominate the market for alternative-energy appliances and similar equipment, but a somewhat larger number sell light bulbs and smaller appliances, most often in conjunction with other environmentally related products, especially recycled paper goods.

Because consumers for most alternative-energy products are scattered around the world—many purchases go to third world countries that do not have widespread power grids—the bulk of the business is carried out by mail order. Toll-free telephone lines and UPS delivery from the seller's warehouse or from the manufacturer make it both easy and efficient to conduct such a business and help to minimize overhead related to storage of products and sales space. Those companies that do operate retail stores in conjunction with their mail-order businesses are typically located in areas blessed with an abundance of sunshine and a concentration of potential customers. Normally, that means the West and the Southwest.

In contrast, companies that specialize in installing the devices, particularly solar thermal systems, primarily deal with a local clientele. Solar thermal energy, furthermore, can be used virtually anywhere in the country, so the number of available locations, and hence of opportunities, is much higher.

Both selling and installing energy conservation equipment requires a fair amount of expertise. As an installer you must have experience dealing with plumbing systems and, if you are also installing photovoltaic panels, electrical systems. Previous experience working with a plumber or an electrician, or with another installer, would thus be desirable, and you will also have to spend time learning the intricacies of the solar systems.

The technical expertise required of the retailer is probably even greater. Customers typically have many questions about both the equipment itself and the installation procedures. And they want to deal with a salesperson who is very knowledgeable about the equipment. If one dealer is not able to answer questions, the customer will probably go to another—and keep trying until all questions are satisfactorily answered. In fact, many companies even encourage such calling around. Dan Brandborg of Sun Electric Co. in Hamilton, Montana, advises clients in his catalog: "If you would like to call *just* to compare information from other companies, please do so."

The best way to learn about the industry is probably to work for another dealer while familiarizing yourself with the field. Short of that, you will probably want to obtain experience by using the equipment you are selling. Many companies encourage their employees to take home various products for testing and familiarization. "We not only sell the products in our catalog, we use them in our homes," says Jonathan Hill of Integral Energy Systems in Nevada City, California.

Most retailers started out with a relatively small amount of cash (under $10,000), usually with just enough money to publish a small catalog, establish an 800 telephone number, and take out some advertising. But the stakes have grown in recent years. The majority of retailers now publish large, expensive catalogs that contain magazinelike articles about the technologies involved in alternative energy, hints for installation, and detailed product descriptions. Real Goods publishes a 320-page *Alternative Energy Sourcebook* once a year, as well as three smaller catalogs with updated information.

Many companies sell rather than give away their catalogs. "When a customer will pay three ninety-five for the catalog, I know that he is as serious about getting the information as I was in gathering it," Brandborg says. "We don't make money on the catalog. I consider it a loss leader. It about breaks even."

Brandborg started Sun Electric Co. five years ago because his home state of Montana was one of the hot spots for solar energy. "I rented a corner of a print shop and spent a couple of thousand dollars for startup. I was told it would be three years before I could take anything out of the business and sure enough that turned out to be true. In most cases, I think a person ought to have maybe fifty thousand dollars in savings to embark on something like this." Fortunately, his wife was working and they were able to finance the growth of Sunelco by pouring profits back into it. In 1990, the company had sales of more than $1 million.

A small number of retailers are helping others get started in the business. One is David Katz, who founded Alternative Energy Engineering in Redway, California, 11 years ago as a retail and mail-order company. After he had been in business for several years, however, many of his customers urged him to become a wholesaler. In 1990, 80 percent of his estimated $1.4 million in sales came from wholesaling. "We sell to the local solar expert, the person who years ago ordered from the catalog we put out," Katz says. "When neighbors told that person they also wanted a similar solar system, he became a dealer. He now runs his own business. We've helped start more than two hundred fifty such dealerships around the country." To help them, Katz now produces a generic catalog with a blank space on the cover for the retailer's name. He thus offers a relatively low-cost way for someone to get into the alternative energy business.

The story is similar for installers. Most got involved in the business in the early 1980's, when solar thermal energy was going through a boom stimulated by high energy costs and government tax breaks. "We didn't need much capital—there was a strong market demand and we didn't need to advertise," says Leigh Seddon, who founded Solar Works in 1980. Similarly, Henry Vandermark started Solar Wave in Charlestown, Massachusetts, in 1978 with almost no money. "We just kind of trickled it in," he says now. Business grew briskly because of the high demand, and neither had to worry much about advertising or any of the other problems of small businesses.

But catastrophe struck in 1985 when the federal government repealed the income-tax credit it had authorized for alternative energy installations. "Nine out of ten businesses failed," Seddon says, and those that didn't had to retrench severely, laying off employees and paring expenses to the bone. Only in the last year has business begun to pick up again, stimulated in large part by the Iraq crisis and the rising price of oil. "But it's going to take a lot of advertising and effort to recreate the market we had before," Seddon says.

Vandermark concedes that he was never very good at marketing solar thermal systems, but the people who were good at selling the systems often needed people to help with installation. That became his niche. In addition, he also built his own solar collectors, starting out by assembling them in the kitchen of his one-bedroom apartment. "It was a classic cottage industry," he says.

After a year, he moved into a warehouse, sharing an inexpensive loft with three artists. Sales were sufficient to cover the loft space.

Through the end of the decade, the surviving companies did so by branching into related areas. Vandermark spent a lot of time repairing systems that had been installed during the industry's heyday, as well as by installing systems in a housing project built by a local contractor. Seddon turned to training other people, particularly engineers from developing countries, in the intricacies of solar energy installation. Much of his work was performed through the Agency for International Development. Now, both have high hopes for the future. "I think we are finally beginning to get on a growth curve as solar energy becomes a little more mainstream," Seddon says.

Marketing Considerations

Retailers of alternative energy products typically advertise in a broad spectrum of publications, including magazines aimed at both environmentalists and outdoorsmen. Real Goods' outlay of 10 percent of sales for advertising and catalog printing and distribution is typical for the industry. A new company competing against those that are already established may have to spend even more to gain a foothold in the market. Alternative types of publicity, such as newspaper, magazine, and television stories, would also be quite helpful. Advertising for installers is somewhat less expensive because it is more locally focused. Installers should also try to develop relationships with the large retailers who can then refer them to customers.

Strategic Issues

Competition

The competition among retailers is expected to be intense, even though the market is rapidly expanding. Established retailers already have a great deal of expertise, established mailing lists of potential customers, and often a highly loyal clientele. Gaining a foothold in the industry may require extensive advertising and, perhaps, the development or acquisition of innovative products that can produce a competitive edge. Even the individual opening a retail store will face competition from the large mail-order companies, which may well be able to offer lower prices and greater technical expertise. Therefore, study the competitive arena carefully before entering the field.

Much the same considerations hold for installers as well. Many existing companies have been in operation for a decade or longer, enduring financial hardships that have forged them into strong competitors. Perhaps the most effective way to enter the field would be installing equipment as an adjunct service to a conventional plumbing or electrical contracting business.

Impact of Government Activities

Federal and state governments have had a strong influence on the alternative energy business during the last decade, and are likely to do so in the future. In the early 1980's, the Department of Housing and Urban Development had a small program that offered a $400 grant for installation of energy-saving systems. Unfortunately, Vandermark says, while applications were made in the first year, people did not receive the money until a year later. Many people thus postponed purchase of solar equipment until they could get the grant, which had an adverse effect on the industry. Many potential customers also were discouraged by the massive amount of paperwork in the program and simply dropped out.

Later, the federal government offered a federal tax credit of 40 percent on purchases of alternative energy equipment up to $10,000. The tax credit could be applied directly to a tax liability, meaning that a $10,000 system cost the customer only $6,000 out of pocket. Many states offered similar credits. Massachusetts, for example, had a 35 percent credit with a $1,000 limit. That dropped the cost of the $10,000 system down to only $5,000. The credits did bring customers out; more than 22,000 solar hot water systems were sold in the state of Massachusetts alone, during that period, according to state officials.

But the credits also brought out a gaggle of operators who sought to make a quick buck selling overpriced, low-quality systems to undereducated consumers. Those systems have often been very expensive to maintain, Vandermark says, and have discouraged many of the people who bought them from continuing their investment. They also put a black mark against the industry in customers' minds.

When the tax credits were repealed in 1985, it shook the industry to its foundations. Many, if not most companies, went out of business and the survivors were forced to pare their operations substantially. Most are just now beginning to overcome their bad images and make a recovery. But the majority also think the future looks bright, particularly with the sharp increases in oil prices that have been triggered by unrest in the Middle East.

Ironically, some states are again offering tax credits for installation of solar and other equipment, and some retailers fear that this will increase competition and perhaps again attract "solar scam artists." Real Goods' Schaeffer says he used to fear such a development, "but I've learned not to get overly excited by the fad element or the sudden popularity of a market. Just make sure you do your own thing right and take your time, and you'll come out okay."

He Saw the Light . . . Bulb

Conventional wisdom says that to succeed in business, you have to be in the right place at the right time. Fred Davis says he was successful because he was in the right place at the wrong time, but stayed with it long enough for the world to catch up with him. Davis is a wholesale distributor for energy-efficient light bulbs, perhaps the only such wholesaler in the country. His company, Fred Davis Corporation in Medfield, Massachusetts, provides bulbs to ecopreneurs around the country, as well as to conventional retailers who want to take advantage of the bulbs' unique characteristics.

"I got into this business because I saw energy being wasted and many opportunities to minimize waste and make this world a better place for ourselves and our children," he says. "It sounds glib, but it's true. It stares me in the face every day." But, he concedes, "the reason this business exists has only tangentially to do with air pollution and the environment. It's simply highly cost-effective to use these bulbs."

Davis originally worked with a company that installed insulation and other energy-saving devices in homes. In 1981, he decided he wanted to be more independent, so he quit his job and started his own company. He began as an independent representative of the VL Service Lighting division of Dura-Test Corporation, selling conventional bulbs and fixtures to businesses in his territory. "They did a lot of training and handholding, providing research, literature, and so forth. The training period would normally have lasted only a few months, but I wanted to take it a lot further and go beyond what they had to teach. So I spent a year of fairly intensive self-study under other professionals because I wanted to feel like I was doing the right thing for customers."

If that sounds like a lot of training just for selling light bulbs, Davis disagrees. "There are hundreds of different types of bulbs and thousands of fixtures. Multiply that by the number of applications and it gets very complicated . . . And when you add energy conservation, that's another level of complexity."

As he began to get more involved with energy-saving bulbs, he started to sell energy-saving products from other manufacturers as well as VL. Eventually, he formed relationships with several of the manufacturers and began wholesaling their products on a limited basis. Initially, his customers were utilities, other resellers, and commercial-scale end-users—companies that purchased large quantities of light bulbs. The utilities would either sell or give the bulbs to their customers as a way to promote conservation of energy and thereby minimize the need to construct expensive new power plants. "From 1983 to 1988, all of our distribution was to commercial end-users," he says. "Four years ago, nobody could have imagined that the residential market would take off like it has."

In addition to running his wholesaling business, Davis offers energy consulting services that include energy audits for large companies. One of his clients is the headquarters of the Environmental Protection Agency in Washington, D.C. He also served on a panel that consulted to the state of Massachusetts on energy efficiency standards for light bulbs. Now, Massachusetts is the first state in the country to have minimum efficiency standards for bulbs.

Davis notes that "lots of people are just starting out selling energy-efficient bulbs. They are starting their own catalogs, operating stores . . . they run the whole gamut." He gets one or two new calls every week, and he tries to help them get moving in the right direction. "I spend time with them, recommending bulbs, sending them literature, holding their hand. I can tell them which types are best, which combination of bulbs is most likely to fit the most sockets." Davis believes that opportunities for selling energy-efficient bulbs and appliances are boundless, as demonstrated by the fact that his own business has grown 100 percent in each of six of the last eight years. "The boom is just beginning," he predicts, "and there are a whole lot of ways to plug into it."

જી

Selling alternative energy devices and energy consulting services has become a viable way of making a living, because of the new environmental awareness and an increasingly unstable political situation in the Middle East. There are numerous opportunities, but there is also significant competition from the pioneers who stuck with the field and are now reaping the benefits of their perseverance. Still, if you like gadgets and like the idea of helping to reduce air pollution and conserve resources, consider how you can make a difference and a good living by starting an alternative energy ecobusiness. In the next chapter, you'll learn about yet another good field for the ecopreneur—water conservation and treatment.

Chapter *Twelve*

The Water Works:
Green Dollars from Brown Rivers

Turning Manure into Gold

Throughout the 1970's, the Sellew family's Pride's Corner Farms in Lebanon, Connecticut, was a simple wholesale nursery—not small, but not overly large either. What distinguished it from most other nurseries was the fact that the Sellews produced their own fertilizer. Peter Sellew and his three sons collected agricultural wastes—primarily horse, pig, cow, and chicken manure, as well as wastes from two large mushroom growers— and composted it. In essence, they laid the waste out in long rows in open fields, allowing it to decompose. About a year later, they collected odorless, but extremely potent, fertilizer.

In the early 1980's, the Sellews began producing more fertilizer than they could use at the nursery, so they began bagging it and selling it as Earthgro, first to their own customers and then through other garden supply centers. But, says Archie Albright, president of International Process Systems (IPS) of Glastonbury,

Connecticut, which owns Pride's Corner Farms and two companies that market the firm's fertilizers, "Here in the Northeast, producing compost on a large scale by an outdoor method is a very tough way to make a living. We had heard about enclosed, automated composting systems in Europe and sent technicians to take a look. But we concluded that they were too high-tech, too complicated mechanically, and none were very reliable."

Next, the technicians went to Japan to study a system that had been in use for more than 15 years, and it proved more to their liking. They adapted it to their own specifications and added a number of design modifications over the past five to six years. In essence, the system (located indoors) consists of long horizontal bays that are agitated daily. Built-in temperature sensors monitor heat output and, when necessary, activate aerating blowers that keep the temperature from rising too high.

As an adjunct to composting agricultural wastes, the company now composts in their two plants in Lebanon yard wastes collected by several local townships and sewage sludge. The company sells 12 to 14 million bags of fertilizer every year throughout the country under a variety of labels. It also sells bulk fertilizer to municipalities under its Allgro label. In addition to selling fertilizer, IPS markets the composting technology.

By the fall of 1990, the company had four operating composting installations. Five more were under construction at the time, and 10 more were slated for groundbreaking by year's end. Several of the firm's composting facilities were purchased by communities. Fairfield, Connecticut, uses an IPS composting system to compost municipal sewage sludge, yard wastes, and certain types of paper that are not readily recycled, such as magazines. The city is now using the resulting fertilizer itself, but plans to begin selling it to residents when its own needs have been fulfilled.

IPS also sells its system to other companies. Beer brewer Anheuser-Busch ordered one for Baldwinsville, New York, to handle leftover mash from the brewing process; the resulting fertilizer is marketed by IPS's Earthgro subsidiary. McCormack-Partyka, a Boston-based landfill operator, has ordered IPS systems to compost yard wastes and other materials from Holyoke and Chicopee, Massachusetts. Both towns are very short on landfill space. Albright sees a rosy future for the company. "We have an acute disposal problem in the Northeast because of bans on ocean dumping of sewage and on landfilling of yard wastes. In most cases, communities are going to have to turn to composting—what choice do they have?"

❧

Sewage—raw human wastes—causes more coastal pollution than any other pollutant. It is also a growing problem in many rural locations where wastes from increasing numbers of vacation homes are released directly into the environment. In most cities and towns, sewage treatment plants separate solid matter (sludge) from the waste stream for burial or dumping at sea. The plants typically treat the remaining liquid with chlorine and other chemical disinfectants before discharging it into rivers or other bodies of water. Despite the treatment, though, both solid and liquid portions of the sewage still contain disease-causing bacteria and high levels of phosphates and nitrates, both of which create problems after disposal. According to the Office of Technology Assessment, more than 500 communities discharge treated sewage sludge directly into estuaries.

The bacteria can kill many types of wildlife, as well as cause disease among humans who eat infected shellfish and crustaceans. The nutrients pose an even more severe problem. Excessive concentrations of nitrates and phosphates in water, a condition known as "eutrophication," overstimulates the growth of undesirable species such as blue-green and red algae, causing algal blooms; a species of marine red algae causes the destructive "red tides." The blooms block sunlight from reaching phytoplankton, which form the basis of the food chain, and other marine vegetation; some of the algae in the blooms produce toxins that kill marine organisms. More important, when the algal blooms die, the process of decomposition strips oxygen from the water, thereby suffocating fish and other organisms.

Another major source of water pollution is so-called "nonpoint-source pollution," a catchall term for contaminated runoff from a large number of miscellaneous sources such as fields, streets, and lawns, rather than, say, discharge from the pipe of an industrial facility or sewage treatment plant. The most common pollutants include fertilizers and pesticides from farmers' fields and residential lawns, sediments from eroding fields, ditches, and construction sites, used motor oil poured into sewers or dumped onto the soil, and toxic pollutants from city streets. Oil is a particular problem; Americans use 1.2 billion gallons of motor oil each year, and at least one third of it is discarded into the environment, creating the environmental equivalent of 35 Exxon Valdez oil spills.

Grass, leaves, and other yard wastes are also frequently dumped in sewers, adding an additional burden to the water supply. More often, they are buried in landfills, contributing to the rapid depletion of available space. According to the EPA, about 17.9 percent of the volume of landfills is now occupied by grass clippings and other yard wastes. Another 7.9 percent is food wastes. Both can readily be composted, eliminating the need for burial.

Going Green in Yard Care

Technical Considerations

The average American home owner uses 5 to 10 pounds of pesticides on his or her lawn every year, a total of about 50 billion pounds. Home owners use about 10 times more pesticide per acre than farmers, and those pesticides cost them about $1 billion per year. They also apply more than half a billion pounds of fertilizers every year, at a cost of another $1 billion. Most of those pesticides and fertilizers are washed off the lawn and down the drain, where they pollute water supplies. Ecopreneurs can help alleviate the fertilizer and pesticide abuse problems by running environmentally conscious yard-care services or marketing naturally occurring pest control materials.

Getting Started

Lawn Care Services

The largest environmentally conscious lawn-care service in the country is NaturaLawn, Inc., headquartered in Damascus, Maryland, just outside Washington, D.C. The founders, Phil Catron and Beecher Smith, had been with ChemLawn for many years before striking out on their own. But that was not their original intention. After ChemLawn turned down their idea for an environmentally friendly lawn care program, they started their own company, NaturaLawn, but were rejected. (ChemLawn apparently had second thoughts and subsequently began test-marketing environmentally friendly lawn services that use manure and no pesticides.)

By 1990, three years after starting the company, the two eco-preneurs could boast more than 3,000 customers and sales of more than $750,000. In addition, Catron and Smith offer franchises for $15,000, which entitle the franchisee to use the name and receive specialized training. As of the summer of 1990, three franchises had been sold, proving that simple ideas like organic yard care can flourish even in high tech times.

Natural Pest Control Products

One of the oldest and largest companies selling environmentally sound pest pesticides and other gardening products is the Ringer Corporation of Eden Prairie, Minnesota. Ringer was founded 30 years ago by the late Judd Ringer, ironically, to market a spot weedkiller containing the potent herbicide 2,4-D. Fred Hundt, Ringer's vice-president for marketing, says "Then he read [Rachel Carson's] *Silent Spring* and realized he was going about this all wrong. He sold off that product line and began moving toward more environmentally oriented products."

Ringer and his partner, a former 3M chemist, Don Lovness, began developing what Hundt calls "a microbial approach to fertilizing that basically enhances the natural process of decomposition of organic material into nutrients." The result was a technique for composting such agricultural wastes as feather meal, bone meal, blood meal, and wheat germ to produce a fertilizer they called Restore. For 25 years, they served a loyal following throughout the Midwest, providing not only the fertilizer, but also starter kits for organic gardeners who wanted to produce their own compost. Their annual sales were on the order of $2 million per year.

Four years ago, the Ringer family sold the firm to a group of venture capital investors who set about building it into a national company that could take advantage of coming environmental trends. The new management group secured distribution for Ringer in chains such as Target, Wal-Mart, Frank's Nursery, and Tru-Value Hardware—9,000 retail outlets in all. In 1989, Ringer acquired a company that produces insecticides made from all natural ingredients. It also began selling bins and other equipment used for composting, as well as a full line of gardening supplies that are listed in a catalog mailed to 3 million homes. Ringer's gross sales were expected to reach $20 million.

In addition to its retail and catalog sales, Ringer is also expanding into producing large-scale composting facilities for cities. In late 1990 the company was constructing a composting facility in St. Cloud, Minnesota, that will be able to handle 250 tons of yard wastes and paper per day.

Other companies have started out on a smaller scale. Bill Wolf was an organic farmer for seven years during the 1970's. To get many of the materials he needed for farming, he had to buy in large quantities—"pallets to railroad cars full"—to get companies to produce it for him. He began reselling the materials to his neighbors to get rid of the excess and, by the end of the decade, was running a large co-op. "By 1977, it had gotten to the point where it was clearly more business than I could run from one room of my house," Wolf says. "Besides, we had a daughter on the way and I was going to have to give up my office for her bedroom. So we leased office space in an unheated cinderblock building in New Castle, Virginia and some storage space in Roanoke and expanded operations."

People were constantly asking what they carried, he says. "I wrote up a description of what it was, why it was made, and what it does for the garden. Pretty soon, it had grown to a hundred pages and the next thing I knew, I was publishing a catalog." Wolf initially financed his firm, Necessary Trading Co., with "a couple of hundred dollars borrowed from friends and relatives." Eventually, he and his wife also remortgaged their farm. Banks were skeptical about his requests for loans, but the president of one bank was a gardener, so Wolf gave him some of their special fertilizer. The fertilizer convinced the president that the business was sound. The president convinced his board, and Wolf got his loan. Today, Necessary Trading's annual sales are approaching $2 million.

Niles Kinerk's story is similar. He had grown up on a farm and enjoyed organic gardening. He, too, had trouble finding the products he needed—products that were described in books about organic farming but that were not readily available. Kinerk had worked for a large mail-order company, and had even operated his own company selling library supplies. So it seemed only natural to combine his two interests and sell organic gardening supplies by mail.

To start up Gardens Alive, Kinerk raised $25,000, most of which went to putting together a 24-page catalog that included extensive instructions about how to use the pesticides and other products. "You need to know what is causing your problem, as opposed to going out and spraying something that kills everything," he says. "Most biological control agents are highly specific and will control only certain things."

Kinerk says that his background in mail-order sales was crucial to his success in his Sunman, Indiana business. "There are a lot of books about how to start a mail-order company, but it's important to have some experience and background. Otherwise, you are quite likely to lose a lot of money. Contrary to popular opinion, it is not a low-cost operation, even though it continues to grow in popularity . . . With the way postage rates have been going up, being a small mailer is a very bad position to be in." But not for him. Gardens Alive now has 50 employees and will fill 150,000 orders in 1990.

Marketing Considerations

Marketing lawn-care services can be a difficult proposition. Local advertising is one approach, but it is often difficult to distinguish your services from a competitor's in a short ad. Some companies thus rely more on direct marketing, such as telephone solicitation, as well as personal contact with potential customers. Brochures that explain the difference in services and point out some of the environmental problems caused by indiscriminate pesticide and fertilizer use are also helpful.

Marketers of alternative pesticides and related products, though, tend to make a large portion of their sales by mail order. In that case, it is crucial to advertise in appropriate national publications such as *Sierra* and *Buzzworm*. Ringer is an exception to this trend, garnering only about 20 percent of its sales through mail order. But it also has a large marketing department capable of getting Ringer products into retail outlets.

Publicity of any sort is extremely beneficial, including write-ups in local newspapers, spot features on cable television, and mentions in the many books on environmental issues that are now appearing. Chapter 4 contains suggestions for using magnet marketing—the lawn-care and natural pesticide businesses are ideal candidates for magnet marketing techniques designed to educate and cultivate customers.

Strategic Considerations

Competition

Your primary competition will be vendors of traditional products and services—often at a lower price than you can afford to offer. Of course, if you are going into mail-order sales, you will also be competing with the existing companies selling similar environment-friendly products via catalogs. In the former case, you will be able to compete only by convincing potential clients of the advantages of your products or services and of their reduced impact on the environment—magnet marketing can be extremely helpful in this regard. One advantage that you'll have is the growing environmental awareness of the problems caused by synthetic pesticides and overuse of fertilizers. This advantage will be lost rapidly, however, if your products or services don't deliver on your promises.

Competing against existing mail-order companies may be even more difficult because you are entering a more limited marketplace. Again, use magnet marketing as a tool. Educate and cultivate, and your customer base may grow to a healthy enough level to sustain your business. Make sure your catalogs include plenty of information about why your alternative products are important and how to use them. Provide plenty of tips that will prove you're the vendor of choice. In short, offer value, don't push products.

Impact of Government Activities

Currently, government regulations have only a small effect on retailers or service providers in the yard and waste area. The greatest positive effect of government action, says Kinerk, occurs when the EPA bans a chemical pesticide because of potential health problems. "That always makes people look to alternatives," he says. In contrast, however, the labyrinthine tangle of regulations that a marketer must traverse in order to bring out a new gardening substance, even one that is completely natural in origin, makes developing new products a time-consuming and very costly proposition.

The companies that are most affected by government activities are those that manufacture or distribute commercial-scale composting equipment. Already, roughly a dozen states, primarily in the Northeast, have banned landfilling of yard wastes and related materials. Many other states are likely to follow suit as landfill space becomes a scarce commodity. That trend should provide a powerful boost to the industry.

Diversification

Some diversification paths in this field are obvious. Companies that provide lawn services might begin selling alternative pesticides and fertilizers, while retailers might expand into lawn care. Other gardening supplies, such as utensils, clothing, and the like, might also be a good way to enhance your business. Composting is another alternative. A yard service company might arrange to collect yard wastes from its customers, composting them and putting them back on the lawns as fertilizer. The operation might then expand to collect wastes from other home owners as well.

Cleaning Up Waste Water

Technical Considerations

Nature does a very good job of cleaning up water as long as humans do not interfere. Unfortunately, in the world's highly populated regions, civilization has overwhelmed the delicate fabric of synergy among bacteria, plants, and animals that accomplishes this task, converting once pristine streams into little more than open sewers. But at least two companies have come up with systems that mimic the action of nature in much smaller space. They use the natural cleansing power of ecological systems to treat wastewater, industrial wastes, and a variety of other types of water, including swimming pools and fishtanks. In the past, one of the problems that has limited the use of such systems has been finding the delicate balance necessary to keep bacteria, algae, and other components of the system alive. When the organisms proliferate to excess, they clog the system and cause it to break down.

The two systems that have been developed so far stand in sharp contrast to each other. Ecological Systems, Inc., of Bethesda, Maryland, has developed a rather simple system, the heart of which is a mat of algae. A pump creates artificial waves to aerate the water, and a light source provides energy for the algae. Ecological Engineering Associates of Marion, Massachusetts, has developed a much more elaborate system that has an integrated community of single-celled organisms, plants, fish, and other aquatic organisms that live in a large greenhouse. But both methods do much the same thing—remove nutrients from water and convert them into harmless chemicals that will not damage the environment. In addition, the plants in the systems remove heavy metals, while exposure to light kills pathogenic microorganisms and breaks down many toxic chemicals.

Getting Started

Using an ecological approach to purifying water requires a high degree of technical sophistication. In both cases, the system was designed by a researcher with extensive experience in ecological systems. Walter Adey, director of the Marine Systems Laboratory at the Smithsonian Institution in Washington, D.C., designed Ecological Systems' Algal Turf Scrubber. Adey originally developed the water-cleaning technology so he could install a living coral reef at the Smithsonian—the first time such a reef has ever been grown in an aquarium. John Todd, founder of the New Alchemy Institute on Cape Cod, designed Ecological Engineering Associates' Solar Aquatics System specifically for water treatment.

Todd and his partner, Susan Peterson, took a conventional route in starting their company, organizing it themselves, and seeking out venture capital (see profile, page 205). But Adey was more interested in staying in his position at the Smithsonian and his venture capital group brought in an outsider, Mark Weinstein, specifically for his entrepreneurial ability. Weinstein runs the company and Adey provides technological expertise.

So far, Ecological Systems' purification process has primarily been used in aquariums, such as the coral reef aquarium at the

Great Barrier Reef Wonderland in Townsville, Australia, which has a one-million-gallon tank. It has also been installed in several aquariums in the United States, including those at St. Louis and Pittsburgh. In addition, it is used for water purification at Biosphere II in Arizona, a large enclosed habitat in which eight volunteers will spend two years completely isolated from the outside world.

Ecological Systems has several other projects in the works. It is working with a large aquaculture company in the Midwest where it hopes to prove its product's utility in a situation with a very high nutrient load in the water. "Fish farming is like a minisewer, with sixty thousand gallons of water filled gill to gill," Weinstein says. No one has previously been able to find a way to purify the water so that a closed system could be used. But Weinstein thinks his company's product will be able to do it. Ecological Systems is also developing products for pools and home aquariums. Its first commercial product will be a small self-contained ecosystem that will purify the water for a 130- to 200-gallon aquarium. Weinstein later plans to develop products that will be used to treat industrial effluents.

Marketing Considerations

The primary method for marketing commercial-scale water purification systems is to build a working plant and demo it to prospective customers. Hence, most sales are made through direct personal contact, either through visits to the company or through contacts made at scientific meetings. But Ecological Systems will use direct mail and magazine advertising to promote its systems for aquariums. "We have to create a market before wholesalers will pick it up," Weinstein says. "Once we're selling them, we can approach selected retailers."

Strategic Considerations

Competition

The primary competition for new water purification systems will be conventional technology. Both Ecological Systems and Ecological Engineering Associates believe they can compete effectively with that technology because they can offer both lower prices and more effective treatment. Furthermore,

Ecological Engineering Associates has a unique approach in that they will build, finance, and operate a sewage treatment plant for a community, thereby relieving officials from most of the tasks involved in constructing a new facility.

Impact of Government Activities

The water purification industry is, to a large extent, driven by government regulations that require a minimum purity for sewage effluent released into rivers and lakes. If the government tightens regulations in the future, facilities like those produced by the two companies will become even more desirable because of their ability to achieve high water purity. Both federal and state governments also have a variety of loan programs to assist in the construction of waste treatment facilities, thereby enabling both communities and private companies to build them.

Diversification

In addition to community waste treatment, possibilities abound for cleaning up industrial effluents, swimming pools, aquariums, aquaculture systems, and anything else where clean water is important.

Greenbacks from a Greenhouse

Susan Peterson sells clean water. It doesn't come out of a bottle, however, but from a specially built greenhouse that, in effect, duplicates the environment a mountain stream encounters flowing down a canyon. Peterson's company, Ecological Engineering Associates of Marion, Massachusetts, has already built three small versions of its innovative water purification system, and she hopes that it will be able to construct such greenhouses all over the country to help communities dispose of their sewage.

An anthropologist by training, Peterson's career took a sharp right turn when she accepted a postdoctoral fellowship to train at the Woods Hole Oceanographic Institution in Massachusetts. "I did quite a bit of research on coastal water quality and we found that the major source of contamination is failed sewage treatment systems and failed septic tanks. We began looking at how to solve the problem." "We" includes Peterson and ecologist John Todd, founder of the New Alchemy Institute and currently president of a research organization called Ocean Arks International in Falmouth, Massachusetts.

The Solar Aquatics System that the two came up with looks like a commercial greenhouse from the outside, but, Peterson says, "They are really rivers of sewage with all kinds of floating and rafted vegetation on the surface." The closed ecosystem contains not only plants, but also bacteria, algae, fish, snails, clams, "and the occasional courageous frog, which volunteers—we don't put the frogs in."

The bacteria and algae attack the sewage, breaking it down into harmless chemicals, and the fish eat the algae to keep populations within bounds. The fish themselves are harvested periodically and sold to pet stores or released as fingerlings into the wild, where they become part of the ecosystem. The plants remove most of the nutrients from the wastewater, in the process producing flowers—such as lilies and narcissus—that Peterson plans to harvest and sell. In effect, the system concentrates the processes that occur in nature into a very small space.

Peterson believes that the firm should not be just an engineering company. "I've toured a lot of waste water treatment plants and many were not operating the way they were designed to. Most engineering firms have nothing to do with the operation of a plant. They design it and walk away, leaving municipal workers to figure out how to run the thing." She reasoned, "If private companies designed, built, and operated waste treatment systems and were paid on the basis of the quality of the water discharged, there would be a powerful financial incentive to make certain the quality of the water leaving the plant is good."

Their plants are designed primarily to handle two different types of materials: sewage and septage. "Sewage is the material that flows out of the household, down a pipe, and into a sewage treatment plant. It's pretty runny stuff. Septage is the material that is collected in a septic tank in the backyard and is typically a hundred times more concentrated." In a septic system, a large underground tank holds solid material, while liquids flow out through a water leaching field composed of porous pipes. Almost half the houses in the United States use septic tanks. The tanks need to be emptied every two or three years. "The contents used to be put out on farm fields and plowed in, but with the suburbanization of America, there's not much local land to spread it on," she says. A lot of communities would like to require that septic tanks be pumped out every two to three years to prevent overflow from contaminating groundwater, but they don't have any place to put it. Peterson says, "We've developed this really elegant system for treating it."

Peterson and Todd used grants from federal and state governments, as well as from foundations, to put together "a couple of pilot plants" to test out their ideas. With these operating units, they were able to attract $5 million in venture capital to start Ecological Engineering Associates in 1988. Much of their time has been spent wading through a morass of legal regulations, but they have built two commercial systems: one for the small community of Harwich, Massachusetts, and one for a business complex operated by Paws, Inc., the Indiana firm that handles franchising for Jim Davis, creator of Garfield the Cat. They recently broke ground for a similar plant in Vermont for Ben & Jerry's Ice Cream.

Peterson is working with a number of other communities where she hopes to build full-scale plants. Some of them want to own their own plants. "That's fine if they want to," she says, "but there's pretty good data that privatized systems are cheaper to build, often thirty to forty percent cheaper, and that they get built faster." In a typical installation, Peterson would expect to get a 15- to 20-year contract and the company would finance, build, and operate the facility for a set charge. In Harwich, which has 10,000 people, the company is charging 15 cents per gallon of septage. To the home owner, that translates to about $50 per year if his or her septic tank is pumped every three years.

If the company gets any contracts, Peterson will have to raise a lot more money, but she doesn't think that will be a problem. The federal government has made money available for low-interest loans through the Small Business Administration, and companies can also apply for money to build sewage treatment plants using industrial revenue bonds. Many states have also developed revolving loan programs to cover the capital costs of sewage treatment plants.

The company's next project most likely will be a system for the town of Marion to use in purifying sewage pumped out of boats. After that, Peterson expects to construct systems for a number of other small towns in New England. Eventually, she would like to be able to work with larger cities. One potential target is Boston, which is now pumping tons of sludge directly into Boston Harbor. And that, she thinks, might be exceptionally appropriate: a revolution in water purification in the same place that wrought a revolution in government.

☙

A variety of other technologies can also improve water quality, but they tend to be so expensive that they can be undertaken only by large companies. Nonetheless, the individual entrepreneur can make many inroads, as has been demonstrated above. Perhaps the area of greatest opportunity involves the use of natural pesticides and fertilizers, which are now applied to only a very limited extent. Composting of yard wastes and sewage is another technology with much room to grow. "I think it is pretty clear that we were on a path to self-destruction because we had gotten away from basic, sensible, sustainable agricultural practices," Bill Wolf says. "But I think we're turning a corner and companies like ours are making the difference."

This concludes the part of *Ecopreneuring* devoted to taking care of the planet. In the next part, you'll learn how you can start ecobusinesses that provide green products and services to an eager marketplace.

Part III

Catering to the Green Lifestyle

Overview

Creating Environment-Friendly Products and Services

Imagine a perfect world from an environmental standpoint. Consumer products would be formulated with nontoxic, noncarcinogenic substances. They would only contain materials that are safe for the environment, and would be developed without animal testing. They would also be packaged with minimal waste and with as many biodegradable, recycled, or recyclable materials as possible.

Food would be free of pesticides, as well as unnecessary additives and preservatives. It would also be packaged sensibly with minimal use of nondegradable or nonrecyclable materials.

In this "green" world, you'd find plenty of people who could help you make sound decisions about your investments, ensuring that your hard-earned dollars supported companies with the best environmental track records. You'd also want to find companies that could help you and your family visit parts of the world untainted by pollution, as well as vendors who could supply your children with environmentally responsible educational materials and games. In short, you'd want a world in which companies catered to a green marketplace.

Those who believe in this vision of the future can actually help to create it. As you'll learn in the next four chapters, opportunities abound for ecopreneurs to get involved with the production and sale of environment-friendly products (Chapter 13) and safe food (Chapter 14), with helping people to make environmentally sound investment decisions (Chapter 15), and with teaching people about the environment through recreation, toys, and games (Chapter 16).

Each of these chapters surveys business fields where you make a mark. You'll learn what you need to get started and get advice from seasoned ecopreneurs as to what works and what doesn't. If you're already in business, you may well find information that will help your company prosper. If you're thinking of going into business, the chapters in this part of *Ecopreneuring* should give you food for thought and point you in a direction that suits your interests and resources. Either way, the goal of Part III is to help you grow a business that works for the environment while working for you.

Chapter *Thirteen*

Green Products:
Meeting the Demand for Environment-Friendly Goods

When Sally Malanga heard the story of primates being sprayed to death with underarm deodorant, something inside her snapped. She had been talking to a laboratory worker for a major company that manufactures a very popular underarm spray deodorant when she learned the shocking tale. The lab worker went into hideous detail about how the primates were tied down and machine-forced to inhale deodorant until they died. The purpose of this "experiment" was to determine the toxicity to humans of the spray deodorants. Malanga had long known that many large companies used animals to test their products, but somehow the vivid description the lab worker had provided, and the phrase "spray till death," stuck with her.

When Malanga heard the story in 1985, she was working for her family's recycling business, traveling around the country in search of scrap computers and jewelry that could be melted down for gold. She enjoyed her work, but had always wanted to do something at the consumer level. After her talk with the lab worker, ideas began to percolate.

"I figured there had to be companies out there who didn't go in for the blinding and burning and poisoning of animals," she recalls. "The tests aren't required by law, they're absolutely not necessary."

She thought to herself, "Why not put together a list of manufacturers who didn't test on animals and list them in a catalog that would appeal to people who didn't want to support companies that engaged in animal cruelty?" She called her catalog and company Ecco Bella, "behold the beautiful."

"We incorporated in 1988," Malanga says. "I was really green. Instinct and trial and error supplied a lot of the business sense I needed. We set up shop in my garage, moved out the cars, and put up shelves where we could stock cruelty-free products."

For the first catalog, she hired three people to help fill the orders. The orders picked up, and she began developing her own line of environment-friendly household goods that were formulated and packaged with the environment in mind. To learn about beneficial ingredients that could be used as substitutes for the toxic ones used in conventional products, she began attending seminars and conventions, and meeting with anyone who offered information on the subject.

Through her networking activities, Malanga met a perfumer who worked for a large company and had gotten seriously ill. "We worked together to develop perfumes that used real flowers, not the synthetic kind of scent essences," Malanga recalls. She also hired a chemist to develop shampoos, hair- and skin-care items that were animal-friendly, environment-friendly, and gentle to the user. The products are expensive to make, but Malanga felt that consumers would pay more for her products because they were buying an idea as well as a product.

Apparently she was right. Ecco Bella outgrew the garage and moved to its present location, where a staff of 25 handles 300 to 500 orders per day. Her first year in business the company grossed $100,000; in 1990 she expects to gross over $1 million. "I decided to let the company blossom, and to plan as though I'll be in business next year," she says intensely.

Competition from the influx of green products into the supermarket doesn't concern her. "We offer something supermarkets can't, and that's the convenience of shopping from the comfort of your home. You can curl up with a cup of tea, a cat on your lap, and go through our catalog."

Currently the Ecco Bella catalog carries 300 products, many of Malanga's own but others as well. Products in her catalog range from cosmetics to food, from pet-care items to household cleansers. Malanga uses the Ecco Bella catalog for education, also. In a letter to her customers published usually on the second or third page, she informs them of the criteria used to choose the products in the catalog:

- Products not tested on animals.
- Products that don't contain animal by-products.
- Products that have minimal impact on the environment.
- Products that use natural botanical ingredients instead of petroleum-based derivatives or synthetic chemicals.
- Products packaged with recyclable materials whenever possible.

Malanga's catalog has a homey touch, similar to a letter from an old friend. She feels this is important, because consumers, when given the right information, will choose to support those businesses that take the extra care to protect the environment and all its living beings.

⁋

What Makes a Product "Green"?

The number of new products entering the consumer marketplace each week is staggering. Among them are products aimed at the environmentally conscious consumer. These "green" or "environment-friendly" products have been appearing on the shelves of supermarkets, drugstores, and department stores. They're designed to appeal to people who are tired of wasteful overpackaging and harmful chemicals, as well as cruelty to animals.

Green products appeal to people who want to cast their vote at the cash register and send a message to retailers and manufacturers. These people don't necessarily want to start a revolution, they're just looking for a cleaner world. And they see the consumption of green products as one means of achieving their goals.

Interestingly, green products appeal to a broad spectrum of Americans, not just yuppies and holdouts from the sixties. A number of surveys have demonstrated that middle America is all too willing to pay a slight premium for products that will help alleviate problems with solid-waste disposal, air pollution, and water pollution.

What makes a product "green"? Since there is no national association of green product standards as yet, the criteria have evolved over the years as various environmental problems have come to the public's attention. But generally green products are those that use alternative ingredients in their formulas, ingredients that serve the same function as the ingredients they replace but are not polluting, toxic to humans, or tested on animals. In a way, green products are "kinder, gentler" products than their commercial counterparts. Here are the major criteria that determine a product's "greenness."

Petroleum. Petroleum is used for a lot more than the manufacture of oil and gasoline. Petroleum derivatives are found in paints, household cleaners, adhesives, and personal-care products such as hair sprays and cosmetics. The use of petroleum in such products creates pollution at the source of manufacture, and creates disposal problems after consumption. By substituting vegetable for petroleum-based ingredients, manufacturers such as Aubrey Organics (personal-care items) and AFM Enterprises (paints and adhesives) do their part in reducing the manufacture and consumption of petroleum.

Phosphates. Phosphates were used by most makers of laundry detergent because they soften the water and prevent the dirt from redepositing on clothes during the wash cycle. Unfortunately, after the rinse cycle they ended up in our waste-treatment facilities or in our rivers and streams, where they are the favorite food of algae and bacteria. Most detergents now contain either little or no phosphates, but according to some environmentalists, even a little is too much. Consumers are becoming more aware of the dangers of phosphates and are choosing not to buy products that contain them. Companies such as Allen's Naturally and Ecover (as well as some leading consumer-product makers) offer phosphate-free products.

Chlorine. Chlorine kills most bacteria and viruses. That's why it's such a good disinfectant. It's also used as a bleach and stain remover in cleaning products. What makes it such a good disinfectant is also what makes it poisonous. A number of companies offer "green" cleaners free of chlorine and other toxic substances.

Bleached Paper. Chlorine is also problematic when used during the manufacture of paper. The process by which paper mills bleach their paper with chlorine creates dioxin, one of the most powerful poisons known (dioxins are by-products in the deadly herbicide, Agent Orange). Also, consumers are becoming aware that the use of such bleached paper products near food, such as coffee filters, may pose a health threat. If consumers can be convinced that unbleached paper serves the same purpose as bleached paper, then paper mills will produce less of it, and the environment will be that much cleaner. Companies like Ashdun and Seventh Generation offer a complete line of unbleached paper products.

Formaldehyde and Other Toxics. Formaldehyde is another toxic and carcinogenic substance, used extensively in paints and solvents as a preservative and disinfectant. Benzene, mercury, and other toxic substances are common ingredients in paints and solvents, too. Again, these ingredients are not only toxic to humans during use, but are difficult to dispose of without polluting the ground or waterways. Several companies, including AFM and Livos, make products without these ingredients.

Packaging. Another area of concern to environmentalists is packaging, because manufacturers waste a lot of energy packaging their products. Also so many products are overpackaged with nonrecyclable or nonbiodegradable materials. "Packaging is my personal nightmare," says Ecco Bella's Sally Malanga. "You think about making a shampoo without using chemicals and without hurting animals or the environment, and you end up putting it into a *plastic* bottle. So what we do is sell our shampoos in a plastic bottle, then offer refills in glass bottles. That way, the consumer can keep the plastic bottle in the shower and refill it from the glass bottle, which can be recycled. That's one way of cutting out unnecessary plastic."

The use of recycled paper for packaging is another way green manufacturers can solve the problem. By using more recycled paper, they increase the demand for it, which will gradually increase production, which will increase the mills' need for postconsumer waste paper. This means less paper will wind up in landfills. Ashdun Industries (see below) produces a full line of paper products using recycled paper.

Green products are available for every area of the home and yard, from food and cleansers to paper supplies, paper leaf bags, and nonpolluting pesticides and fertilizers. Chapter 12 covered the manufacture and sale of safe yard and garden supplies. This chapter focuses on opportunities to make and sell general household and personal-care items. The first part covers the manufacture of green products, while the second focuses on their sale.

Making Green Products

You don't have to be a chemist to make a green product, but it helps to have access to one. A layperson can certainly devise new formulas for cleaning products, foods, even paints and solvents. You just have to look at the list of ingredients and know what each one does, then figure out an alternative. Most of the information is available at local libraries or universities. University professors are usually eager to talk about their subject to someone other than students, so they make a good resource. But a chemist, or at least someone skilled in the applied sciences, is necessary to actually mix the ingredients and test their performance.

Usually an ecopreneur and chemist work hand in hand to develop the product. Tom Chappell teamed up with chemist Dr. Blaine Tewksbury to formulate a toothpaste, shampoo, and deodorant with all natural ingredients. That was 20 years ago. Today, Tom's of Maine toothpaste, shampoos, and deodorants are found in supermarkets and drugstores across the country.

Household Detergents and Cleansers

Commercial detergents and cleansers contain many ingredients that are not good for the planet. Either they are harmful to humans or they create problems when disposed of, fouling our land and water. This state of affairs bothered Allen Conlon. Conlon had become quite familiar with the natural-foods market from his work with Coop Warehouses. "What was missing from the natural-food store offerings was a line of cleansers that met sound environmental criteria," he says. "That means no petroleum by-products, no dyes or perfumes, no animal ingredients, and no testing on animals."

In addition, Conlon wanted to see highly concentrated cleaning products. "The best thing for the environment," he says, "is to reduce usage. If you can create a superconcentrated cleaner, then you have something people can use but end up using less of without even knowing it. One ounce of my product equals four ounces of a commercial liquid laundry detergent. So a quart bottle of mine is the equivalent of a gallon of theirs. Over a period of time, it adds up to less used."

Conlon wasn't a trained chemist, but he had ideas. He ransacked the local libraries, paying close attention to history. "How did they get things cleaned up in the old days," he asked. Next, he brought his research findings to a chemist who helped him devise modern-day counterparts that had the same cleaning power, but without the modern environmental hazards.

Starting Allen's Naturally cost Conlon about $50,000. He made the actual detergent and laundry soap at his home at first, eventually contracting it out to other manufacturers who had the equipment to make bulk quantities.

After three years Allen's Naturally earned nearly half a million dollars in sales. This might be a mere drop in the dishpan compared to the big commercial soap makers' sales, but that's okay with Conlon. "I'm not out to take over the market from Proctor and Gamble," he says laughing. "We're content with slow and steady growth, sticking to the market we know, the niche where we belong."

Interestingly, technology may prove to be the catalyst to propel the use of nontoxic cleaning products into the mainstream. Because homes are built so tight, and so well insulated, the EPA has issued several warnings about "indoor air pollution" (see Chapter 10 for more details). The pollutants in these cases are often the cleaning agents and solvents we have lying around the house. In the old days, with house air changing every hour, there was no problem. But with modern well-insulated homes, the air inside a home may change only four or five times a day or less. Thus fumes, undetected by our noses, can congregate in our living spaces. This may be good news for manufacturers of green household cleaning products.

Building and Construction Products

Back in the late 1970's, AFM Enterprises in Riverside, California, was well entrenched in the building materials industry, manufacturing an array of products such as sealers, paints, and solvents. But AFM president Nester Noe began to get concerned about the contents of his products and asked the company chemist to explore ways of making their products without toxic substances. He broke down the formulas into their component parts and for each one asked, "What can we replace this ingredient with?"

In 1980 AFM introduced Waterseal, a water-based sealant. Shortly after Waterseal's introduction, a nearby armed services clinic approached Noe to test out Waterseal in the waiting room; fumes from the walls were making the clinic's highly sensitive patients ill.

"So we gave them the stuff," Noe recalls. "And they applied it to the waiting room walls and ceilings, painted over everything. Because the fumes had come from the concrete and insulation in the walls, it had been leaking out. This sealer bonded and sealed the fumes inside."

The clinic then brought in patients who were ill and had them sit for several hours in the newly painted waiting room. Remarkably, their symptoms cleared almost immediately. The clinic immediately ordered more Waterseal and painted the entire facility with it, giving AFM strong credibility for its new product.

Noe and his chemist soon began looking at other products they made—paints, varnishes, de-greasers, wood and floor finishes, detergents, shampoos, and even shoe polish. They reformulated the basic mix, replacing toxic with nontoxic, or at least less toxic ingredients, and made products water-based so they could be disposed of more easily and cleanly. Positive response was immediate.

"I didn't have to go out looking for the market," Noe says. "It came to me. Word got around. I began attending seminars—building seminars, medical seminars. I told the people there was an alternative, that you could build a home without the use of toxic materials. You could keep your house clean without the use of toxic materials."

Noe had years of experience in the oil industry and as a builder and developer. He was already a successful businessman when he decided to take a chance and change his formulas. "I had faith the market was out there and would respond," he says. Today AFM Enterprises makes 40 different nontoxic products, from paints to shoe polish. The company does all its own manufacturing and packaging and employs 12 people full time.

At least two other companies also offer nontoxic household and building materials: Livos Plantchemistry in Santa Fe, New Mexico, sells a line of imported German products, as does Auro Natural Plant Chemistry, distributed by Sinan in the United States.

As more people become concerned about the harmful substances in paints, thinners, solvents, and other common workshop products, the market for products like AFM's, Livos's, and Auro's will surely expand.

Personal-Care Products

Personal Care at Who's Expense?

Personal-care products represent a significant opportunity for ecopreneurs. Most commercial personal-care products aren't packaged with the environment in mind, and many contain petroleum-based and/or other harmful substances. In fact, alternative personal-care products, formulated without animal testing and without substances that tax or harm the environment, make up the majority of green products found in mail-order catalogs and natural-food stores.

In the cosmetics industry petrochemicals are used mostly to provide a base or emollient to help in the application of other ingredients and to keep those ingredients in the proper solution. But these functions can be performed by other substances, such as beeswax or vegetable oils, without a loss of effectiveness. For example, Autumn Harp produces a product, Unpetroleum Jelly, made with vegetable oils and beeswax, that serves the same function as the conventional petroleum-based products.

Solutions More Than Skin-Deep

Aubrey Hampton, founder of Aubrey Organics, never had to make a choice about what kind of cosmetics he wanted to make.

"I was raised on a farm, and back in the 1940's, most farming was organic simply because that's the way farming was back then, before the oil companies began pushing their fertilizers and such. So I came from an organic background, I guess you'd say, even though at the time it was nothing special."

From the beginning Hampton seemed ahead of his time. In 1967, before most people had ever heard of organic, or natural, he produced his first product, Relaxorbath, a formula of herbal bath salts. Hampton produced it in a rented storefront in New York City, packaged it himself, and made the rounds of natural- and health-food stores to find shelf space. Though times have changed and his company, Aubrey Organics, has built itself a solid niche in the personal-care products industry, Hampton still does almost everything himself.

"We don't sell to distributors," he says, "because we emphasize the freshness of our product and its purity. Stuff that sits around in a warehouse, even for just a week, has lost its freshness . . . lost something, so I don't want to sell it. We sell directly to stores so we can ship fresh batches as soon as they're made."

Armed with a degree in organic chemistry, Hampton started Aubrey Organics with certain criteria in mind, criteria that reflected his personal values: his products would not require testing on animals, would not contain synthetic chemical ingredients, and would be ecologically safe. He doesn't hide his attitude toward other cosmetics manufacturers who market their products similarly when in fact they have compromised.

"Nothing new about that," he says. "Unless it's important to you, what happens is that you set out to make a pure product, but then along the way you compromise here, compromise there, and soon your product is no longer what you say it is. I've seen a few companies start out with those ideals, only to change midstream for one reason or another. Some just get too big, or they're bought out by large companies who think only of the bottom line."

Hampton has seen his competition come and go during the 20-odd years he's been in the industry, and feels comfortable in his niche. Unlike some manufacturers of green products, he has no desire to get too big, to enter the mass market. "I'm perfectly content to stick with the small natural-food stores. We've worked well all these years and I don't see any reason to change that."

Tom's of Maine, based in Kennebunk, began 20 years ago marketing its natural brands of personal-care items exclusively to natural-food stores. But after 12 years the company's annual sales were approaching $2 million. Tom and Kate Chappell, the founders of the company, realized they couldn't keep growing if they continued to sell only to natural-food stores. So in 1982 they brought in marketing experts with the goal of expanding into mass market outlets.

Despite their entry into the mass market, Tom's of Maine continues to support the environment. The company uses recyclable toothpaste tubes and recycled paper for their labels, boxes, and stationery. It makes all its own products in a 5,000-square-foot factory, except for dental floss, which is contracted out. In 1989 the company's sales passed $8 million, demonstrating that ecopreneurs can break into the mainstream market without losing their vision.

Whether they grow or stay small, entrepreneurs entering the market for personal-care products will find a ready and vocal customer base. As environmental and health concerns increase among the general public, products that are kinder and gentler promise to do well.

Treating Baby Gently

Baby products are another area of personal care that requires attention to the environment. Although polls show that about 87 percent of Americans prefer disposable diapers to cloth, the use of disposables strains local landfills. In fact, diapers represent the largest single component in the waste stream, after newspapers and beverage containers. An average baby uses 6,000 disposable diapers by the time he or she is toilet-trained. That's about two tons of trash going into the landfill. Disposable diapers make up about 2 percent of our trash. They also contain human waste, which cannot be handled safely in landfills.

Despite the claims of manufacturers, there's no such thing at this time as a completely biodegradable plastic diaper. To make degradable plastic diapers, manufacturers mix vegetable starch from corn or potatoes in with the plastic. The starch does help the diapers decompose more quickly, but the plastic breaks down into tiny pieces, which don't degrade. Thus, landfills, even after years of being capped, will still have soil laden with plastic.

Fortunately, there are alternatives. One need only go back one or two generations to the days before disposable diapers, when every community had a local diaper service. These businesses delivered a load of fresh diapers each week and carried away the soiled ones. Now diaper services are on the rise again; home diaper service usage increased 39 percent in 1989. This also opens the door for ecopreneurs interested in starting their own diaper services. If you're interested in starting such a business, the National Association of Diaper Services will sell you a startup kit (see page 295).

Diapers offer other ecopreneurial possibilities as well, evidenced by the success of products such as Bumkins, Biobottoms, and Nikkys. These products try to combine some of the features of disposable diapers while still using cloth. Bumkins, for example, joins a cotton diaper inner layer with a waterproof nylon shell. When the diaper is dirty, you just roll it up and close the tabs until you get home. Biobottoms takes another approach, offering a disposable paper diaper made for use with a diaper cover.

What's needed is a perfect disposable diaper made of a renewable material that decomposes several days after use. Perhaps a future ecopreneur will devise one, and millions of parents will sigh with relief.

Recycled Paper Products: A Paper Moon in a Cardboard Sky

Paper has been around since ancient times. But at no time in history has the demand for paper products been so overwhelming as it is now. True, paper originates from a renewable resource. But as described above, the manufacture of paper, especially bleached paper, produces dangerous environmental consequences.

One company that set out to make paper in a way less harmful to the environment is Ashdun Industries, headquartered in Fort Lee, New Jersey. The company was founded in 1988 by Greg Phillips, who along with his partner, David Labovitz, had extensive experience in the mass-market food industry. The partners noticed that in Europe, companies already existed that were marketing environment-friendly products. Labovitz had formerly worked for the paper industry, so the partners began by concentrating on marketing paper products that were environmentally safe. Their formula for success includes the use of recycled paper, the use of an oxygen bleaching process instead of the traditional chlorine process, the use of water-based dyes, and recyclable plastic packaging.

The two began by taking each paper product and breaking it apart, ingredient by ingredient, process by process, to see where they could substitute environmentally safe and ecologically sound ingredients and processes. Next, they contracted with a commercial paper mill to manufacture the product to their specifications. Finally, they approached large supermarket chains and variety stores, offering them the reformulated products under private labels. Ashdun makes over 40 products under various labels: Earthsafe, Envirocare, Project Green, Consumer Action to Restore the Environment (C.A.R.E.), and others.

"The reason for using this technique, private brands, is to give the retail stores some involvement with the community," says Labovitz. "They can educate the consumer about the environment, and with their own brands on the shelves they have some incentive to do that."

Labovitz and Phillips have expanded their product line to include such things as cleaning and laundry concentrates, light bulbs, and baby wipes, but the bulk of their output is still paper.

When they started with their paper products, Phillips and Labovitz used 25 to 40 percent recycled, postconsumer wastepaper (PCW) as the basis of their manufacturing process. In the future the company wants to develop products containing 70 percent PCW.

What seems to set Ashdun apart from other companies making and selling green products is its experience in business and marketing. Equally important, the two ecopreneurs realized that business and the life of the planet were interconnected.

Says Labovitz, "We took a product, like paper towels, and thought about the hierarchy of disposal—where it goes after it's used. One thing that's important, and which the consumers must be educated about, is the concept of concentration. For example, when manufacturers pump air into their paper towels to give them that 'nice feel,' they can sell 'less' that looks like 'more.' We go the opposite direction, compressing our paper towels so that they take up much less space. Now that has repercussions. In 1989 two and a half billion rolls of paper towels were produced in this country. If they had been compressed, we could have saved sixty-five thousand truckloads of corrugated cardboard used for packaging, and five hundred fifty thousand gallons of gas used to truck the stuff to warehouse!"

As Labovitz pointed out, taking one environmental action leads to a host of others, a ripple effect spreading out from one action to another. Using recycled paper, especially PCW, affects not only the paper mill producing it, but the local landfill and the community recycling center. Compressing paper towels cuts down on usage of gasoline and other paper used in packaging. This multi-dimensional effect is one of the beauties of promoting green products.

Selling Green Products

As an ecopreneur with a green product to sell, you have several choices: sell direct to the consumer through a direct-mail catalog, as Sally Malanga does with her products; find a distributor to sell your product to retail establishments; or open a retail outlet.

Malanga discovered that creating a catalog requires a lot of upfront capital, enough to see you through the long wait for a return. But the advantage of selling your product through a catalog is the control you have over every stage of the marketing process. If you're not in the producing end in a major way (for example, if you've created only one or two products), you can use your own goods to initiate the catalog, adding other products that fit in. Both the Ecco Bella and Seventh Generation catalogs carry their own products along with those made by others.

If you have only a small number of products, finding a distributor to market them may be the easiest and most cost-effective choice. Finding a place on an already existing catalog page is one way of getting the product out to the potential consumer. You would choose what market you want to reach—natural-food stores, gift shops, supermarket chains—and find out who distributes to them (see Chapter 14, "The Green Grocer," for details about locating distributors).

Opening a retail store would be the last choice for an entrepreneur interested in making his or her own product, because of the costs involved. But for an entrepreneur interested in selling products made by others, retailing offers exciting possibilities. The remainder of this chapter discusses the retail and catalog end of green business.

The Green Retail Operation

Small retail outlets are one of the newest wrinkles in green product marketing. "Green stores" are springing up in large cities and small towns across the country.

Charles Hugus decided he wanted to make a difference by offering people in the Charlottesville, Virginia, area alternatives to products that harm the environment. So the small magazine publisher turned store owner by opening Earthwise, a retail outlet that sells energy-saving devices, unbleached paper products, unbleached cotton products under Earthwise's own label, and water-based cleaning and laundry detergents.

Hugus's startup costs were met in a unique way. He needed $50,000 but managed to borrow only $10,000. To make up the deficit he sold credit coupons to customers. For $100 they would get a coupon worth $120 in merchandise in 90 days, or $130 in 120 days (see page 46 for more details).

Up in New England, cellist Annabelle Ship was moved by her own environmentally induced asthma to seek green products. Figuring that other people would also be in need of such products, in 1990 she opened up The Green Planet store in Newton, just outside Boston, Massachusetts. Ship sells products that are environmentally sound, not tested on animals, and that have minimal packaging. Like Hugus, she plans to introduce her own line of personal-care products for environmentally sensitive people. Her marketing approach was an outreach program in which she visited homes and groups and talked about environment-friendly products. She has also developed education programs that she plans to use during school visits.

The decision to start a retail or catalog company selling green products should not be made overnight. Like Ship, Hugus pounded the pavement months before he opened his store. First he got a list of local paper companies. Then he visited their mills and talked to them about using recycled paper.

Next he took his pitch to the community. "I went everywhere during that time," Hugus recalls. "I spoke to schools, to church groups, just about everybody who'd listen. I told them what I was up to, and asked for their support. I wanted them to start using the recycled paper products I was going to order from the mills."

Hugus placed small orders with the paper mills at first, buying in just large enough quantities to make it worthwhile. His first customers were the church groups and schools he had spoken to earlier. This base of small groups ordering recycled paper allowed him eventually to move into a storefront on the main street in Charlottesville.

Both Ship and Hugus are on the cutting edge of an ecopreneurial trend. Consumers concerned about the environment and their health can feel secure walking into a store such as The Green Planet or Earthwise because much of the decision making and research has been done for them. They have only to choose, knowing their choice will not harm the planet, animals, or human health.

The New Bottom Line

Alan Newman and Jeff Hollender are known around the Colchester, Vermont, offices of Seventh Generation as the "Birkenstock and pinstripe team." Sounding like an old vaudeville duo, the two unlikely partners have parlayed a rather romantic vision into a dynamic business success. Newman is the guy in Birkenstocks, a self-described "holdover from the Woodstock generation." He's also the embodiment of the counterculture come of age, a denim-clad iconoclast who hasn't quite lost his enthusiasm for activism. Hollender is the pinstriped partner, the guy who looks like a banker. But he, too, shares a history of activism. He may have exchanged his jeans for a suit, but he still enjoys shaking the world up a bit.

The belief these two ecopreneurs shared was that the government acting alone would never solve the environmental problems facing our planet. They also felt that it was necessary for business to take responsibility for its contribution to the ecological mess and to offer consumers products and services that solve, rather than create, environmental problems.

Newman and Hollender came at the vision from very different directions. Newman had previously founded Niche Marketing

Services, a direct-mail fulfillment and consulting company. Before that he had been a cofounder and director of Gardener's Supply Company, a direct-mail firm with over $15 million in annual revenues.

Hollender's background included community involvement, starting in 1976 with his first venture, the founding of the Skills Exchange of Toronto, a nonprofit adult education program that taught people about alternative health care and political activism. In New York, he established the Network for Learning. Later Hollender was director of Social Venture Network, a group of socially conscious business executives.

How did these two dissimilar types get together to create a path-breaking company? It began with Newman. While oversee-ing Niche Marketing Services he helped a client, Renew America, a national advocacy group, to produce a small catalog of energy conservative products. The catalog was just a sideline, and one day Renew America's directors offered to sell it to Newman so the group could get out of the business. Newman took them up on the offer.

"It was a gut decision," he recalls.

The first catalog he produced cost him little except time. Newman was known in the community, so when he went to the printer and asked him to extend credit, the printer agreed. Newman saved money by creating all the art and graphics him-self. The first catalog was digest size (the size of *Reader's Digest*) because Newman couldn't pay to have the photographs resized; instead he reduced the page size to accommodate the pictures.

Newman financed subsequent catalogs by going to the bank "with his hands out," borrowing money for the substantial mail-ing costs. When orders would come in, he'd use that money to pay back the loan. This became tiring to Newman and the bankers, and eventually the banks gave him a credit line. Despite his ability to secure cash from the bank, the first few catalogs were merely hybrids. By now he had changed the name to Seventh Generation, which comes from the great law of the Six Nations Iroquois Confederacy, "In our every deliberation we must consider the impact of our decisions on the next seven gen-erations"—but it still wasn't the kind of catalog Newman felt it could be, it didn't quite fit his vision.

In 1989 Newman and Hollender met for the first time. They discussed how Hollender could help by raising money to upgrade the catalog, so that it could truly feature "products for a healthy planet." As they saw it, the catalog would be "one hundred percent philosophy and one hundred percent business."

With Hollender's financial savvy, the two raised $850,000 to upgrade the Seventh Generation catalog, increasing the piece from digest to standard 8.5-by-11-inch size. The first large-format catalog came out in the spring of 1989 and featured 150 products on 24 pages. Less than a year later, after two more mailings, the company had grown by about 800 percent and had fullfilled 150,000 orders. As of 1991, Seventh Generation has a core staff of 70 people (which swells to about 140 during peak season) and occupies a 50,000-square-foot facility. Newman explains the positive response to his catalog this way: "We hit a nerve."

Popular acceptance and rapid growth haven't occurred without problems. One of the casualties of such rapid growth, Newman feels, was customer service. "We would have huge back orders, problems in shipping," he says. "We had already moved twice to accommodate the extra business and things were in total chaos." One day, Newman walked in and saw two unfamiliar faces at phone-answering desks. One of the strangers seemed to be teaching the other how to take orders. He thought he knew everyone working for him, but he'd never seen either of these people before. So he asked someone he knew who they were and what they were doing.

"The tall one is training the other one," the employee replied.

"And how long has the trainer been working here?" Newman asked.

"He started yesterday."

Experiences like that forced Newman and Hollender to make a decision: they had to control their growth. "Our phase one goal," Newman says, "was to become a household name and establish ourselves in the marketplace. That meant rapid expansion and constant marketing. I think we've done that—order processing is now rapid and efficient, customer service is topnotch, and backorders are almost nonexistent. Now we can work on phase two, developing a strong financial base to achieve our ultimate objective of balancing social responsibility and profitability. I see Seventh Generation becoming a $100 million a year company.

And that would be good for *both* bottom lines. One bottom line involves profits and losses; the other involves social and environmental goals. The two go hand in hand, and that's what this business is all about."

☙

The manufacture of green products offers ecopreneurs an excellent opportunity to balance what Alan Newman refers to as the two bottom lines, profitability and social responsibility. People will always need food and personal-care and other products, and if you can get them to vote with their conscience at the cash register, you'll make a contribution to the planet while building a strong business. The next chapter describes another way to get people to vote out of conscience—making or selling pesticide-free food products.

Chapter *Fourteen*

Green Grocer:
Satisfying the Hunger for Safe Foods

The True Vision Building in Burlington, Vermont, got its name because it houses an optometrist. But in the summer of 1984 it served as the birthplace of another kind of vision. In the attic of the building, twin brothers Ron and Arnie Koss had rented an office and begun talking about an idea that had been brewing in Arnie's mind for years: developing a line of baby food made from organically grown fruits and vegetables, baby food that was pure, without added salt, sugar, or preservatives.

Having managed a natural-food store in the early 1970's, Arnie had seen first hand how many new products appeared on the shelves week after week. He was especially impressed by such products as organic pet food and all natural snack foods.

"It seemed to me back then," Arnie remembers, "that our priorities were somehow messed up. We were feeding our pets better than we were feeding our babies."

He figured that someone, somehow, would eventually come up with a natural baby food, one that parents would feel secure about feeding to their children. But by 1984 no such product had appeared. While discussing that fact with his brother Ron, who was a new father, something clicked in Arnie's mind. The next morning at the breakfast table, he told his wife that he was going to develop and make a pure baby food that was simply . . . the earth's best.

What the brothers had in mind was nothing short of a revolution, a David-vs.-Goliath battle with the likes of Beech-Nut, Gerber, and Heinz, the giant trio of mass-market baby-food producers. They envisioned a complete line of baby foods made from healthy, organically grown fruits and vegetables. No additives. No sugar. No salt. No flavorings. No preservatives.

As good as the idea sounded, the task was formidable; there were good reasons why only three big makers of baby food had survived. For one thing, manufacturing baby food requires a substantial investment in equipment, research, development (making up recipes and testing them), and distribution. The maker of a food product must invest heavily in quality control, ensuring that the product will taste the same, batch after batch. The baby-food maker must also pay high insurance premiums and worker's compensation, since to make food in volume requires heavy machinery.

Undaunted, the brothers began at the grass roots level. From the start, they wanted control over the product from the plant seedling to the finished, packaged product. After locating organic farmers, they consulted with university nutritionists to formulate high-quality, good-tasting, baby-food products made from food grown without the use of synthetic fertilizers or chemical pesticides.

Next, they pitched their idea to a group of Vermont investors and lenders and raised $900,000, making Earth's Best one of the largest startup deals in the state's history. With the funds in hand, the Koss brothers built a small processing plant in Middlebury, Vermont, and in the fall of 1987 began manufacturing a product line consisting of six puréed fruits and vegetables and two cereals. By early 1991, Earth's Best products were being carried in natural-food stores and supermarkets in 20 states, and the company could point to the following accomplishments:

- It was the first to introduce the concept of commercial organic baby food in the United States.

- It was the first to distribute organic baby food nationally in natural-food stores and supermarkets.

- It was the first to obtain shelf space in the baby-food aisle, not in the specialty or health-food aisles, for such a product.

- It was the first to produce an entire line of juices for babies without using concentrates.

- It was the first to develop whole-grain instant cereals for babies.

In 1989, the Koss brothers sought and obtained venture capital to increase production capacity and to expand the number of products from 8 to 20. The money went to good use; by the end of 1990, the company spawned from a casual chat in an attic overlooking Lake Champlain boasted revenues exceeding $5 million, and a product line that could be found in supermarkets in 25 percent of the nation.

"The industry was begging for improvement," reflects Arnie Koss with a smile. "The products were stale, the companies complacent. We changed all that."

છ્ર

If, like the Koss brothers, you're concerned about additives that pose a health hazard and pesticides that threaten the environment, then an ecobusiness in the growing natural-foods industry might by for you. If so, you can get into the field in one of three ways: make or produce food, distribute food, or sell food.

Of these options, the second, distribution, offers the least potential for ecopreneurs. Distributing natural food is a tough business—relatively easy to get into, but it slips away from you just as easily. During the health-food boom years of the late seventies and early eighties, natural-food stores sprouted across the country like mushrooms after a fall rain, followed by a bumper crop of distribution companies. This boom made it easy to get into the business of distributing food. All you needed was a pickup truck.

Barcley McFadden, who bought a struggling distributorship called Llama Trading Company in 1976, recalls that in 1973 Llama began just that way—with $15,000, a pickup truck, and two or three natural-food stores in and around the Brattleboro, Vermont area. The original owners saw the company grow so rapidly during those boom years that by 1976 it was foundering, as rising gasoline prices and the need for storage space created a burgeoning overhead.

McFadden bought the company and streamlined the operation, cutting costs while still maintaining a competitive edge. In 1979 he bought Stow Mills, a distributor of vitamin and mineral supplements in Massachusetts, which he merged with Llama under the Stow Mills banner, a move that allowed him to expand his product base to include not only foods but supplements. Two years later he bought Erewhon's distribution business as that company withdrew to concentrate on food manufacturing. In the late seventies and early eighties distributors in New England were struggling to keep up with a growth rate of 25 percent in the natural-food retail business. After the dust had settled by the mid-eighties, however, the distribution field had shaken itself out as the smaller companies either went under or were taken over by the larger companies.

McFadden warns fledgling entrepreneurs about the deceptive nature of the distribution business. "It doesn't take much to get started," he says. "But it's also difficult to make a profit, the margins are low. It's very easy to lose money, and lose it fast."

McFadden remembers how the blizzard of 1978, which hit Boston and New England with over three feet of snow and knocked power out for days, proved a factor in Erewhon's decision to abandon distributing. Unforeseen events such as snowstorms, oil crises, and hurricanes can ruin a distributorship that has little or no reserve.

Given the difficulties with the distribution end of the business, the two best alternatives for the fledgling ecopreneur in the organic-food industry lie in manufacturing/processing and retailing. The rest of this chapter will concentrate on those activities.

Making Organic Food

Market Overview

"Health-food" stores have been around for years, selling mainly vitamin supplements and processed foods. But since World War II they have been overtaken by the natural-food stores, which emphasize whole foods but also carry vitamin supplements, cosmetics, body-care items, and organic produce. Some even carry meat, poultry, and fish. What differentiates natural foods from those you would find in a supermarket is how they're made and what they're made of.

You can find a box of Super O's oat bran rings in a natural-food store that looks just like what you'd find in a box of Cheerios, but if you read the label you'll see that the Super O's, made by U.S. Mills, are sugar- and additive-free, whereas Cheerios contains sugar and salt and various additives. From a marketing standpoint, the differences are highly significant; the lack of sugar in a child's breakfast is becoming increasingly important to many parents, as the Koss brothers demonstrated when they began Earth's Best.

Foods and other products found in a natural-food store genrally:

- Go through minimal processing, and consist of either whole grain or whole-grain flour.

- Contain no chemical preservatives, such as BHT, or additives, such as food coloring, sugar, or salt.

- Use ingredients grown without the use of pesticides or chemical fertilizers.

- Provide a healthy alternative for people unable to tolerate certain substances; for example, wheat-free bread for those allergic to wheat, soy milk for those unable to digest cow's milk.

- Reflect certain values generally held by both the store's owner and its customers (e.g. not tested on animals).

The market for natural-food products has been expanding, and experts think that growth will continue. Gil Johnson, analyst for New Hope Communications, publishers of *Natural Foods Merchandiser* trade magazine, sees the market expanding to include not only foods but other products such as cleansers, recycled paper products, and other "green" merchandise.

In 1970 gross sales of foods sold in natural-food and health-food stores totaled around $300 million. In 1989 it hit $4 billion. Since 1980 the industry has grown at a 7 percent yearly rate, which doesn't seem that remarkable except for one factor. Johnson points out that those figures don't include natural foods sold in supermarkets and other outlets, so many of the products such as yogurt and whole-grain breads, once found exclusively in natural-food outlets, have since migrated into the mainstream.

"The natural-food business keeps losing its best stuff," Johnson says, "as products make the transition from entry level to supermarket shelves."

"Organic" vs. "Natural"

The year 1988 represents the "Trafalgar" of the organic movement. That was the year of the Alar scare. Alar is a growth regulator used by most commercial apple growers, and in 1988 news stories across the nation trumpeted the results of laboratory tests indicating that the substance may be carcinogenic. Growers maintained that without Alar apples would not look the way consumers want them to look. Apples, of course, are a favorite food for children. Applesauce is also one of baby's first solid foods, and apple juice is a staple for the toddler's bottle.

Suddenly, consumers worried that the food they were buying might not be safe. Since companies didn't have to list Alar on labels—which need only cite the ingredients added to the product for processing—even "100 percent natural" apple products—not to mention fresh apples—could conceivably contain Alar residue. As a result of the Alar scare, a growing number of consumers began reading labels and seeking proof of a food's organic claim to be free of chemicals during both growth and processing. Suddenly the producers and growers of organic foods moved into the main arena, as commercial producers scrambled to assure a frightened public that their products were safe to eat.

As a result of the uproar over Alar, the 1990 Farm Bill was approved by Congress in October of that year; it defined the first national standards for the production, processing, and certification of organically grown foods. Introduced by Vermont Senator Patrick Leahy, chairman of the Senate Agriculture Committee, the Organic Food Production Act was drafted, debated, and adopted within 12 months, despite strong opposition from agribusiness and the U.S. Department of Agriculture.

But what does it mean? What is "organic"? Basically, organic agriculture involves a soil-based system of farming that avoids the use of synthetic pesticides and chemical fertilizers. For the past 20 years there has been much confusion over terminology. Only the most well-versed, alert consumers were able to sort through the many terms—"organic," "certified organic," "natural," "unprocessed," "100 percent natural,"—to determine which foods were actually grown and processed without the use of chemicals. For example, many products labeled "natural" may not be grown organically. In many states, the "natural" label must mean only that the food was not treated with chemicals after harvest.

Before the 1990 Farm Bill, various private organizations and state agencies shouldered responsibility for determining standards for organic farming. But "organic" in Michigan wasn't necessarily "organic" in Maine, and vice versa. California farmers, to have their produce certified "organic," must prove that their fields have not been chemically fertilized for at least three years. In other states the time period may be only one year, but the labels from food grown in those states will still list the ingredients as "organic." With the new national standards, some of the confusion should end.

Growing Organic, Selling Commercial

Organic agriculture now represents one of the fastest-growing segments in American agriculture, with a market value of $1.25 billion in 1989 and an annual growth rate of 40 percent projected through the nineties. Nevertheless, it has been a tough battle for organic farmers to withstand the pressure to abandon their principles in favor of larger profits. A typical organic farmer is not necessarily an idealist or radical agriculturalist. Take Dan Patenaude, of Wisconsin. Patenaude began farming 17 years ago, raising dairy cows. One day, as he was spreading his corn fields with a fertilizer, he happened to read the label. It was full of warnings, even a skull and crossbones. Patenaude decided there and then that the contents couldn't be healthy for people or the environment, and that he would grow organically.

It took a number of years, but in 1988 Patenaude won certification by the Organic Crop Improvement Association, an international organization of organic farmers based in Ohio. Unfortunately, the market hasn't kept up with him, and currently he must sell most of his milk to conventional dairy distributors who mix his milk with nonorganic milk from other farmers.

Perhaps the granddaddy of organic agricultural enterprises is the Lundberg Family Farm in the Sacramento Valley of California. The four Lundberg brothers moved to California in 1937 from Nebraska and began farming organically, not out of idealism but because back then that's the way everyone farmed. It wasn't until the 1960's that the so-called "chemical boom" occurred in the farming sector.

According to Lundberg spokesperson Gordon Brewster, the family farm was certified organic in the late 1960's and has remained so ever since. The family sees itself as stewards of the land. The Lundberg farm produces nothing but rice, eleven varieties, on a total of 3,100 acres, 2,700 of which are certified organic. The other 400 acres are used to grow some "low-input" commercial rice.

Twenty years ago the Lundbergs made the commitment to experiment with new rice varieties and develop a market in the United States. They acquired seed from the gene bank in Maryland, and now are part of a handful of rice growers producing such exotic varieties as Basmati, Wehani, and Black Japonica. Lundberg supplies manufacturers and sells directly to wholesalers, packaging their rice for retail trade.

For the Lundbergs and Patenaudes, organic farming makes sense for consumers, processors, and farmers. Chemicals aren't good for the body, and chemical fertilizer runoff pollutes nearby water. No one will be safe from the consequences of such hazards unless more farmers heed the warnings that prompted Dan Patenaude to take action.

Manufacturing and Processing Organic Food

A major barrier to anyone wanting to enter the organic food processing market is the high capital investment necessary. The Koss brothers spent $900,000 building a processing plant from scratch. Given the complex nature of food processing, and the high sanitary standards required, much of the expense goes toward ensuring the quality of the product.

The major portion of the Koss brothers' startup expenses fell into three categories. The first and most easily calculated expense involved buying and installing the equipment. They would, of course, foresee and plan for that expense in advance. According to Arnie Koss, what foils most inexperienced entrepreneurs is the other two categories: getting the facility running with trained employees, and the working capital needed to keep the company going while developing the market.

"Most beginning entrepreneurs are unrealistic about what it will cost to start up," Arnie Koss says. "After sitting down and making out a budget, we added forty or fifty percent as a cushion to take care of unforeseen circumstances."

The Koss brothers took more than two months to train their employees and test the equipment, and they hired their employees in stages, first the supervisors, then the plant workers. They spent several weeks engineering test runs of the product, beginning with as small an amount as they could process, and running it through the system so the workers could learn on the job.

Still, even after the plant was running, money delays occurred before income started coming in. "The lag time between receiving orders and getting paid can be several months," Arnie Koss warns. "We would get an order from a distributor for a thousand cases, but we wouldn't get paid for two or three months. On the distributor's side they needed that lag time to prepare a new catalogue, or to prepare their retailers for a new product. So we were fortunate that we had budgeted enough working capital to take care of such time lags."

The key, then, is to plan realistically. Don't assume that you can go from groundbreaking to stocking store shelves overnight. If you don't have enough capital to get through a protracted period of building customer acceptance, you may find yourself with product in the distribution channels, yet no cash to whip up your next batch. As explained in Chapters 3 and 5 and reinforced by the experience of the Koss brothers, make that "plus 50 percent" rule a guiding principle.

Ecopreneurs contemplating an organic food-making business should think about liability. Nothing makes the heart of a food processor stop faster than the threat of tainted food making its way to someone's dinner table. Fortunately, since the American food industry enjoys a relatively good track record, liability insurance rates are reasonable. Most food processors belong to the National Food Processors Association, a trade organization that provides insurance for its members.

Purity Gives the Marketing Edge

Not all the manufacturers of organic or natural foods began by building state-of-the-art plants. Back in 1968 Bob Bergwall and John Paino were fraternity brothers at Hartwick College in Oneonta, New York. The two had moved out of their dormitory and into the fraternity house because of the institutional food

served in the dorm. They both worked in the kitchen, helping prepare and serve food for their fraternity brothers. Since both were
interested in what they considered "good food," meaning whole,
unprocessed food, they started a subtle, covert operation, infiltrat-
ing brown rice and millet into the steak and hamburgers on the
menu. Within a year their "brown rice revolution," as Paino calls
it, was discovered, and they were kicked out of the house.

But the two friends had the last laugh. After college, they
became brothers-in-law, and later business partners as well. Paino
had been especially intrigued with making and cooking tofu, the
fermented soy cheese that has been as common as bread in the
Orient for thousands of years. Whenever he served it to friends
and relatives, he got a favorable response. After attending a lec-
ture by Michio Kushi, the leader of the macrobiotic movement,
Paino and Bergwall decided that they had to find something to do
with their lives that would integrate their values and their livelihood. Since food played an important part of their belief system,
the question became whether to make it or sell it. And since
Paino was already making it on the side, the answer was obvious.

In 1977 they leased an abandoned dairy farm outside
Leominster, Massachusetts, and moved into the milk-processing
barn, where they began making tofu under the brand name
Nasoya. Paino estimates startup costs to have been about
$50,000, "plus one whole year of free labor from me and Bob."

Although another manufacturer of tofu was operating in the
area, Paino knew his tofu was better. First of all, he used pure
well water. Secondly, he insisted on using only organic soybeans,
which made Nasoya more expensive than the competition. "It
cost me about a hundred thousand dollars to stay organic during
that time," Paino remembers. "Even some of the people on staff
here thought we maybe should bend a little. But that wasn't the
way I wanted to go. So we stuck it out."

Sticking it out enabled Nasoya to outlast the "nonorganic"
competition. Bergwall and Paino, like the Koss brothers, claimed
victory because they stuck to their principles, never sacrificing
the purity of their product.

Anyone contemplating the manufacturing of organic food
items used to have difficulty finding a source for the raw material. Most organic farms are small scale, not like the vast agribusiness farms in the Midwest and California, where most of the

nation's produce and grains are grown. By the late eighties, though, many of the large farmers in the Midwest and South were beginning to find that going organic actually made them more productive in the long run. Sure, yields were smaller at first, but they also saved money by not having to buy chemical fertilizers.

At the same time, organic farmers were organizing, forming co-ops and other organizations to facilitate the marketing of their products. Trade groups such as the Organic Food Production Association of North America (OFPANA), the Organic Farmers' Association (OFA), and the Organic Food Alliance (OFA) help producers like the Koss brothers find suppliers for their factories.

To ensure quality, the founders of Earth's Best instituted its own requirement: suppliers' fields used to grow fruits, vegetables, and grains must be free of all chemicals and pesticides for three years. The company demands a certificate from all growers, and inspects each field to corroborate the certification. Part of Earth's Best certification program entails testing by a qualified independent third party to ensure compliance.

Nasoya also insists on documentation from the growers of their soybeans. During the past 10 years, Paino has worked with some of his supplying farmers to produce a special type of soybean grown exclusively for the making of tofu. Regular soybeans have a high oil content, whereas the soybeans delivered to the Nasoya plant have a low oil content, resulting in tofu with a much more delicate taste than it would have otherwise.

It may seem like a lot of trouble to foster such a close relationship with the farmers supplying you, but from a marketing standpoint, the key to success is product purity. Earth's Best and Nasoya feel confident that their products meet the highest standards of purity, all the way back to the ground on which it grows. Ensuring quality thus maintains a competitive marketing position that has helped Nasoya tofu outlast its rival.

This sort of attention to detail sets the organic food processors apart from their commercial counterparts, and increases the cost of such items to the consumer. But recent polls have shown that consumers now are willing to pay a bit more for organic food, a trend that can only increase as they become more educated about how organic agriculture helps the environment and their bodies.

Selling Organic Food

Market Overview

The modern natural-food store reincarnates the American Dream. Years ago, when a family wanted to run a business, one of the most accessible avenues open to them was the grocery store. In fact, many of us have at least one relative who has been involved with a neighborhood shop that sold packaged goods, produce, meats, pickles and grains, jars full of spices, and fresh produce sitting in wooden baskets on shelves of ice or in coolers.

After World War II a new concept appeared in the retail food industry: the supermarket. Of course, the supermarket wouldn't have worked without the car, since the idea was that you could do your entire week's shopping in one shot, in a large, well-lit store with wide aisles and attractive displays. As the car became more deeply embedded in American life and suburbs began to dot the landscape, the supermarket soon replaced the neighborhood grocery store.

Still, the dream of a family store remains ingrained in our national character. Despite modern technology, despite all the benefits that advances in food processing and distributing have brought us, there seems to be in everyone a longing for simplicity, for getting back to the basics.

This became apparent in the 1970's, when another retailing concept, the food co-op, began to emerge. This wasn't new, but rather an outgrowth of the 1960's. Food co-ops, organizations of people that buy in large quantities to save money for its members, sprang up in big cities among young, educated professionals, and in rural areas among those trying to get back to the land or save money on food for their families.

Co-ops work by buying direct from wholesalers or distributors, providing their own trucks to transport the food, then having members "break down" the orders and distribute them. Co-op members save money because there is little or no overhead, and their labor partially pays for the food. The motivation behind most co-ops is not only to save money, but to buy unprocessed, pure food.

From the co-op it was only a small step to the retail storefront. In fact, many of the natural-food stores today trace their beginnings to co-ops, or else their owners got their experience through co-op memberships. (In the Minneapolis–St. Paul area co-ops still dominate the natural-food retail market, with 16 stores in the metropolitan area grossing a combined $12 million annually.)

For the ecopreneur, a natural-food store represents a relatively easy entry into the organic food industry, because the principles of success are tried and proven.

Starting Up

Linda Harris, one of the four founders and the first manager of the Center Street Grainery in Bath, Maine, remembers the advice she received from a member of the Small Business Administration when she told him she wanted to open a natural-food store: "There are three important things to look for when you open a food store, location, location, and location."

Fortunately for the Grainery's owners, the Bath economy at the time was going through a slump, making several downtown storefronts readily available. They decided on a shop just off the main street, a block away from the state's largest employer, Bath Iron Works, and, most important, on a street with a low enough density of shops that parking was not a problem for shoppers.

For retail-food stores competing in areas with large supermarkets, parking is a deciding factor in choosing location. Nancy and Rob Auerbach learned this lesson the hard way, when they opened the Rainbow Blossom Natural Food Store and Café in downtown Louisville, Kentucky, in 1977. The store survived, helped along by the Auerbachs' catering service and the popularity of the café; however, Nancy says, "It was a wonderful, wonderful place but it just never supported itself."

In 1981 the Auerbachs closed the café and moved off the beaten track, not far away from downtown but on a side street with plenty of parking. What the store lost in foot traffic it picked up from offering additional parking. Sales zoomed.

Starting a natural-food store is relatively easy compared to starting a food-processing plant. The major startup expenditures go toward initial inventory and capital outlays for freezers, coolers, displays, and so forth. The costs can vary according to what you want to do and how much you want to spend. The Auerbachs started Rainbow Blossom with about $80,000. They gutted the storefront they had leased and even went so far as to buy woodworking machinery so they could make their own tables and chairs for the café.

Such an initial outlay need not be the norm. In general, you can open up a natural-food store for as little as $20,000, assuming the retail space you rent or buy offers almost everything you need. If you're taking over an existing natural-food business, your outlay will mainly be for inventory. If you must buy equipment and renovate the store, your costs can rise to $40,000 and more, depending on your location.

Many natural-food store owners hire out the plumbing and wiring to meet code regulations, but do the interior work, such as the shelving displays, themselves. If you can afford to bring in professional help, do so—you'll probably wind up with a more appealing store. At Rainbow Blossom the owners hired an outside contractor to renovate the space when they made the move to a new storefront. The contractor worked on a consulting basis, providing the design and layout. Nancy Auerbach feels the input of the contractor was invaluable. "I would definitely recommend to anyone who is expanding or starting out to get professional help with the design and layout."

In most communities opening a retail food store entails few legal twists and turns. Unless you serve food customers will eat on premises, moving you into the restaurant category, all you need is a simple victualer's license from local authorities. If you begin serving soup, sandwiches, and other prepared food, you'll have to meet health and sanitation department standards, which are easy to comply with in most areas. Depending on your area, you might need to install two- or three-basin sinks, a hot-water heater capable of heating water to sterilizing temperatures, and an exhaust system over the working area. Also, the food preparation area itself will likely have to conform to certain standards of cleanliness.

Again, these regulations differ from area to area. In Louisville the Rainbow Blossom store needs an egg inspector from the state health department, since the eggs it uses are grown by local small farmers and gardeners and not by large processors. But in Maine such egg inspection is unheard of. Find out the specific requirements well ahead of opening day, so you won't find yourself in a red-tape bind.

Once you've acquired your storefront, you can begin contacting distributors. You can find these by reading through trade magazines or by studying other natural-food stores in the area and asking which distributors they use. (By and large natural-food store owners eagerly share information.) Each distributor will follow different policies regarding credit for new accounts; however, in general be prepared to pay cash upfront for your opening inventory. Usually after two or three orders, you'll be able to establish a credit basis, provided you make timely payments.

Marketing a Natural-Food Store

Large supermarket chains go to great lengths to create a competitive edge. The latest trend is toward the "super" supermarket, warehouse-sized emporiums where the shopper can buy just about everything, from small household appliances and automotive supplies to milk, fresh-baked bread, and imported olive oil.

Some natural-food retailers, such as the Bread and Circus chain in Massachusetts, have met the supermarkets head on by expanding to become natural-food supermarkets. Bread and Circus, which began as a small shop in Cambridge, now has several stores in the Boston area and one in Rhode Island. But most natural-food sellers will take the opposite approach, focusing on a segment of the market that prefers the kind of service that only a small shop can offer.

Unfortunately for the small store owner, with the growing awareness among consumers of the advantage of organically grown foods, it's only a matter of time before such foods begin appearing on supermarket shelves. In fact, many products formerly relegated to the natural-food stores are now readily available in local supermarkets. Products such as rice cakes, whole-grain cereals, and sugar-free jams and preserves have already entered the mainstream market, with more sure to follow.

To survive you want to take care not to define your store too narrowly, catering to a small, select group of customers. The natural-food store that survives the marketing muscle of large supermarkets will serve the needs of a variety of lifestyles and tastes. If your customers want organically raised chicken and beef, or nitrate-free hot dogs, but such food items fly in the face of your conception of a natural-food store, then you might face a tough decision. Offering those items might even cause some hard-core vegetarian customers to shun your store. Still, to compete with large supermarkets, you may have to decide between your own vision for the store and the realities of the marketplace.

"Over the years," says Taffy Field of Bath's Center Street Grainery, "we've had many long sessions about what our policy should be. There have been lots of foods coming down the pike that we're not sure of. Basically, what we try to offer are foods that are free of additives and chemicals, that are processed minimally, that are not tested on animals, that are kind to the planet, that are healthy and nutritious and that our customers can feel good about eating and serving."

Throughout the industry such policy discussions occur constantly. Most natural-food store owners agree that service should inform their basic policy, because service is the one benefit a small entrepreneur can offer that a supermarket can't. Nancy Auerbach of Rainbow Blossom welcomes competition from supermarkets.

"We feel that supermarkets advertise for us. It gets our products out there in the mainstream. When customers want to know more about a product they see on the supermarket shelves, they come to us."

Service can mean many things: special ordering of hard-to-get items for customers, cooking classes, answers to questions about vitamin supplements, assistance in helping a customer decide which kind of brown rice to buy, or how to cook certain foods— services far beyond the capabilities of the harried checkout clerks at your local supermarket.

At Rainbow Blossom service takes the form of personal contact with customers. The store mails its own newsletter and copies of its distributors' fliers to over 2,500 customers. The company has also instituted community outreach programs such as working with a local PTA on educating children about nutrition, and holding cooking classes in the fall.

As the Tofu Rises

In the spring of 1978, two couples met over dinner in rural Maine to discuss the possibility of pooling their resources to buy a rotary tiller for their gardens. The dinner took place at the home of Taffy and Eliot Field, nestled among wild blueberry fields atop Blinn Hill, about 12 miles from the coastal city of Bath. The other couple, Linda Harris and Bob Kalish, lived about three miles downhill, in the town of Whitefield, in a house deep in the woods along the shores of the Sheepscot River.

These two couples had met three years earlier while both were enrolled in the Shelter Institute, a school in Bath that teaches neophytes how to build their own homes. While working on their respective homes they had visited each other's work sites and had become friends. After dinner that evening in the spring of 1978, the couples sat around the table talking of gardening. But then the subject changed, with the talk meandering as it often does among friends chatting around a table after dinner. Linda had been a teacher, but had burned out. Someone at the table asked her what she would do if she could pursue her dreams.

"Open a health-food store," Linda replied, "so we wouldn't have to drive all the way to Portland to get tofu."

By the end of that dinner, the two couples had agreed to explore the feasibility of opening up a natural-food store in Bath. They never did get around to buying a rotary tiller.

Twelve years later, the Center Street Grainery is a thriving business in the little town of Bath. Located next door to the Shelter Institute in downtown Bath, it has undergone several transformations, shedding skin like a molting snake as it has sometimes struggled to keep up with a changing and often volatile market. The story of the Grainery mirrors the larger story of the natural-food industry, as its consumer base grew from a small, specialized clientele on the fringes of society to mainstream buyers.

With startup costs in 1978 of $20,000, borrowed from friends, the original owners were able to renovate the space and pay for a basic inventory (about $10,000 worth) from Boston-based Erewhon Foods. In the beginning, the store occupied only about 900 square feet, small enough for manager Harris to do everything—order the items, stock the shelves, wait on customers, and keep the books.

From the start, the Grainery founders planned on serving sandwiches and other food items, so they included a sink and a stove in their renovations, all designed to meet health department standards. They also put a lot of time and thought into the look of the store.

"We figured that's what would make people come back," Taffy Field says. "So we wanted to create a warm, comfortable kind of feeling. We chose incandescent lights for the main area, and wood, lots of wood. Lots of earth colors like brown and greens. I think that's what was most satisfying in the early days, that when we were through with all the hammering and building and so on, the place looked great."

The central focus of the store was a beautifully crafted set of 24 bins, constructed by a local boatbuilder. Into those bins the proprietors poured 50 pound bags of rice, beans, nuts, and pasta. The bins were important, for what set the Grainery apart from other stores, what became its theme, was bulk foods. Like the old-fashioned family market in an old neighborhood, the store displayed bulk food in bins so customers could buy as much or as little as they desired. Not only does it make sense from the consumer's point of view, but such a policy helps cut down on the use of plastic packaging. The bins were a great hit with people from all walks of life.

"When we first opened, we were surprised at the number of older people who came in, mostly women," Field says. "And their reaction was so heartening. For instance, we had a bin full of kasha, roasted buckwheat groats. Well, those women knew what kasha was and they were thrilled to see it just sitting there to be scooped into their bags. Some of the younger people, people my age, were just learning about the health benefits of kasha, and of whole wheat, and corn, and so on."

The immediate, positive reaction to the new store gratified the owners. Within three years they had paid back the $20,000 in loans and were operating at a profit. Unlike most fledgling businesses, the Grainery had succeeded.

During that time the store's original manager, Linda Harris, moved away from the area. Business still grew. The store hired more employees. No longer was it possible for one person to do everything. Grace Goldberg came aboard to assume management duties.

"When the store was four years old," Field recalls, "we were out of debt completely, making a small but steady profit, and our accountant told us we should think of going into debt again, it was good for business. So we decided to expand. The storefront next door was vacant. We hired a firm to do the expansion. They broke through the wall, doubling our retail space. No problem. We borrowed the money from a local bank, and had a grand reopening in December of 1982, and went on our way."

But the owners made a common mistake: they underfinanced the expansion. Although they figured out what the work on the vacant storefront and the extra inventory would cost, including those sums into the operating budget, they forgot the length of time it would take for the extra expense to be made up by extra sales volume. In other words, their cash flow took a turn for the worse.

Unskilled in business, they struggled for two years before realizing that something was seriously wrong. Despite an increase in gross sales they were still having trouble meeting their expenses. So they fired their accountant and found a new one who could lead them to a positive cash flow.

After months of meetings and pouring over the books and analyzing sales figures, Goldberg, herself now a stockholder, instituted a tighter system of buying inventory and controlling labor costs. The Grainery had been lucky, managing to pay back its startup loan almost immediately, making a profit from its first day, never having to worry about whether or not its costs exceeded its income. This seat-of-the-pants entrepreneurship was fine in the early days.

But when the store expanded it operations, increased its inventory and labor costs, it found itself overextended. This might have appeared obvious to someone who had studied business, but like most entrepreneurs, the owners of the Grainery were nonbusinesspeople with a good idea who had been lulled into an illusion created by their seemingly effortless initial success. The solution entailed some painful cutbacks.

After a two-year austerity diet, the Grainery found itself once again on a steady growth curve. Now, the pressures come more from without than from within as the large purveyors of food eye the lucrative organic market. Even so, Goldberg treats supermarket competition philosophically: "The best thing that could happen is for us to be out of business because there's no need for our service. When every little town has a supermarket that carries nutritious food grown with care and respect for the planet, when they carry organic foods, chemical-free foods, then we'll gladly close our doors."

ও

From seat-of-the-pants planning to thoughtful execution, the Center Street Grainery owners' story is similar to those stories of many people who believe that marketing or selling healthy food is an important environmental statement. You start out with an idea, based on a particular belief system, and through trial and error find how to balance your ideals with a firm business foundation.

Chapter *Fifteen*

Greenbacks:
Helping People Put Their Money Where It Will Do Some Good

On Carsten Henningsen's tenth birthday, his parents gave him what every boy wants—two shares of Mattell stock. Maybe it was a whim, or maybe it was a plan, but the effect of the gift on Henningsen's life was undeniable. He began to follow his stock avidly, and he soon had his own broker at the local Dean Witter office, where he would hang out after school (mostly with retirees six times his age) and watch the ticker tape spew out the latest quotes.

Henningsen's entrepreneurial bent emerged three years later. While on a family trip to Vancouver, British Columbia, he noticed that the local banks offered 10 percent interest on savings accounts. When he returned home, he assembled a modest "brochure" from the literature he collected at the banks, then placed a classified ad in the *Saturday Evening Post*. The headline screamed, "Guaranteed 10% interest—send $2 for information." As people responded to the ad, he'd mail out his brochure about the Canadian banks. Had his mother not stumbled onto the books, shut down the business, and returned whatever money she could trace, Henningsen's enterprise probably could have soared far beyond the $25 in revenue it collected during its first month of operation. He recalls with a grin, "My parents were quite horrified, with visions of their son being charged with mail fraud or securities fraud or who knows what."

Henningsen acquired more stocks during high school and college, but kept his entrepreneurial urge in check—he focused his energies on his studies and getting some experience of the world. By the time he graduated from college with a bachelor's degree Henningsen had visited about 40 countries, including many in the third world. He had even spent some time studying at a monastary run by the YMBA (the Young Man's Buddhist Association), an experience that had a strong impact on him.

Seeing poverty, hunger, and death in the third world and comparing it to affluence in America left him feeling that something was out of kilter. He also began to think about incidents like the Bhopal, India, disaster, in which more than 2,500 people died from a chemical leak at a Union Carbide plant, and the controversy surrounding Nestle's marketing infant formula throughout the third world. How could he make a difference, combining his knowledge of investing and his urge to help redress the inequities between the developed and the developing world?

At the time, he'd never heard the term "socially responsible investing," let alone met anyone doing it. But in the spirit of his first entrepreneurial adventure, he jumped in with both feet. Henningsen rounded up $20,000 in investment capital from friends and relatives, to start Progressive Securities. His first year, 1984, was a succcess, judging from the 40 percent return he realized for his clients. But at the same time he knew that he had to formalize his business; until then he had been making all of the investments under his own name and social security number and operating out of a back bedroom in his Eugene, Oregon, house. It took him six tries to find a securities lawyer who would seriously consider his idea of starting a mutual fund (he was 22 years old at the time). The lawyer he finally found (and still retains today) convinced him that a mutual fund would probably be too complicated an undertaking, and suggested an investment partnership instead. Although an investment partnership has more limitations, such as being restricted to operating in only one state, it would enable him to take his business to the next level and begin soliciting investments from clients.

In 1985 Henningsen obtained a broker's licence, and began to use his attorney's office twice a week to meet clients. A year later he opened his own office, and then expanded to Portland. Expansion allowed Henningsen to staff up, which in turn enabled him to offer more financial services to his clients. This was an important step, because it allowed Progressive Securities to earn fees for services, whereas before it could only earn commissions from selling load funds (A load fund is a fund that carries a commission to the financial person who sells it. A 4 percent load means a 4 percent commission to the originating seller. A no-load fund is typically sold by fee-only financial planners who do not rely on commissions.)

Since its first year of operation, Progressive Securities has shown spectacular growth. In 1984, a new client came to Henningsen with a check for $10,000, which seemed like an outrageous amount of money. Just a year later, a large corporate client showed up with a check for $600,000, and in 1988, Henningsen's company saw its first million-dollar account. By 1990, Progressive Securities was servicing 1,200 clients, with investments totaling over $40 million. The company now handles investments ranging from $250 to $3 million.

In 1970, when Carsten Henningsen was a junior high school student, he bought his first magazine subscription. It was to *Money* magazine. In 1990, the company he founded was written up in that same magazine as part of a profile on socially responsible investing. Not bad for a kid who started with two shares of toy company stock.

℘

Guides for the Perplexed

As environmental consciousness sweeps the country, an increasing number of investors will seek financial advisers who can steer them in the right direction and sort through the relevant information. Investing in environmentally sound companies may seem simple at first glance, but the search for worthy companies, and the right broker/financial adviser, is fraught with difficulties.

To begin with, there is a distinction between "clean" companies and companies that are in environmental services. A company might, for example, be involved with waste management, but have a horrendous record of pollution violations. Such a company is far from clean, but at the same time can be said to be an "environmental company."

Determining culpability can get pretty complicated for an investor who wants to evaluate a company's environmental record, not to mention the financial risks of their liabilities for the cleanup effort. Answering these questions often becomes the job of the socially responsible investment adviser.

In some ways, socially responsible investing (SRI) or ethical investing is nothing new. Some trace its roots to the early 1900's, when religious groups stopped buying stock in companies associated with sinful activities like drinking or smoking.

In recent years, that approach to making a statement and bringing about social change has become a highly refined investment technique. According to the Minneapolis-based Social Investment Forum, individuals and corporations plunked down an estimated $40 billion dollars in 1984 according to ethical guidelines. By 1990, that number soared to $500 billion.

The Social Investment Forum is a key resource for the ecopreneur who wishes to get involved in the SRI field. This organization, founded in 1981, serves as a national clearinghouse for information. Its members are involved in various aspects of socially responsible investing, and include officers of mutual funds and foundations, information providers, loan fund officers, research organizations, and individuals. In addition to publishing a newsletter, the Forum holds quarterly meetings and publishes a directory of financial professionals and organizations. (See page 295 for the Forum's address and telephone number.)

A good measure of the interest in socially responsible investing is the proliferation of mutual funds that adhere to some social guidelines in building their portfolios. A number of these have an environmental component, and some focus exclusively on the environment.

On the Job

First and foremost, an SRI advisor must have broad expertise in finance. Joel Diskin, of Worldview Financial Services, Inc., in

Birmingham, Michigan, stresses the importance of providing comprehensive services to clients. Diskin's clients see him as a full-resource provider who understands the details of their portfolios. By drawing on his background as an insurance agent, he can develop comprehensive plans that deal with environmentally responsible stocks, bonds, life insurance, annuities, and real estate investments.

Once an environmental investment adviser is confident that he or she understands the financial needs of a client, the next step is to ascertain the client's ethical goals. To assess those goals, some financial planners use questionnaires to help determine where the client's particular concerns lie.

Progressive Securities uses a four-page social survey that probes some tough issues. According to Henningsen, this gives him the oppportunity to truly customize a portfolio, especially for his larger clients. "It makes them think about their priorities and put them in categories. It's frustrating for a lot of people, but it's a healthy and necessary exercise." One question asks the client to consider 10 issues—everything from the environment to gay and lesbian rights—and to rate them on a 1–10 scale.

At first blush, it doesn't seem there should be any conflict among the issues—they all reflect a liberal mind set. But this assumption doesn't necessarily hold up when it comes to investing. "None of us are perfect," says Henningsen, "and I haven't found the perfect company out there yet to match everyone's needs. So we're constantly having to balance and weigh a company's positive and negative actions in terms of a client's preferences."

Just as important as understanding clients' goals is understanding their risk tolerance, and explaining to them how *you* interpret it. Don't let political and social enthusiasm undermine the foundation of sound financial advice. For example, a 60-year-old client preparing for retirement should be considerably more cautious about investing in a high-risk company than a 30-year-old in good health with a secure job. And many of the public companies at the cutting edge of the environmental field are exactly that—risky. They can be subject to political and regulatory whims—look what happened to solar companies after the government dumped its tax credits programs and cut research into solar energy. It would therefore be better to steer clients who can't afford to take chances toward a "risk-aversive" environmental company with a proven track record.

Types of Investment Opportunities Available to SRI Advisers

SRI advisers take advantage of a variety of investment opportunities for their clients. Many rely on mutual funds, especially for individual clients. Mutual funds offer two main advantages to the SRI specialist. First, they help solve the daunting problem of researching individual stocks. Second, they tend to fit better with the financial needs of most small investors. In general, small investors shouldn't build a portfolio by buying individual stocks in a field like the environment because of the risk; they can use mutual funds to acquire diversified holdings. This doesn't mean that the SRI adviser simply sits back and lets the fund do the work; on the contrary, the adviser must understand the background of the fund—its screening criteria and investment philosophy—and then determine how well it fits into the client's financial picture. This again entails careful investigation and a weighing of pros and cons.

A number of mutual funds focus on environmental issues; the Schield Progressive Environmental Fund and the New Alternatives Fund rigorously screen their investments for polluters.

Some socially responsible funds include environmental litmus tests as a part of their stock-picking criteria, while not focusing exclusively on environmental concerns. Such funds can provide a more diversified alternative while still paying attention to environmental criteria. The Calvert Social Investment Money Market Fund researches environmental citations.

An alternative to mutual fund investing is a "money manager" such as Clean Yield Group. A money manager is a person or company retained by an individual to oversee the investment of some part of the person's assets. A money manager can have the authority to make investment decisions without consulting with the client, or that authority can be restricted to meet the principal's requirements. Money managers can do the actual investment management for their clients according to their criteria, and build a stock portfolio.

Skills and Background

You can't simply hang out your shingle and begin offering SRI advice—it's critical to get a lawyer before offering a word of investment advice, to determine whether you have to comply with federal or state laws. For example, in many states, you must register with the state securities division before doing business. Also be aware that the Securities and Exchange Commission (SEC) has asserted jurisdiction over newsletters that even hint at discussing securities.

If you are going to sell insurance products you have to be licensed by the state in which you plan to do business, and you must pass separate tests in order to sell annuity products as well. Fixed annuities, which are basic insurance products, require licensing at state levels. Variable annuities include stocks and bonds, and as such will in addition require federal securities licensing. To meet the licensing and registration criteria, you'll have to undergo a great deal of training—which is as important for the quality of service you will provide as it is from a regulatory standpoint.

The most practical approach to the training issue is to get a job at an existing investment firm, especially one that has a well-established training program. In addition, you want to surround youself with experts, not the least of which is a good securities lawyer. Try to find one through recommendations from people already in the business, such as other investment advisers of the type you want to be. In addition to helping you sort through the regulatory morass, a good securities lawyer should be able to help you understand what you can and can't tell your clients, and what kinds of disclosures you are required to make.

Marketing and Opportunities

A person seeking SRI advice should be sure that his or her adviser is competent. The best advertising is from personal referrals and common experience. To that end, it is important to consider an investment advisory service a networking business.

Fortunately, it's easy to tap into existing networks. The people most likely to use the services of an SRI adviser are usually involved with causes; one of the best ways to meet investors concerned with environmental issues is to join environmental organizations, attend meetings, and participate in such organizations' activities. Not only are these activities important for getting the attention of potential clients, but they will provide you with information and contacts that can help you do a better job screening investment options for environmental flaws.

Another good way to gain exposure is to make yourself available for speaking engagements at civic, church, and community groups. Your audience is really a pool of potential clients. Moreover, each engagement increases your credentials as an expert in your field, which is essential to cultivating clients over the long term. You will not find people rushing the podium with fistfuls of cash to invest after each speech. But repeated exposure will gradually position you in a potential client's mind as an adviser to trust when it comes time to invest.

Speaking engagements and other magnet marketing techniques (see Chapter 4) designed to cultivate and attract customers can pay off handsomely. Investment adviser Joel Diskin's press release campaign led to a spate of articles that built credibility and attracted new clients. Similarly, Progressive Securities has been able to parlay its expertise into a weekly radio program on the local NPR affiliate and into regular columns in local newspapers.

Joel Diskin has done a half-hour television interview on the *Global Connections* program, which is aired on over 30 cable television stations. Diskin found his way to the program after he was interviewed as an expert in socially responsible investing for an article in *Financial Services Week*. This led to a two-page feature about his company in *Michigan Business Magazine*. The manager of the TV station that produces *Global Connections* saw the article in *Michigan Business*, and a year later Diskin was a guest on the show. How did it all start? With a good magnet marketing press release campaign (see page 65 for details).

Information as Power

Some ecopreneurs have created successful businesses by providing information rather than offering specific investment counseling. Accurate information about particular investments is critical to the SRI adviser, and is also a high-priced commodity because of the difficulty in obtaining it. Unlike financial-performance data, which is easy to secure, information about environmental performance can be buried and masked in many different ways.

Consider the problems with a seemingly easy research task, determining whether an environmental enforcement agency has cited a particular company for violations of environmental laws or regulations. Since citations can be issued by several enforcement agencies operating at both federal and state levels, the task of uncovering information becomes enormous.

To further confuse the issue, nobody is accumulating citation data nationwide. What data exists from the EPA and the Department of the Interior deals mainly with alleged violations, not proven cases or consent decrees. Also, the company's public reports required under the securities laws only have to acknowledge cases in which the company's potential liability exceeds $100,000. In short, getting information is not as easy as it may sound.

Company Reports/Profiles

All this seems like the perfect opportunity for researchers with a passion for digging and the patience of a saint. It does offer a challenge, but as an ecobusiness, it also has its shortcomings. If you're trying to sell the information to brokerage houses, banks, and large institutions, you'll be competing against these organizations' own internal research staffs. Since they are probably trying to answer a limited number of questions about a narrow pool of companies, they can focus their efforts on getting that specific information. For you to sell information across a broad base, you'd need to have a veritable supermarket of studies in order to meet the demands of any single client.

Newsletters

Another way to get involved with socially responsible investing is to publish a newsletter. Consider *Good Money*, published by Good Money Publications in Worcester, Vermont. This publication began almost by accident in 1982. Its founder, sociologist Ritchie Lowry, became interested in SRI after inheriting a sum of money from his parents. He subsequently wrote an article titled "Doing Good by Doing Well" for *The Futurist* magazine.

Lowry found himself besieged with requests from people all over the world who were seeking information about companies worthy of their investment, and soon after launched the bimonthly *Good Money*. The newsletter is geared to individual investors, and provides general social information on publicly traded companies. In addition, Lowry's company publishes a mutual funds guide and upon request can provide issue papers on a variety of social topics.

While the opportunities seem ripe, beware of the difficulties that newsletter publishers in general face, and the particular problems with starting a newsletter in the SRI field. First, starting a quality newsletter requires a great deal more expertise than just knowledge of the subject area. Most newsletters fold because the publisher does not have an adequate understanding of direct mail.

Many, for example, plan for a 10 percent or higher response, when 1 or 2 percent would be considered excellent. They plunk down all their funds on the mailing, then shut down because they do not have the capital needed to research, write, produce, and mail the newsletter—it takes time to build a subscriber base and collect the cash for subscriptions. Also, some people who said "Yes! Sign me up" will inevitably cancel or refuse pay up, leaving gaping holes in your cash-flow projections. The fact is, far more newsletters fail than succeed, and you can minimize your chances of becoming a statistic by proceeding with caution and getting expert help each step of the way.

From a competitive standpoint, new SRI newsletters will face the publications of investment firms that use them to attract new clients and service existing ones. These firms are not counting on the financial success of their newsletters to keep them—or the newsletter—afloat. Franklin Insight, an affiliate of Franklin Research and Development Corp. in Boston, Massachusetts, publishes the monthly newsletter *Investing for a Better World* (subscription cost $19.95) which provides profiles of socially responsible companies and mutual funds, as well as business news of interest to environmentally conscious investors. The firm also offers a more comprehensive service that includes equity briefs, quarterly reports, investment advisories, as well as social profiles, and the monthly newsletter. This service costs $195.00 per year.

Yet another source of competition for newsletter publishers are the publications offered by nonprofit organizations such as the *The Corporate Examiner*, published by the Interfaith Center for Corporate Responsibility. This publication, which costs $35 for 10 issues, analyzes general issues and developments relating to shareholder resolutions and SRI concerns.

In short, the need for information is great, but so are the competitive pressures. If you believe that you have a unique angle and people would be willing to pay for it, proceed cautiously. Talk to experts in the publishing field. Study the competition. Link up with a direct-mail marketing expert. And above all, only proceed if you have the cash to sustain your operation for at least a year. You may be the most savvy SRI adviser on the planet, but if you can't afford to keep the presses rolling, your publication will have a readership of one.

A Hybrid Information Business

Kinder, Lydenberg, Domini & Co., Inc., has hedged its bets in the information field by offering a wide range of products and services to a variety of customers. The firm publishes the Domini Social Index (named for Amy Domini, a nationally recognized expert on SRI), a common-stock index whose 400 companies pass multiple social-responsibility screens, one of which is environmental. The firm provides a monthly report on the performance of the companies in the Domini Social Index (DSI) and detailed social profiles of companies in the DSI 400 and the Standard & Poor's 500. Kinder, Lydenberg broadens its customer base by providing customized screening on a consulting basis to investment firms, mutual funds, private companies, and institutions. (For more details on the founding of this company, see page 264.)

According to Peter Kinder, the firm's president, the more detailed the information an environmental research firm can provide, the broader its market will be. If you can provide details about case settlements, your research may be of interest to environmental lawyers, as well as social investment professionals. The caveat though, is that such clients may well have topnotch resources for doing their own research, so don't plan your whole business around acceptance into a market that may be able to secure its own information.

Kinder explains that to start any type of information service in the SRI field, you must first decide what information you are selling, then determine if there is anyone who would be willing to pay for it. You must also determine how you will get the information you wish to sell. In the example of environmental citations, you would have to go directly to the citing agency.

You will definitely want to secure information from national environmental organizations such as the Sierra Club and Greenpeace. But more important, you will want to keep in close touch with their local chapters. (The National Toxics Clearinghouse is an excellent direct route to local groups concerned with hazardous wastes.) Otherwise, you will have to track locals down through the nationals and your own networks. As with most products and services, the key is to identify a specific niche and then market to it successfully. If you can do that, you've cleared the most difficult hurdle in getting going.

A Bright Green Investment Future

In her book *100 Predictions for the Baby Boom—The Next 50 Years*, Cheryl Russell points out that people in their middle years are more likely to take risks in order to have their money grow. The first baby boomer hits age 45 in 1991, and as the boomers swell the ranks of the middle-aged, America will see greater numbers of investors looking for big wins in the stock market. When you consider this along with increasing concerns about the environment and quality of life, there appear to be a lot of opportunities in green financial planning and information services. Some investment professionals, like San Diego–based Michael Stolper, are skeptical. Stolper told a reporter from *The Wall Street Journal* that environmental investing is "just the latest marketing gimmick in a business with too much competition," Nevertheless, the emergence of mainstream investment vehicles such as Merrill Lynch's EcoLogical Trust 1990, and the continued success of companies such as Progressive Securities, seems to indicate that the environmental branch of socially responsible investing is here to stay.

☙

Fish Tails and Corporate Trails

Tourists have always loved to watch fishing boats returning to harbor—it's so, well, picturesque. Even on Lake Erie. Even in 1972, when public health agencies banned the sale of Lake Erie bass because its flesh contained high levels of mercury.

Inspectors from Ohio's Department of Natural Resources (DNR) did not share vacationers' romantic reaction to one corporation's homeward-bound vessels, which brought in cargoes of banned fish and sold them to the public. The inspectors, who were stretched to the limit, could catch but a few of the offenders, who would pay a fine in court, only to set sail the next day.

In the midst of this fishy business, Peter Kinder was a second-year law student at Ohio State University and the junior member of the DNR's five-person legal division. "Surely," his section chief mused, "there must be a way to stop these guys. Can't we put them out of business? Maybe lift their corporate charter?"

Off to the library went Kinder. A week later he returned with an astonishing answer: no. Except in one very restricted circumstance, all the DNR could do was fine the corporations and turn them lose for another day of bait and tackle. The memory of that revelation would eventually shape the course of Kinder's professional career.

After passing the bar exam, Kinder stayed on with the state. At that time, Kinder worked in the attorney general's office, where he participated in dozens of lawsuits that attempted to hold corporations responsible for their violations of state law—charitable and consumer frauds, environmental and energy violations, and illegal campaign contributions. When he left state government in 1977 he knew one thing for certain: suing corporations was not going to change corporate behavior in America.

What *was* changing corporate behavior, Kinder determined, was public opinion. "A board member of two Fortune 500 companies put it this way," he says. "'No company is going to change what it's doing until not changing hits the bottom line or senior management has to spend more than three percent of its time responding to the issue.'" It's hard for consumers to affect the bottom line, he admits, and boycotts are hard to organize and sustain. "But," he says, "consumers *can* force senior management to spend more than three percent of their time dealing with an issue. Management simply has to confront an issue when well-informed consumers press it."

Today, Kinder's company, Kinder, Lydenberg, Domini & Co., Inc. (KLD) arms people with the information they need to pressure corporations to change. "Social research affects corporate behavior," he insists, "first, because the researcher acts as a proxy for social investors simply by asking about corporations' actions. Second, the research enables other social investors to raise issues in other contexts. For instance, it may be the basis of a resolution placed on the proxy statement at the annual meeting of the shareholders."

KLD identifies companies that have positive records and creative approaches to the environment, product quality, employee relations, community involvement, and hiring of women and members of minorities. The firm's research also identifies companies with interests in South Africa or revenues from weapons, nuclear power, alcohol, tobacco, or gambling.

Kinder and his wife, Amy Domini, launched the company in March 1988, funding it with a home equity loan and a large loan from a very generous friend. Given the capital-intensive nature of starting a research firm—you have to have research in hand to sell—and the current state of the economy, Kinder does not recommend this course. "Look for partners who'll bring equity. If you have to go the debt route, be sure to keep enough in reserve to cover Maalox and physical therapy for stress-related injuries."

In developing an information product to sell, Kinder recommends relying on as few "munchkin researchers" as possible: "Hire quality, not quantity," he says. "Don't hire anyone on a permanent basis until you've tried them on a contract basis. Test their work. Be honest with yourself about how you like having them around. There's nothing worse than working under incredible time and money pressure next to someone you don't like—especially if he or she is being paid out of your home equity loan."

Perhaps the most important piece of advice Kinder has for information providers relates to product. "You can't make it by just selling information. No way. You have to find ways to package the information in other forms that expanded audiences will buy." One answer Kinder's firm has arrived at is book writing. The firm is currently working on two new titles; a social investment primer (to replace Kinder and Domini's groundbreaking book, *Ethical Investing*) and an almanac of social investing. The firm is also using its database to provide consulting services to firms that want information on trends in American business.

Will Kinder change the world? "Certainly not overnight," he says with a smile. "Social change is incremental and erratic in speed. That's the lesson of the twenty years following the first Earth Day. But who, even in 1987, would have thought that Du Pont, Dow, and Monsanto would be positioning themselves as environmentally conscious companies in the 1990s?" The millennium, he notes, is only nine years away.

∽

The investment business is complicated and fraught with legal complications. But as people like Carsten Henningsen and Peter Kinder prove, there are many ways to get involved. If you really believe in bringing about environmental as well as social change, then you may find the investment field a powerful lever for reshaping our society. In the next and final chapter, we'll focus on bringing about change through something a bit lighter—literally, fun and games.

Chapter *Sixteen*

Educate, Entertain, Ecotain!
Have Fun While Doing Good

By the time that most of us reach adulthood and settle into careers, we find ourselves doing things far afield from our childhood dreams. John Bangs and Richard Yost are two exceptions. In 1973, they realized their fantasies of being the first Westerners to raft down the Awash River in northeast Ethiopia. The Awash at that time was a little-known river that scoured the Ethiopian escarpment, plunging down from the 8,000-foot plateau to the Danakil Desert.

Smitten by their Indiana Jones–style expedition, Bangs and Yost decided to integrate their love of the wild with their careers, and concocted the idea for an adventure travel company, Sobek Expeditions (Angels Camp, California). Their assets consisted of $500 in cash and a strong seat-of-the-pants intuition, the same kind of intuition needed to steer a raft through white water. "We had no grand scheme, no grand vision," Bangs recalls. "We sort of began it as a lark, to see if we could do it, what would happen."

That was back in 1973. Later that same year they went back to Ethiopia with 20 people to raft down the Omo River. During the following year they organized more trips, exploring such rivers as the Baro, in Ethiopia, and the Blue Nile. By 1976, Sobek moved to Angels Camp in the Sierra Mountains, keeping an office in Oakland. Today the company employs a staff of 30 to 40 at the Angels Camp site. It hires guides for the trips on a per-job basis, and most of the guides live in the area where the trip will take place.

Sobek's trips run a wide gamut and appeal to a broad spectrum of individual abilities. The company offers rafting trips down the Tatshenshini River in Alaska, trips to Africa, Antarctica, and South America. Their excursions run from one day to six weeks, and cost anywhere from a few hundred to several thousand dollars. Sobek has become the General Motors of the ecotourism field, grossing $6 million in 1989 and guiding 17,500 clients to the outdoors.

Some trips appeal only to experienced outdoors people, others to more sedentary people. Applicants are screened to avoid the catastrophe of someone winding up on a trip he or she can't handle—but sometimes the screening process doesn't work.

Bangs tells the story of one trip down the Colorado River when a lawyer showed up at the site carrying his briefcase, dressed in a three-piece suit and wing-tip shoes. He had just finished an intense trial that had been going on for weeks. When he told his secretary two days before to "book me on a Grand Canyon cruise," she had signed him onto Sobek's rafting trip down the Colorado. The lawyer went ahead, but halfway through the trip had to be helicoptered out.

With the success of their trips the two began to market the "soft adventure" concept. This concept takes travel a step further than simple sightseeing and nights around the hotel bar. Bangs and Yost were persuaded that more had to be done by an incident that happened while they were leading their second expedition down the Omo River back in 1975.

As the rafting party floated down the river, Bangs and Yost, along with the 40 people on the Sobek expedition, were amazed to see one little boy clad only in a loincloth but wearing a pair of sunglasses adorned with studded flamingoes, and a man with the animist markings on his cheeks wearing a T-shirt proclaiming

Indiana University, NCAA Champions. What was going on there in this remote part of the world that had seldom, if ever, seen Europeans or Americans, a pristine area completely cut off from world marketplaces?

Then it all became clear; six months before, they had led a group of 20 tourists down the same river. Now the villagers were wearing the clothes and sporting the accoutrements the tourists had traded to them for items such as gourds and beads during their first trip. Bangs and Yost felt as guilty as if they had left a load of plastic milk jugs in the middle of the rain forest.

When they arrived back in the States, Bangs wrote to scores of anthropologists recounting what had happened and soliciting their responses. What should he do? The answers he received ranged from the fatalistic—"There's nothing you can do, these people will have to enter the twentieth century someday"—to scoldings for going over there in the first place. As the hard-liners saw it, such cultures should be studied by anthropologists only—no one else admitted.

Bangs finally worked out a solution. "With the help of some sympathetic anthropologists, we made up a policy to allow only low-impact trading between our clients and the native peoples. What that meant was we set up certain criteria regarding what could be bartered with the villagers—fish hooks, edible food, anything biodegradable, was okay. But no sunglasses, no T-shirts with faddish stencils on them, nothing that could enter their economy and cause culture shock."

Today, Sobek's "soft adventures" have given thousands of people the opportunity to see remote areas of the world, and to interact with native peoples without exploiting them. Sobek has taken tourists to such far-flung places as Borneo, Siberia, and Antarctica. In every case the policy is to leave the area as they found it.

"We want to give people the opportunity to see these parts of the world as they exist and as they existed before we arrived. They come back from these trips and they have a better understanding of different cultures, a better understanding of how interconnected the world is."

☙

There are infinite ways to educate and entertain people about environmental issues. You can take them to the rain forests and out to the ocean to see for themselves the trees and whales. You can write articles and books, make video- and audiotapes, or create games that educate people on ways they can help the environment. You can open a store selling only items produced in environmentally safe ways. You can sell such items through the mail via catalogs. In each case you give your product or service a "green twist," aimed at educating as well as entertaining your customers. This chapter focuses on only a few such opportunities, but these just might stimulate you into starting a business that entertains, educates, or ecotains.

Ecotourism: The New Adventure

The environment-friendly "alternative safari" may be the travel equivalent to organic foods in the food industry—a concept whose time has come in the 1990's. According to industry figures, two million Americans each year are choosing vacations in the wild armed with cameras and binoculars instead of guns. The 1980's saw an incredible boom in the travel industry, as affluence and competitive transportation rates put almost the entire globe within easy reach. Americans began seeking out-of-the-way places, the opportunity to do more than simply sightsee or relax around a hotel pool.

But along with the easy accessibility came problems, new concerns from environmentalists about the impact of modern human traffic on wildlife areas and native peoples. Travelers do tend to disturb the peace of natural places, befoul the environment with their waste, and even interfere with the local communities.

For a time, many conservation organizations denounced groups like Sobek that promoted excursions into the world's pristine locations as just another form of pollution. But that thinking has changed, in many ways thanks to the efforts of people like Richard Bangs and John Yost.

Bangs and Yost are not the only ecopreneurs to make a living teaching people about the jungle; the Amazon rain forests also support ecopreneur Mark Baker. In 1982, Baker, a woodworker in Cambridge, Massachusetts, wanted to get into the sales end of the wood business and make use of his knowledge of tropical woods. So he started Amazonex Lumber Company, which worked with several sawmills in the Amazon basin of Brazil. Amazonex placed orders, and the local people cut and shipped the wood to Massachusetts.

When Baker went to Brazil to visit the sawmills, he saw first hand where they got the wood he was selling back in the United States. That experience changed his outlook. "I was never unaware of the issues with rain forest conservation," he recalls. "But with each visit I became more aware of the pace of destruction. I began to get concerned with what was going on, and finally concluded that I should use my knowledge to somehow contribute to conservation."

Baker spent an afternoon in Washington, where he talked to several environmental groups about jobs, but soon realized that his entrepreneurial spirit was leading him in other directions. In 1988 he founded Ecotour Expeditions (Cambridge, Massachusetts), and in 1989 led the first tour group of six to the rain forests of Brazil. Ecotour Expeditions has organized 10 more tours since then, all of them to Brazil to study the rain forests. In addition to Brazil and Ecuador he plans to develop more tours, until he can offer 40 per year, and to expand to other parts of the world, such as Borneo and Madagascar.

While ecopreneurs like Richard Bangs, John Yost, and Mark Baker guide tourists through the remote jungles of the world, other ecopreneurs have taken to the seas. In Provincetown, Massachusetts, Aaron Avellar runs the Dolphin Fleet, a business started by his father, a Portuguese fisherman who pioneered the conversion of operations into sightseeing excursions. The senior Avellar has even gone to Norway and Japan to help whalers there seize the opportunity to make a living by preserving an endangered species. The Dolphin Fleet has created satellite ecotainment opportunities for others, such as Cetacean Videos, which videotapes trips for passengers. On each trip, scientists from the Center for Coastal Studies talk to passengers about efforts to save the whales, and information generated by the whale sightings is fed into the Center's database. The boats also sell the Center's T-shirts and educational materials to support their investigations.

Ecotourism can mean many things, depending on the tour operator. Some operators may call themselves ecotours by making a meager donation to conservation causes. Other tour companies are simply eager to cash in on the latest trend and feel no real motivation to conserve the environment they exploit. Some large travel companies have created smaller divisions with names that include "nature" or even "ecotour." Even so, they have taken a small step forward toward protecting the environment.

Companies specializing in ecotourism, however, take the environmental aspect very seriously. For Mark Baker, the "eco-" in Ecotour Expeditions has a precise meaning: every one of the company's tours includes an ecological narrative. For guides, Baker hires biologists or scientists who are involved in ongoing field work in Amazonia. During tours, these scientists talk about the ecology of the particular forest type the group is visiting. Most of Ecotour Expeditions' tours tend to focus on a single environment and to study that area in depth.

"We take walks, not treks," Baker says. "The purpose of our tours is to study the ecology of the forest, not to get to any particular place."

An entrepreneur thinking of entering the tour business will quietly discover some pros and some cons. On the plus side, you don't need tremendous amounts of capital to set up a tour company. But you need contacts, you need to know where to rent equipment, where to hire guides, and you have to be familiar with the places you're going to visit. Much of any tour business's reputation comes from word of mouth, and there's nothing like a trip that goes wrong to give a company a bad name.

Bangs and Yost certainly had done most of the preliminary work to make Sobek the instant success it was: they shared years of rafting and outdoor experience, they knew other outfitters and tour companies so they could link up with them if necessary, they had a deep respect for what they were doing, and they both had a true love of the outdoors and the environment. They were thus able to start up with only $500, scraping together what they needed by borrowing or tapping credit. But at the time they weren't starting up a business—they were starting up an adventure, a trip to Africa to raft down an unexplored river.

In addition to using advertising, Bangs offers journalists and photographers free or discounted trips so they can write articles for major magazines and newspapers. Sobek has hosted a number of well-known writers and has been the subject of several television documentaries.

Once you get started, can you support yourself through ecotourism? "You don't really make a lot of money in this business," says Bangs, "but we're not in it for the money. For me, it's a matter of how I want to spend my life. This is ideal, I get to do what I love and I can support myself doing it. But if you're thinking of going into it, you have to ask yourself what's important in your life. If being rich is important, then this is not the business to go into."

Seeing the World Through Sound

There's a common notion that says technology and the environment can't coexist peacefully. Ecopreneurs, however, know that environmental awareness and technological know-how sometimes work hand in hand. Take the field of audio and video recordings. With advances in technology, you can pack up the equivalent of a quality recording studio on your back and trek to the most remote areas of the world to record sights and sounds.

Richard and Sharon Hooper did just that when they created Nature Recordings, which provides a stressed-out and harried world with soothing images and natural sounds. Before melding his love of nature with technological know-how, Richard Hooper made a living as an ordained Lutheran minister in Pacific Grove, California. Hooper describes himself as a "different kind of minister," one who hosted and produced his own radio show in his home. The show featured interviews of various "new age" personalities—such as gurus and psychologists.

From contacts made producing his radio show, Hooper created a catalog featuring various "counterculture" items. Eventually Hooper left the ministry to concentrate on making audio and visual recordings, but that business folded, and in 1986 he began looking for something else to do. He also began speculating that with the "new age" movement in full swing, there might be a market for recordings of "environments."

For his first recording he chose the sounds of the sea. After making his recording, he asked his wife, Sharon, to quit her job as director of the Fort Ord Child Development Center, one of the largest day-care centers in the world, and take over the marketing of the sea tape. Sharon was reluctant to quit her job, but on weekends she packed her car with tapes and headed down the coast. On her first trip, to Santa Barbara, she sold the tape to 12 of the 15 shops she visited. Before long, she had won 50 accounts, with all of them reordering.

"The response was so terrific, so immediate," Sharon recalls. "It was such a simple idea, just going out and recording the sounds of nature. But I guess the idea hit a chord among certain consumers."

The success of the *Sea* recording convinced Sharon to quit her job and take over the marketing of the tapes full time. At that point, Nature Recordings was up and running.

From the beginning, the Hoopers avoided the usual music outlets, instead focusing on gift shops, natural-food stores, and bookstores. Their tapes weren't really aimed at the music-buying public, but at the kind of people who browse through bookstores and gift shops. Sensitivity to their market made their success that much more immediate. Had they tried to break into the music stores with recordings of "nature," the response probably would have been disappointing.

"That first year we were lucky in some ways," Sharon says. "We already had the recording and duplicating equipment from Richard's studio, so we were able to start up with about fifteen thousand dollars. For an entrepreneur looking to start such a business now, it would cost at least thirty thousand dollars because of the expensive tape duplicators. We also kept our costs down by doing everything ourselves—creating the covers and labels, writing ads, and so on. The only thing we contracted for out of house was a graphic artist to do some of the artwork."

In 1989 the Hoopers moved their operation to Friday Harbor in the San Juan islands in northwest Washington state. That year their company grossed over a million dollars, and supported a staff of 10 full-time and two part-time employees. In 1990 the Hoopers expanded to include several "music" titles, with new age recording artists.

Their "environments" include such titles as *The Jungle*, *Thunderstorm*, *Wilderness*, and *Bamboo Waterfall*. For these recordings the Hoopers visited rain forests in Central and South America, Africa, a Japanese Buddhist temple, and the forests in their own backyard. The expansion into music recordings represented a natural extension of their work with the environment.

"We're selective," Sharon Hooper says, "we choose only certain kinds of artists to record. I guess you'd say we specialize in what's called new age music, a bit like Windham Hill Records." To help market the music recordings, the Hoopers created a separate label, World Disk Productions. Richard Hooper also plans to introduce videos into the company's product lines.

The Hooper's business has changed the couple's way of thinking. "We found ourselves becoming more and more aware of the environment and how important it was," Sharon recalls. "Making the sound recordings made us extremely sensitive to how the sounds of nature were becoming increasingly extinct. We could see it in our own backyard in California; you had to trek deeper and deeper into the mountains to pick up what you wanted."

This change led them to a policy of donating a percentage of their profits directly to organizations involved in conservation, such as Rainforest Action Network (RAN), Greenpeace, and others. But the Hoopers' commitment goes even further. They have tried to change things within their own organization. For example, they no longer use "blister packaging" to send their tapes, and are exploring ways to make their own company more environmentally responsible.

Subverting the Retail Ethic

Like many entrepreneurs, Paul Dzerinski and Will Anderson had no intention of becoming business partners. In fact, going into business was a notion that neither partner entertained when they talked of the future back in 1983. Dzerinski was a physical therapist and artist, interested only in supporting himself so he could paint. Anderson had worked at various jobs in the construction field, but had gained some retail experience when he had helped Greenpeace set up its first retail outlet in Portland, Oregon, in 1980.

What motivated the two men was a strong commitment to the environment, summarized by Anderson as "a belief in living in harmony with the global environment, and in actively striving to eliminate those practices that impede such harmony."

This belief system moved the partners to open Ecology House, a retail store specializing in items that were produced with an awareness of the environment, that didn't exploit animals, that educated consumers about ecology, or whose proceeds from sales supported environmental efforts.

From the beginning, Anderson and Dzerinski had definite ideas about what products they wanted to carry. "We wanted products that would express our value system," Anderson recalls. "Usually, places of business are value-free. That's the prevailing philosophy of business, create a value-free space for the transactions of business. But we didn't want that. We wanted a place where the consumer *would* get a dose of our values we call it retail it 'retail subversive'."

The two partners started their store with $30,000 borrowed from friends and family and personal credit cards. Anderson had made contacts while setting up the retail outlet for Greenpeace. After the first Ecology House opened in 1983 (on the island of Maui), the business grew until the partners began franchising the operation in 1988. By 1990, Ecology House operated six stores, three in Boulder, Colorado, one each in Portland, Oregon, and Portland, Maine, and one in Denver.

Franchising helped spread the Ecology House values. For a fee of $20,000, the franchisee receives hands-on training, trade sources, computer software, advice on site location and store layout, and opening support. In return, franchises pay 5 percent of gross sales to the company.

The concept has proved successful, not only for Anderson and Dzerinski and Ecology House, but for others as well. Another operation, Nature Company, now has 39 stores located across the United States.

For an entrepreneur entering the market, a knowledge of suppliers is essential, since you can't rely on the conventional gift shop vendors for your special inventory. Will Anderson went into the business already armed with a list of contacts he had made while with Greenpeace, but a newcomer would do well to study the market constantly, seeking distributors' catalogs and asking hard questions of people running similar shops.

Despite the apparent ease of opening a retail store, Anderson cautions against taking anything for granted. He has discovered some difficult truths about running a retail business. "You have to be prepared to give over your life to the business. It's not a nine-to-five job. It's also not enough to have great intentions and to have these altruistic ideals—your store won't go anywhere unless you follow sound business practices. That's the most basic truth about get started and succeeding."

Education Can Be Fun, Too

Perhaps in no other endeavor has environmental awareness found such willing audiences as in the educational field. After all, it's so much easier to nurture and instruct a child's instinctual love for nature than to reeducate an adult. In most schools across the nation, the natural sciences now contain an ecological component. It's getting harder to find grade-school children who aren't aware of ecological disasters like the Exxon oil spill, or the destruction of the rain forests. It's also hard to find a science class that doesn't in some way address the issues of environmental pollution.

Education and games go hand in hand. Children love games, and if the games can teach a lesson or two, so much the better. In recent years a growing number of educational games with an environmental twist have begun appearing in specialty stores such as Ecology House as well as in commercial toy and gift shops. Entire catalog companies, such as Music for Little People, The Geode Catalogue, and Hearthsong, feature an assortment of games, toys, video- and audiotapes, art and craft supplies, all with qualities that make them appealing to the most rigorous environmentalist.

Many of the toys in these catalogs do not use batteries, because of the environmental problems associated with battery disposal. Many of the toys are also made of wood or other natural materials instead of plastic. Likewise, the dolls and stuffed animals do not use real animal fur. Also, many of the companies making such products have embarked on a policy of not selling any toys made from tropical wood in an effort to help save the rain forests.

For an ecopreneur with a good idea for a game or toy, the market is ready. Every year at Christmas time, manufacturers and retailers are hoping for the next Trivial Pursuit or Monopoly, or for the latest toy to capture the imagination. Once you've developed the game or toy, and protected your work (see a good patent attorney), you have two choices. You can make and market it yourself, or you can sell the idea to one of the existing toy and game manufacturers. Whatever route you decide on, the way to go about it is to rent some space at the annual International Toy Fair in New York City. This event usually occurs in February. All the toy and game buyers in the country attend this fair to scout out new products and complete their purchasing in time for the Christmas season. You'll find various regional toy fairs as well, but the New York event is the place to break into the national market.

On the retail side, not all stores selling toys and games fit into such neat categories as "green" and "commercial." Many children's stores have been unwittingly "green" for years because their focus on quality steers them toward toys made from natural materials and with a more educational bent. In Brunswick, Maine, Ask Your Mother has been in business since 1976. Owner Becky Cuthbert has seen a trend in recent years for stores like hers to find themselves carrying more science kits, more environmental games, and toys.

"We've never been just a toy store," she says. "We opened as a quality place, where parents could find good quality toys and games, not the usual stuff they saw advertised on television. Our products would last." Even 14 years ago Cuthbert emphasized wooden toys over plastic. Now her store carries solar energy kits, science projects, hug-the-planet cuddlies, and all kinds of reading material with an environmental slant. She has also seen her products take on a global aspect, with toys and games emphasizing global awareness, such as the hug-a-globe and world map puzzles. Stores like Ask Your Mother are ready outlets for your environmental toys and games.

The Conscientious Objector of the Computer World

Imagine this scenario: You have been appointed UN Commissioner of the Environment, which means you can levy taxes on activities that impact the planet, and can use the money so derived to grant subsidies to environmentally beneficial activities. Consequently, you are responsible for many aspects of human life on earth, and must make some difficult tradeoffs.

For example, you could tax industry for polluting the air, but at the same time you'd raise unemployment and reduce the standard of living improvements gained from industrial development; you could cut fertilizer use to control water pollution, but risk lowering crop yields; or you could levy a tax on beef production to limit destruction of the rainforests, but this will have strong economic consequences.

Saving the planet isn't easy, is it? That's what Chris Crawford hopes to teach people with his sensational software game, Balance of the Planet. Crawford, now regarded as the best designer of "high-minded" computer games, got his start in 1979 after receiving a master's degree in physics. At that time, he was hired by Atari to design computer games that went *pow* and *splat* and featured fireworks. Meanwhile, he dreamed of designing a game that would offer something more than an adrenaline rush as alien craft careened off the screen and fighter planes demolished each other in mock dogfights.

Atari folded, and Crawford found himself on the free-lance circuit. While on his own, he created a game that fulfilled his dream, one with meaning, substance, and merit. "Balance of Power" quickly became a classic. It explores many of the manifestations of power on a global scale, giving players a feeling for how wars occur and what can be done to prevent them.

"Balance of Power" was picked up by Mindscape, a software publisher, and sold over 250,000 copies in its first year, 1985, giving Crawford an instant reputation. He then went on to produce several more games for Mindscape. The success of "Balance of Power" encouraged Epic Software Publishers to approach Crawford in 1988 for an environmental game to coincide with the twentieth anniversary of Earth Day in 1990. The game designer thought about it for a couple of months, then called back to say he couldn't do it. But the publisher kept calling him every couple of months, until gradually some ideas began flitting around in Crawford's mind.

"They knew how to handle me," he recalls. "Giving me the challenge of doing something that couldn't be done. So I started working on it, over quite a few months, until I thought I had something." Unfortunately, by the time Crawford had something on disk, the publisher had gone out of business. That's when Crawford made an important decision: to publish it himself.

"Frankly, self-publishing was something I had thought about a lot. I'm a guy whose work has been terribly mutilated by publishers. I never had a desire to be an entrepreneur, but after seeing what publishers did to my stuff, I figured it was the only way to keep my integrity."

Crawford tells the story of how one publisher handled a game he designed called "Guns and Butter." The game was a clever amalgam of economics and war. In it, the operator tries to strengthen the economic system in order to amass the largest army so he or she can conquer the world. But the publisher wasn't sure anyone would understand the title (economics teachers often use it to illustrate supply and demand). So they changed the title of the game to "Global Dilemma," and slapped a picture of the earth on the cover. Crawford was disgusted. He figured he could do a better job.

His chance came in 1990 when he finally self-published his Earth Day game, "Balance of the Planet." There were times after he released the game, however, when he regretted his decision to self-publish. "We were stampeded by distributors," he says. "They were so excited, part of it was my reputation. Having no business sense, I responded to their enthusiasm by going overboard on production. The result was I had too much inventory. I had cases and cases of games sitting on shelves in my warehouse, so I may have to eat a few."

Unshaken by the inventory buildup, Crawford continues to believe in his product. "People who play my game should come away from it with an understanding of the inter-connectedness of this planet," says the wizard of the computer. In the past we've looked at problems microscopically. But that isn't the way things are. We must look at problems in a macroscopic way, seeing the big picture. We worry about the death of one whale while in Africa forty million die of hunger. We worry about one endangered species without considering others. I want people to change their personal values, I want people to see things from a global perspective. And that's what my games do, I hope."

❦

Ecotainment is a field limited only by one's imagination. To educate, inform, entertain all with one product or service can be very satisfying. As we've seen with the case studies in this chapter, the entrepreneurs interviewed sought to merge their beliefs with their livelihoods. Ecotainment may be just the field for those who hold such integration as the highest goal in life.

Think locally, sell globally, but above all, follow an old Chinese maxim that exhorts adults to retain the heart of the child. Which is just another way of saying that work and play should be one and the same.

Part IV

The Ecopreneur's Resource Guide

Ecopreneur's Resource Guide

The entries in this section are designed to help you start your business and stay in business. You'll find a variety of books, magazines, newsletters, and organizations that can help you with general business issues as well as technical issues relating to your field.

Basic Business Bibliography

General

The McGraw-Hill Guide to Starting Your Own Business: A Step by Step Blueprint for the First Time Entrepreneur, Stephen C. Harper, McGraw-Hill, 1990.

How to Leave Your Job and Buy a Business of Your Own, C.D. Peterson, McGraw-Hill, 1989.

Your Family Business: A Success Guide for Growth and Survival, Benjamin Benson, Business One Irwin, 1990.

Going Global: An Entrepreneur's Guide to International Business, Lawrence W. Tuller, Business One Irwin, 1991.

Financial

Starting on a Shoestring (2nd ed.), Arnold Goldstein, John Wiley, 1991.

When the Bank Says No—A Complete Guide to Small Business Finance, Lawrence Tuller, TAB/McGraw-Hill, 1991.

SBA Loans: A Step-by-Step Guide, Patrick D. O'Hara, John Wiley, 1990.

Financing Your Small Business, Jeff Seglin, McGraw-Hill, 1990.

Directory of Financing Sources, Venture Economics, Inc., 1989.

Marketing

Magnet Marketing: The Ultimate Strategy for Attracting and Holding Customers, John R. Graham, John Wiley, 1991.

The McGraw-Hill 36-Hour Marketing Course, Jeff Seglin, McGraw-Hill, 1990.

Total Marketing: Capturing Customers with Marketing Plans That Work, Don Develak, Business One Irwin, 1989.

Guerilla Marketing: Secrets for Making Big Profits from Your Small Business, Jay Conrad Levinson, Houghton Mifflin, 1984.

Building a Mail Order Business (2nd ed.), William A. Cohen, John Wiley, 1990.

The Unabashed Self-Promoter's Guide, Jefffrey Lant, JLA Publications, 1983.

Miscellaneous

The Presentations Kit: Ten Steps for Selling Your Ideas, Claudyne Wilder, John Wiley, 1990.

Front Line Customer Service: Fifteen Keys to Customer Satisfaction, Clay Carr, John Wiley, 1990.

Marketing Sources and Tools

Direct Mail

Direct Mail Marketing Association (DMA)
11 W. 42nd Street
New York, NY 10036-8096
212-768-7277
FAX: 212-768-4546

Directories of Newspapers, Magazines, and Radio and TV Stations

Bacon's Publicity Checker
332 South Michigan Avenue, Suite 900
Chicago, IL 60604
800-621-0561
312-922-2400

Standard Rates and Data Service (SRDS), Inc.
3002 Glenview Road
Wilmette, IL 60091
708-256-6067
800-323-4601

Business Organizations

General

The following organizations can provide valuable management
information and networking possibilities. Some also provide
group insurance rates.

American Federation of Small Businesses (AFSB)
407 S. Dearborn Street
Chicago, IL 60605-1115
312-427-0206

American Small Businesses Association (ASBA)
P.O. Box 612663
Dallas, TX 75261
800-227-1037

National Association for the Self-Employed (NASE)
2330 Gravel Road
Fort Worth, TX 76118
817-589-2475/800-736-NASE
FAX: 817-595-5456

National Business Association (NBA)
15770 N. Dallas Parkway, Suite 260
Dallas, TX 75248
214-991-6973

National Small Business Benefits Association (NSBBA)
9933 Lawler Avenue, #120
Skokie, IL 60077
708-679-1499
FAX: 312-679-6737 (in Chicago)

National Small Business United (NSBU)
1155 15th Street NW, Suite 710
Washington, DC 20005
202-293-8830/800-345-6728

Network of Small Businesses (NSB)
5420 Mayfield Road, Suite 205
Cleveland, OH 44124
216-442-5600
FAX: 216-461-7988

Business Assistance

Service Corps of Retired Executives Association (SCORE)
1825 Connecticut Avenue NW, Suite 503
Washington, DC 20009
202-653-6279

Small Business Assistance Center (SBAC)
P.O. Box 1441
Worcester, MA 01601
508-756-3513

Small Business Service Bureau (SBSB)
554 Main Street

P.O. Box 1441
Worcester, MA 01601-1441
508-756-3513

Environmental Organizations

General

Environmental Action, Inc.
625 Broadway
New York, NY 10012
212-677-1601

Environmental Defense Fund
257 Park Avenue South
New York, NY 10010
212-505-2100

Environmental Protection Agency
401 M Street SW
Washington, DC 20460
202-382-2090

Friends of the Earth
218 D Street SE
Washington, DC 20003
202-544-2600

Greenpeace USA (Main Office)
1436 U Street NW
Washington, DC 20009
202-462-1177 or 462-8817

House Interior Committee
U.S. House of Representatives
Washington, DC 20515
202-224-3121

House Merchant Marine and Fisheries Committee
U.S. House of Representatives
Washington, DC 20515
202-225-4047

National Wildlife Federation
1400 16th Street NW
Washington, DC 20036
202-797-6800

Natural Resources Defense Council
40 W. 20th Street
New York, NY 10011
212-727-4400

The Nature Conservancy
1815 N. Lynn Street
Arlington, VA 22209
703-841-5300

Recycling: General

National Recycling Coalition
1101 30th Street NW, Suite 305
Washington, DC 20006
202-625-6406

Recycling: Paper

American Paper Institute
260 Madison Avenue
New York, NY 10016
212-340-0600

Recycling: Glass

The Glass Packaging Institute
1801 K Street NW,
Washington, DC 20006
202-887-4850

Recycling: Aluminum

Aluminum Recycling Association
1000 16th Street NW, Suite 603
Washington, DC 20036
202-785-0951

Recycling: Plastics

The Council for Solid Waste Solutions
1275 K Street, NW, Suite 400
Washington, DC 20005
202-371-5319

The National Association forPlastic Container Recovery
5024 Parkway Plaza Boulevard, Suite 200
Charlotte, NC 28217
704-357-3250

The Plastic Bottle Information Bureau
1275 K Street NW, Suite 400
Washington, DC 20005
202-371-5200

Plastic Bottle Institute
The Society of the Plastics Industry, Inc.
1275 K Street NW, Suite 400
Washington, DC 20005
202-371-5200

Plastic Recycling Corporation of California
3345 Wilshire Boulevard, Suite 1105
Los Angeles, CA 90010
213-487-1544

Plastics Recycling Foundation
1275 K Street NW, Suite 400
Washington, DC 20005
202-371-5200

Air Pollution

Acid Rain Foundation
1410 Varsity Drive
Raleigh, NC 27606
919-828-9443

Acid Rain Information Clearinghouse
46 Prince Street
Rochester, NY 14607-1016
716-271-3550

Greenhouse Crisis Foundation
1130 17th Street NW, Suite 630
Washington, DC 20036
202-466-2823

National Clean Air Coalition
801 Pennsylvania Avenue SE
Washington, DC 20003
202-797-5436

National Oceanic and Atmospheric Administration
14th Street and Constitution Avenue NW
Washington, DC 20230
301-443-8910

Energy

Alliance to Save Energy
1725 K Street NW
Washington, DC 20006
202-857-0666

Department of Energy
Federal Energy Regulatory Commission
825 N. Capitol Street
Washington, DC 20426
202-208-0200

Energy Conservation Coalition
1525 New Hampshire Avenue NW
Washington, DC 20036
202-745-4874

Environmental and Energy Study Institute
122 C Street NW, Suite 700
Washington, DC 20001
202-628-1400

Office of Conservation and Renewable Energy
1000 Independence Avenue SW
Washington, DC 20585
202-586-9220

Office of Technology Assessment,
U.S. Congress

Washington, DC 20510
202-225-3121

Passive Solar Industries Council
2836 Duke Street
Alexandria, VA 22314
703-371-0357

Safe Energy Communication Council
1717 Massachusetts Avenue, NW
Washington, DC 20036
202-483-8491

Solar Energy Research Institute
1617 Cole Boulevard
Golden, CO 80401
303-231-1000

U.S. Department of Energy Conservation
and Renewable Energy Division
1000 Independence Avenue SW
Washington, DC 20585
202-586-9220

U.S. Department of Energy
Energy Information Administration
1000 Independence Avenue
Washington, DC 20585
202-586-8800

Water

Clean Water Action Project
317 Pennsylvania Avenue SE
Washington, DC 20003
202-457-1286

Clean Water Fund
317 Pennsylvania Avenue SE, 3rd Floor
Washington, DC 20005
202-457-0336

National Coalition Against the Misuse of Pesticides
530 Seventh Street SE

Washington, DC 20001
202-543-5450

Water Pollution Control Federation
601 Wythe Street
Alexandria, VA 22314
703-684-2400

Green Products

Household Hazardous Waste Project
901 S. National Avenue, Box 108
Springfield, MO 65804
417-836-5777

Pennsylvania Resources Council
25 W. Third Street
P.O. Box 88
Media, PA 19063
215-565-9131

Food

Center for Science in the Public Interest
1501 16th Street NW
Washington, DC 20036
202-332-9110

Department of Agriculture Soil Conservation Service
14th Street and Independence Avenue SW
P.O. Box 2890
Washington, DC 20013
301-627-3661

Senate Agriculture Nutrition and Forestry Committee
U.S. Senate
Washington, DC 20510
202-224-2035

Other Associations

National Business Incubator Association
1 President Street

Athens, OH 45701
614-593-4331

National Association of Diaper Services
2017 Walnut Street
Philadelphia, PA 19103
215-569-3650

National Food Processors Association
1401 New York Avenue SW, Suite 400
Washington DC 20005
202-639-5900

Social Investment Forum
430 First Avenue North, Suite 290
Minneapolis, MN 55401
612-333-8338

Periodicals

General Business Periodicals

Business Week
1221 Avenue of the Americas
New York, NY 10020-1001
212-512-3896
FAX: 212-512-2821

Entrepreneur
2392 Morse Avenue
P.O. Box 19787
Irvine, CA 92714-8234
714-261-2325

Forbes
60 Fifth Avenue
New York, NY 10011-8802
212-620-2200

Fortune
Time-Life Bldg.
Rockefeller Center

New York, NY 10020
212-522-1212

Nation's Business
1615 H Street NW
Washington, DC 20062
202-463-5650
FAX: 202-463-3178

National Home Business Report
P.O. Box 2137
Naperville, IL 60567-2137
708-717-0488

Environmental Periodicals

General

Environment
4000 Albemarle Street NW
Washington, DC 20016-1851
202-362-6445

Environment Report
National Press Bldg.
Washington, DC 20045
202-393-0031/202-393-1732

Garbage
P.O Box 56519
Boulder, CO 80322-6519
800-274-9909

In Business
P.O. Box 323
18 S. Seventh Street
Emmaus, PA 18049
215-967-4135

Air and Water Pollution

Pollution Abstracts
7200 Wisconsin Avenue

Bethesda, MD 20814-4811
301-961-5700

Pollution Engineering
1935 Shermer Road
Northbrook, IL 60062-5319
708-498-9846
FAX: 708-498-0376

Pollution Equipment News
650 Babcock Boulevard
Pittsburgh, PA 15237-5821
412-364-5366 or 364-5667

Solid Waste Management and Recycling

Packaging
1350 E. Touhy Avenue
P.O. Box 5080
Des Plaines, IL 60018-3303
708-635-8800
FAX: 708-635-6856

Packaging Digest
400 N. Michigan Avenue
Chicago, IL 60611-4104
312-222-2000
FAX: 312-222-2026

Recycling Times
1730 Rhode Island Avenue NW, #1000
Washington, DC 20036-3196
202-659-4613
FAX: 202-775-5917

Recycling Today
4012 Bridge Avenue
Cleveland, OH 44113-3320
216-961-4130

Resource Recovery Report
5313 38th Street NW
Washington, DC 20015
202-298-6344

Resource Recycling
P.O. Box 10540
Portland, OR 97210-0540
503-227-1319
FAX: 503-227-3864

Reuse/Recycle
P.O. Box 3535
851 New Holland Avenue
Lancaster, PA 17604
717-291-5609

Solid Waste Report
951 Pershing Drive
Silver Spring, MD 20910-4432
301-587-6300

Waste Age
1730 Rhode Island Avenue NW, #1000
Washington, DC 20036-3196
202-861-0708
FAX: 202-775-5917

Waste-to-Energy Report
1221 Avenue of the Americas
New York, NY 10020-1001
212-512-6310 or 512-4914

Wastetech News
131 Madison Street
Denver, CO 80206-5427
303-394-2905
FAX: 303-394-3011

The Bennett Information Group

The Bennett Information Group is a consulting consortium whose members include experts in business, science, and the environment. Prior to developing *Ecopreneuring*, the Group assembled *The Green Pages: Your Everyday Shopping Guide to Environmentally Safe Products*, and *Save the Earth at Work: How You Can Create a Waste-Free, Non-Polluting, Non-Toxic Office*.

Executive Director **Steven J. Bennett** has written more than thirty business books, including *Playing Hardball with Soft Skills* and *Executive Chess*. He assisted John Graham in the writing of *Magnet Marketing*. In addition, Mr. Bennett has written numerous business computing books. Prior to forming The Bennett Information Group, Mr. Bennett served as a science and medical writer and then as the president of a technical advertising and publishing firm. He holds an M.A. in Regional Studies from Harvard University.

The following members of the Group worked with Mr. Bennett on *Ecopreneuring*.

Tom Maugh: Dr. Maugh holds a Ph.D. in chemistry and is a science writer for the *Los Angeles Times*. He frequently writes about air and water pollution, as well as other environmental topics. Dr. Maugh drafted the chapters in Part II, "Taking Care of the Planet."

Richard Freierman: A graduate of the College of Environmental Science and Forestry, State University of New York, Mr. Freierman has conducted extensive field and wildlife research. He is currently a free-lance researcher and writer in Cambridge, Massachusetts. Mr. Freierman researched and drafted Chapter 15, "Greenbacks."

Bob Kalish: A novelist and journalist, Mr. Kalish holds an M.S. in education and currently oversees Writer's Ink Communications Consultants in Bath, Maine. With senior NASA scientist Jack Fishman, he is the coauthor of *Global Alert*, and has written numerous technical publications about the paper industry. Mr. Kalish drafted Chapters 13, 14, and 16, "Green Products," "Green Grocer," and "Educate, Entertain, Ecotain!"

Nancy Schmid: Ms. Schmid holds an M.B.A. and serves as a free-lance researcher and analyst to small consulting groups. She conducted the initial phase of research for *Ecopreneuring*.

Mike Snell: Mr. Snell is a leading book developer and literary agent specializing in business, science, and the environment, among other topics. He collaborated on such best-sellers as *Creating Excellence*, *Europe 1992*, *The Future 500*, and numerous other seminal business books. Mr. Snell helped develop the concept for *Ecopreneuring* and coordinated resources.

Dorian Yates Kinder: Ms. Kinder has worked for a number of environmental organizations as a researcher and writer. She also owns and manages Pure Podunk, Inc., which manufactures nontoxic, chemical-free bedding. Ms. Kinder conducted background research on the ecobusinesses described in *Ecopreneuring*.

You can write the Bennett Information Group at P.O. Box 1646, Cambridge, Massachusetts 02238.

Index